# POCKET ANNUAL 1998

## Bruce Smith

*4th Year of Publication*

Virgin

# Formula 1 Grand Prix Pocket Annual 1998

Copyright © Bruce Smith – Author 1998

ISBN: 0 7535-0295-X

First published in March 1998 by *Virgin Publishing*.

Virgin Publishing Ltd
332 Ladbroke Grove
London
W10 5AH

Typeset by Bruce Smith.

Edited by Mark Webb.

Printed in Great Britain by Caledonian International Books

## Disclaimer

In a book of this type it is inevitable that some errors will creep in. While every effort has been made to ensure that the details given in this annual are correct at the time of going to press, neither the editor nor the publishers can accept any responsibility for errors within.

Contact: Bruce-Smith@msn.com

# CONTENTS

Introduction ... ... ... ... ... ... ... ... ... ... ... ... ... 5
Car Changes '98 ... ... ... ... ... ... ... ... ... ... ... 7
Annual Key ... ... ... ... ... ... ... ... ... ... ... ... ... 8

**Review 97** ... ... ... ... ... ... ... ... ... ... ... ... 9
Diary – Month by Month ... ... ... ... ... ... ... 10
Race Procedures ... ... ... ... ... ... ... ... ... ... 22
Flags and Signals ... ... ... ... ... ... ... ... ... ... 26
GP Results '97 – Race by Race ... ... ... ... 27

**Records** ... ... ... ... ... ... ... ... ... ... ... ... ... 46
FIA Drivers' Championship Placings '97 ... ... 47
Constructors' Championship Placings '97 ... ... 47
Drivers – Finishing Positions – Race by Race '97 ... 48
Drivers – Qualifying Positions – Race by Race '97 ... 49
Drivers – Points Tally – Race by Race '97 ... ... 50
Constructors' Points Won – Race by Race '97 ... 51
Constructors' Total Laps – Race by Race '97 ... 51
Drivers – Laps Completed – Race by Race '97 ... 52
Drivers' World Championship Winners 1950-1997 ... 53
Drivers' World Championship Wins by Number ... 54
1997 Drivers All-Time Records ... ... ... ... ... 55
1997 Drivers by Completion % ... ... ... ... ... 56
1997 Teams by Completion % ... ... ... ... ... ... 57
Three-Year Driver Points Record 1994-97 ... ... 57
World Championship Drivers with 100 Points or More ... 58
World Championship Last Race Deciders ... ... ... 58
Drivers with Five or More Grand Prix Wins ... ... 59
Drivers with Five or More Pole Positions ... ... 60
Drivers with Five or More Fastest Laps ... ... ... 60
Drivers Who Have Completed 100 GP or More ... 61
Drivers with More than 5 Pole Positions in a Season ... ... 62
Drivers with 3+ Successive Grand Prix Wins in a Season ... 62
Drivers to Win Their National Grand Prix ... ... 63
Grand Prix With Driver Fatalities ... ... ... ... ... 64
Constructors' Cup by Car Type ... ... ... ... ... 65
Constructors' Cup Winners ... ... ... ... ... ... ... 65
Grand Prix Wins Per Car Type ... ... ... ... ... ... 65
Grands Prix Completed Per Car Type ... ... ... ... 66
Grand Prix Pole Positions Per Car Type ... ... ... 66
Grand Prix Fastest Laps Per Car Type ... ... ... 66

# A-Z Formula One Drivers .................. 67

Introduction .................. 68
Team and Driver Number Allocation 1998 .................. 68
Driver Race Summaries .................. 69
A-Z Drivers .................. 70

# Team Directory .................. 137

Arrows .................. 138
Benetton .................. 142
Ferrari .................. 146
Jordan .................. 152
McLaren .................. 156
Minardi .................. 161
Prost .................. 164
Sauber .................. 168
Stewart .................. 172
Tyrrell .................. 176
Williams .................. 180
Retired Teams: Lola .................. 185

# Circuit Directory .................. 187

A1-Ring .................. 188
Buenos Aires .................. 191
Catalunya .................. 194
Hockenheim .................. 197
Hungaroring .................. 200
Imola .................. 203
Interlagos .................. 206
Kyalami .................. 209
Magny Cours .................. 211
Melbourne .................. 214
Monaco .................. 217
Montreal .................. 220
Monza .................. 223
Nurburgring .................. 226
Silverstone .................. 229
Spa .................. 232
Suzuka .................. 235
Zhuhai .................. 238
107% Times .................. 239

# Race Diary '98 .................. 240

## Introduction

AT THE BEGINNING of the 1997 season there was some expectation that the domination of Formula One by the Williams team might be under threat, from Michael Schumacher and Ferrari, perhaps from a revitalised McLaren duo, even from Damon Hill when his fans closed their eyes to reality. And by the end it was indeed a close-run thing.

The decision to remove Schumacher from the Drivers' World Championship placings, following his coming together with Villeneuve, was greeted by derision from most of the world's press. Had the Ferrari driver ended up by winning the race and championship then it would have indeed been significant punishment. Although the FIA state they have set a precedent, it would seem to be a very dangerous one, and one that seems to have been missed by most commentators. Consider a similar situation again, but this time the team's number-two driver takes the front runner out, thus enabling his teammate to go on to glory. Under the FIA's precedent the number two would lose his place, but his number one would win the championship. Team tactics were after all at the fore in 1997.

Away from the track a few sideshows played in courtrooms, behind closed doors and perhaps even at Number Ten Downing Street. The trial concerning the death of Ayrton Senna at Imola on 1st May 1994 was ongoing throughout the season, coming to the surface whenever drivers were called to give evidence. The first day of the trial was adjourned after only fifteen minutes when more than 75 camera crews, photographers and journalists packed the courtroom which was set up in a discotheque.

At various stages, Formula One teams were rumoured to be ready to announce boycotts of future Italian Grands Prix.

Those concerned were Williams team boss Frank Williams, Williams technical director, Patrick Head, Williams chief designer Adrian Newey, Belgian race director Roland Bruynseraede, Imola race track director Federico Bendinelli and former track official Giorgio Poggi. Evidence would revolve around a possibly faulty steering column and debris on the track. In the end charges were dismissed and common sense prevailed.

Tobacco controversy raised its head in the latter stages of 1997. It is a subject for debate for many people. At present the money is vital for the sport, yet there can be no dispute that the plant causes disease and death. Many countries already impose bans on tobacco advertising – the French government for example have legislation called *Loi Evin* and thus teams are forced to come up with new methods to get recognition for their sponsors. Jordan and Williams were particularly innovative in this area last year. There seems little doubt that direct tobacco advertising is on its way out – will that mean the loss of races from Europe and a movement of F1 to satellite TV?

During an intense eight months there were the usual rumours about new teams and driver changes, fuelled by injuries, potential retirements and mismatches of drivers and cars. Perhaps because teams other than Williams experienced some success during the season, a surprising number of driver combinations remained intact for 1998.

The new regulations will create some confusion during the early part of the season as each team evaluates its own and its competitors' new designs. The key to the season may well be in the slow corners where the new car modifications will probably have the most impact (in all senses of the word!). The team and driver that is quickest through the slow corners will probably indicate the ultimate destination of the silverware.

## Deadlines '98

In response to many requests, this year's annual has been produced with a view to publication prior to the start of the 1998 season. As such, the cut-off for information was the 20th January 1998. At that time there were still a number of issues to be decided, not least the provision of circuits for the season. The future of races at Spa and Magny Cours was still being debated.

## Thanks '98

I would like to thank all the Formula One teams for their co-operation in producing this annual, in particular: Lindsay Morle (Williams), Jessica Walker (Benetton), Claudio Berro (Ferrari), Giselle Davies and Claire Walker (Jordan), and Stuart Sykes (Stewart). Photographs courtesy of ICN.

Many thanks also to Mark Webb who wrote the season's review and helped edit and proof read these pages – also to Ben Dunn at Virgin.

## Contact '98

If you have any comments or ideas for future editions of this annual you can E-mail me at:

Bruce-Smith@msn.com

# CAR CHANGES '98

Recent years have seen a number of changes to the specifications laid down by the FIA that govern all factors regarding car safety and design. The 1998 season, though, sees some of the most radical changes yet, and not all of these have been met with enthusiasm by teams or drivers. World Champion Jacques Villeneuve has been particularly outspoken in this respect. While the FIA's aim has been the safety of drivers, many drivers have suggested that the proposed changes will make the cars less stable and racing less of a spectacle. Time will tell.

## Groovy Tyres

Probably the most talked, about change is the introduction of grooved tyres. The 1997 season saw Bridgestone arrive to take on Goodyear, who had enjoyed having the marketplace to themselves for many seasons. The need to produce reliable tyres saw lap times increase slightly. However, it has been estimated that the introduction of grooved tyres might add as much as ten seconds per lap on some circuits!

The introduction of grooves means that there will be less actual tyre runner in contact with the track surface. This means less grip and an increase in braking distances. Cars will therefore need to brake earlier and turn through corners and bends more slowly than before. Corners often provide some of the best points for overtaking, with drivers looking to brake later than one another to get that bit of additional speed. The changes might result in more cars spinning as they brake later into corners, due to lack of grip. The change could benefit the more skilful drivers.

One benefit that looks certain to come about with the introduction of the grooved tyres is more 'off-line' racing. Grooved tyres should pick up less dirt and also generate less in the way of rubber 'marbles'. Cars should therefore be able to drive, and possibly overtake, on the straights away from the main racing line, where the track will always be cleaner.

The FIA argue that grooved tyres will also make the force of any accident impact less than that with cars running with non-grooved tyres on the basis that 'energy impact is directly proportional to the grip of the tyres'. In other words, the more grip a tyre has, the greater any pending impact.

The minimum complete widths of tyres is 305 mm for front and 365 mm at rear, while the number of dry weather tyres that can be used has been increased by four to forty for each event.

## Size and Shape

Cars will look narrower in 1998, because they are. The overall width of cars has been reduced by 200 mm to a maximum of 1800 mm. The minimum width at the front wheel axis line increases to 350 mm. Despite the new narrower configuration, the size of the driver's monocoque (that's the safety shell which they are positioned inside) has been increased to a cross-section of 300 mm each way – an increase of 50 mm. The front of the cockpit opening has been modified slightly so that it becomes much wider and flatter with a view to making driver egress – assisted or un-assisted – much simpler and quicker. To aid this further, there is now a ten-second time-limit imposed for drivers on being able to evacuate the cockpit and replace the steering wheel! Padding on the cockpit headrests must now extend as far forward as the steering wheel.

Up until 1997, the fuel inlet adapters have been exposed to the elements; now, they have to be fitted with a cover which is strong enough to prevent them coming open when an accident occurs – they must also be locked in place when the car is on the track. This will make pit stops slightly longer for refuelling as the cover has to be opened and closed.

Other minor changes include a 20 mm increase in the width of mirrors to make their size 50 mm high by 120 mm wide. Each car must carry two cameras – be they working or dummy units – one of which must be mounted on top of the main roll hoop.

# ANNUAL KEY

The *Formula 1 Grand Prix Pocket Annual* is divided into several clear sections that arrange information, statistics and reviews in relevant sections which are clearly defined in the Contents list on pages 3 and 4.

At the start of each section you may find a small guide or key to specific information and abbreviations used.

Through the Pocket Annual a set of country abbreviations is used and the key to these is listed below. Thus *Jap* signifies a Grand Prix in Japan.

## Key to Races

| | | | |
|---|---|---|---|
| Arg | Argentina | Fra | France |
| Aus | Australia | GB | Great Britain |
| Aut | Austria | Ger | Germany |
| Bel | Belgium | Hol | Holland |
| Bra | Brazil | Hun | Hungary |
| Can | Canada | Ita | Italy |
| Dal | Dallas | Jap | Japan |
| Esp | Spain | Mex | Mexico |
| Eur | Europe | Mon | Monaco |
| Fin | Finland | NZ | New Zealand |
| | | Pac | Pacific |

| | |
|---|---|
| Pes | Pescara |
| Por | Portugal |
| SA | South Africa |
| San | San Marino |
| Swi | Switzerland |
| USA | United States of America |
| USAE | USA (East) |
| USAW | USA (West) |

# Grand Prix Review 1997

As always, it was a very busy pre-season run up to the start of the 1997 Show. Sauber and Ferrari agreed to set up an independent company to develop V10 engines for Sauber. Larini signed to Sauber for 1997. Jos Verstappen signed to Tyrrell. Japanese Driver Shinji Nakano, who finished sixth in the 1996 Formula Nippon series in Japan, accepted a one year contract to drive for Ligier-Mugen for 1997.

The 'will he, won't he' rumours continued to surround Damon Hill and when he failed to join Jordan, it seemed to be between Brundle or Fisichella. The name of Nigel Mansell resurfaced as a possible stop-gap as the great man indicated that he had not yet retired from Formula One. He tested with Jordan in Spain and reportedly asked for £7 million to do the drive.

The FIA approved the use of black boxes in all Formula One cars. The boxes, developed by Delco Electronics, record technical information about the cars which can be reviewed and used to find out what went wrong after accidents.

Hill announced his signing with Tom Walkinshaw's Arrows team. Walkinshaw claimed that Damon was faster than Michael Schumacher and predicted that his new team would give Hill the chance to win at least two races in the coming season. Hill was awarded the BBC Sports Personality of the Year for the second time.

New team Lola announced that Ricardo Rosset and Vincenzo Sospiri would drive for them. Rosset and Sospiri drove together in F3000 for the SuperNova team in 1995 with good results, Sospiri claiming the Championship and Rosset runner-up spot.

The Malaysian Government pushed ahead with its objective of running a Formula One race in 1999. They contracted a German company (Tilke Ingenieure Fur Umwelttechnik) to build a track, reportedly worth over $US99 million.

Ligier confirmed that they were joining the Bridgestone camp for at least the 1997 season. The Bridgestone versus Goodyear tyre battle was one of the most interesting technical changes for the season as commentators debated the respective merits of the manufacturers.

To the swirl of bagpipes, Jackie Stewart unveiled his team's new Royal Stewart coloured car (as used by Jackie during his racing career). It took just nine months in production and was the first car released for the 1997 season. Jackie said that he would be happy to score one World Championship point in 1997 and would be very happy with some top 10 qualifying and finishing positions.

Benetton team boss Flavio Briatore said that he would consider boycotting the Monza and Imola grands prix if the charges against Frank Williams and other members of the Williams-Renault team led to convictions. He cited the risk of taking his team to a country that might bring charges over a racing accident.

It was announced that Formula One cars will have modifications to the tyres and brakes for the 1998 World Championship season. Dry weather slicks will be replaced by grooved compounds and the brakes will be modified to increase braking distances. The maximum overall width of the cars will be reduced from 200 cm to 180 cm to reduce cornering speeds and assist in overtaking.

Williams announced that they would continue to use Renault engines after the French company quits Formula One at the end of the 1997 season. A company called Mecachrome, which has been a Renault partner for 22 years, will supply engines to Williams under their own name.

The new Jordan-Peugeot 197 and the Tyrrell 025 (using a Ford V8) were launched. The team boss of the former, Eddie Jordan said that he was very happy with their new car and that Ralf Schumacher would have a very good season with it.

The new TV commentary dream team for UK television was revealed: Martin Brundle alongside Murray Walker. Other members of the team, included Louise Goodman, who was brought in from the Jordan press office to do reports.

Winter changes were carried out at Silverstone to make the track faster and more flowing. The Copse corner was opened out with an earlier entry and the complex before Woodcote was extensively re-worked to allow the cars to be quicker into Woodcote and the pits straight with more variety of lines into and out of the complex.

## January

The start of January saw the unveiling of the new Ferrari F310B. Damon Hill, an OBE in the Queen's honours list, launched his A17 TWR Arrows car at a Birmingham trade show. Williams signed a new sponsorship deal with Henderson Investors. Ferrari announced that they were to move their car design to Maranello. Team boss Luca de Montezemelo said "Our aim is to bring most of the activities to Maranello."

Jarno Trulli was confirmed as number two driver for Minardi, joining Katayama and Marques. Trulli was a test driver for Benetton and also won a Formula Three Championship in Germany. Martin Brundle became a director for the TWR Arrows team.

Testing in Jerez and Silverstone during January revealed problems with the Arrows' gearbox and the Ferrari engines. Michael Schumacher announced that Ferrari would be using last year's engines for the beginning of the '97 season. This was due to the consistent problems the team had been experiencing with the new V10 engines.

## February

The February crop of new cars included the Williams-Renault FW19, the Minardi M197 with new Hart V8 engine and Bridgestone tyres, the Sauber and McLaren. Lola, the new boys on the block, revealed their T97-30 with Ford Zetec to the public.

McLaren signed a five-year deal with British Aerospace to share technical expertise. Tyrrell announced a new sponsor in ICL. John Byrne joined Ferrari as chief designer, replacing John Barnard and linking himself once again with ex-Benetton technical director Ross Brawn.

Alain Prost bought the Ligier team. The deal was finalised after Jordan and Peugeot agreed to the terms of the engine supply contract. Magnussen was rushed to hospital after crashing his Stewart-Ford during testing at Estoril.

The Ayrton Senna manslaughter trial started. Rubens Barrichello got married to his girlfriend Silvana in Sao Paulo.

Protesters dumped oil over a 500-metre stretch of the Melbourne Grand Prix track at Albert Park. Victoria Premier Jeff Kennett wasn't pleased, but race chief Ron Walker assured race fans that the race would go ahead as planned after a cleaning operation.

## March

Formula One fans turned their attention to the first race of the season – the **Australian Grand Prix**. Michael Schumacher immediately made his mark with comments about the track, adding to worries over a public transport strike on the big day. A new seat for Damon Hill was cobbled together when it became apparent that his seat might not make it across the world in time for the first practice session. As it turned out, the top teams dominated practice and Damon Hill only just got in under the qualifying time. The Lolas didn't even manage that and, whatever the expectations for the new season, some realism now set in.

When it came to the race, Damon pulled off in the parade lap with electrical problems, Villeneuve and Herbert went off early and Irvine was out soon after with collapsed front suspension and a flat front left tyre. Ralf Schumacher and Verstappen went out as Frentzen opened up a big gap between himself and Coulthard in the McLaren. Frentzen regained the lead after his first pit stop but failed to pull out enough time to retain the lead after his second. Alesi defied team orders to pit for four laps and eventually pulled off the track out of fuel. Frentzen and Schumacher swapped second place, but neither was in a position to challenge Coulthard who went on to win the second grand prix of his career and McLaren's first win since Senna won Adelaide in 1993, 49 races previously.

Bernie Ecclestone announced plans to float Formula One on the stock markets in London and New York. Ferrari signed a deal with Finmeccanica who own the helicopter-making Augusta company. The two companies will share technical information with each other.

Lola announced that their season was over unless more money was forthcoming. Bic signed a four year contract with the re-named Prost team.

Five different constructors filled the top five grid positions in the **Brazilian Grand Prix**. Villeneuve slid onto the grass as he and Michael Schumacher fought their way into the first corner. The first corner also saw some contact between other drivers including Hill, Fisichella and Irvine. Luckily for the field, Barrichello stalled on the grid, causing a re-start. Villeneuve overtook Schumacher Senior at the end of the first lap and went on to win the race. Berger finished second, followed by Panis, to give Prost and Bridgestone their first podium place. Then came Hakkinen, Michael Schumacher and Alesi. Hill ran in the points for quite a few laps, getting as high as fourth position, but retired from the race three laps from the end with an oil fire.

## April

The black box from Senna's car was scrutinised in Italy when the trial continued. Rumours began about a new team being built around Villeneuve for 1999, just as Rothmans extended their contract with Williams for another year and Villeneuve signed for Williams for 1998.

Gerhard Berger's wife Ana gave birth to a new baby girl, named Heidi. The inline skates company Roces signed a new sponsorship deal with Minardi.

Stewart-Ford introduced revised bodywork for both SF1s in time for the Argentine Grand Prix. Giancarlo Fisichella returned from South America to shake down the fourth Jordan 197 at Silverstone. Technical director Gary Anderson explained that Fisichella was also testing some minor components in preparation for the Buenos Aires race. Jean Alesi was also back at Silverstone, at the wheel of the Benetton B197 test car, preparing new front suspension geometry.

The organisers of the **Argentinian Grand Prix** were handed a $10,000 fine for showing a red flag after the first-corner incident that took Schumacher and Coulthard out of the race. Although Villeneuve's victory was predictable, Irvine and Ralf Schumacher joining him on the podium was not. Jordan's other driver, Fisichella, was reported to say that he would pursue only a professional acquaintance with Ralf Schumacher (or words to that effect) after the latter caused him to crash out.

It became apparent that Adrian Newey would leave Williams for McLaren later in the season. The Canadian Parliament passed Bill C-71 into law, severely restricting tobacco advertising, including that on cars, presaging the debates in Europe.

After a test drive with grooved tyres (standard for 1998), Villeneuve was reported to comment that it was like driving a Formula Ford car, with a bit more power and downforce.

Villeneuve and Frentzen took the front of the grid at the **San Marino Grand Prix**, but it was Frentzen who won this time, his first grand prix victory and his first points of the season. A frustrated World Champion Damon Hill was handed a one-race ban, suspended for one race, for dangerous driving. Hill had rammed into the back of Shinji Nakano's car. Lola finally went bust with debts of more than £6m.

## May

Michael Schumacher received the Silver Laurel Leaf, the most highly regarded award given to German sportspersons. The 'Damon Hill to move' stories began just as top designer John Barnard agreed to become technical director at Arrows. Barnard replaced Frank Dernie, who left the team.

The proposed Malaysian Grand Prix in 1999 will take place only just after the monsoon season, which should suit spray-specialist Michael Schumacher, who won the **Monaco Grand Prix** after two hours of rain to give him the lead in the Drivers' Championship and Ferrari their first win at Monaco since 1981 when Villeneuve Senior won for them. The Williams team took a gamble by starting their drivers on slick tyres, only to see Frentzen and Villeneuve slipping back through the field and both eventually failing to finish. Jackie Stewart's team scored their first podium finish with Barrichello an excellent second, confirming Stewart-Ford as the most promising new team since Jordan. Irvine rounded up the top three to give Ferrari fourteen points for the day, and the lead in the constructors' standings.

Damon Hill survived a high-speed crash during testing at the Magny-Cours circuit in France. His Arrows car was badly damaged when it went into the barriers at the Estoril Curve. Pedro Diniz fared no better, suffering an engine failure. Tyrrell began a two-day test at Silverstone, with Salo running the new Ford ED5 engine for the first time

In the **Spanish Grand Prix,** Williams put their drivers onto the front of the grid, but in the race only Villeneuve could make it count with Frentzen dropping out of the points with tyre problems. Panis put in a charge and reduced the gap to 9.913 seconds by lap 61 in the Bridgestone-equipped Prost car, taking the tyre manufacturer close to its first win, and Goodyear's first failure in more than ten years. Ten points put Villeneuve top of the drivers' tree, and made Williams' earlier problems seem like a temporary blip.

It became apparent that the last race of the season would be at Jerez in Spain. Designated work at the Estoril track was behind schedule and wouldn't be ready in time for the race.

As the propaganda war over tobacco sponsorship continued, there were rumours that Craig Pollock and Julian Jakobi would buy the Tyrrell Formula One team from Ken Tyrrell, with financial backing from British American Tobacco. Villeneuve got a slap on the wrist for openly criticising the introduction of grooved tyres for 1998.

Going into the **Canadian Grand Prix**, Gerhard Berger was forced to pull out because of a sinus infection. He had undergone surgery two weeks previously for his sinus problems but it worsened on the way to Canada and his doctor ordered him to rest. Alexander Wurz was brought in as his replacement.

Michael Schumacher won a race which was prematurely ended due to a crash involving Olivier Panis. The Frenchman was helped from his car and medical attention was soon on the scene. The pace car was called for the second time in the race, but it was soon apparent that it would take time to clear Panis and his car from the track, so the race was stopped. Alesi and Fisichella completed the top three. Coulthard was in a race-winning position, but he stalled his car on his final pit stop minutes before Panis crashed.

After it was established that Olivier Panis had sustained double fractures to each leg, the press lined up a number of possible replacements – including Rene Cavel and Yannick Anseaume, two drivers of the French Formula Three Championship, Emmanuel Collard, Shinji Nakano and the Minardi driver Jarno Trulli.

The Italian Sauber driver Gianni Morbidelli broke his arm during a test run at the French Magny-Cours circuit. Noberto Fontana was recruited as stand-in. Wurz continued deputising for an incapacitated Berger.

Following a successful test at Magny-Cours, Jarno Trulli was released from his contract with Minardi to compete for the rest of the 1997 World Championship with the Prost team. Trulli's seat at Minardi was taken by Minardi's test driver Tarso Marques. Gian Carlo Minardi said, "It's a great opportunity for Jarno, which confirms the Minardi Team as an excellent springboard for young talented drivers."

Damon Hill and Rubens Barrichello topped the times for the first practice session of the **French Grand Prix**, helped by rain and Bridgestone rubber, but in the afternoon session, and with a drying track, it was a different story with Michael Schumacher and Fisichella topping the times. Michael Schumacher eventually claimed pole position ahead of Frentzen.

Rain started falling towards the end of the race proper, but leader Michael Schumacher and second placed Frentzen stayed out on slicks. Villeneuve spun off while chasing Irvine for third on the last lap, but managed to avoid the wall and keep his engine running to come home in fourth; a vital recovery in hindsight.

The Jordan team signed a major commercial sponsorship with Esat Digifone, with the company also becoming the telecommunications partner of Jordan Grand Prix Ltd. Benetton signed a major sponsorship deal with Federal Express. Gerhard Berger's father, Johan, died in an aircraft accident in Tirol, Austria.

Villeneuve stole pole in the last minutes of qualifying for the **British Grand Prix**. Damon Hill set a good time to sit twelfth on the grid, but when he crossed the line in sixth you could have been forgiven for thinking he had won from the way Damon and his supporters celebrated. Villeneuve slid from first to seventh after a 33-second pit stop due to a wheel nut problem. Michael Schumacher had the race in the bag but retired on lap 38 with brake troubles. Villeneuve fought his way back to second place behind Hakkinen who was in line for his first career win when his engine blew to hand the race back to Villeneuve who celebrated Williams' 100th victory. Alexander Wurz drove another great race finishing third behind his teammate Alesi.

Villeneuve was issued with a suspended one-race ban for failing to maintain the correct distance behind the safety car at the beginning of the race.

The 24-year-old Italian Jordan driver Giancarlo Fisichella signed a one-year contract with Benetton for 1998, triggering another Formula One court case. Alain Prost was given the go-ahead to switch his team's headquarters from Magny-Cours to Versailles. He wanted to move from the grand prix circuit site to be nearer Peugeot. Patrick Head announced that Frentzen would be staying in the Williams camp for the '98 season.

Gerhard Berger took the chequered flag at the **German Grand Prix**, three years after his last victory. Formula One's most experienced driver drove a faultless race and used a two-stop strategy while most other top runners ran a one-stop. Gerhard hinted that his father, who died two weeks previously, was looking after him and had to wipe a tear from his eye during post-race interviews. Michael Schumacher finished second to edge Ferrari further ahead, and Hakkinen finished a strong third, his first podium finish since Australia. Fisichella would have finished second but for a blown tyre. There was a minor Williams slump as both drivers failed to finish. Frentzen clashed with Irvine on the first corner, all but ending both their races, and Villeneuve spun off, seemingly unable to move up through the field. Damon Hill finished a strong eighth.

The Tyrrell Racing Organisation confirmed that its Formula One cars will be powered by Ford V10 engines during 1998. The management and development of the engine would be handled by Cosworth Racing, Ford's technology partner in Formula One, with whom Tyrrell's engineers worked closely throughout the 1997 season. Tyrrell stated that this move was part of their Racing towards the Millennium programme which was designed to put in place all the agreements for the team to become a title challenger by the year 2000.

## August

Michael Schumacher claimed pole for the **Hungarian Grand Prix**, from Villeneuve's second on the grid and Damon Hill's surprise third on the grid.

In the race, Hill had a blinding start and was second going into the first corner behind Michael Schumacher who he chased down and overtook after a few laps. He held his lead until pit stops and when all the top runners had stopped Hill was back in the lead. Again after the top runners pitted a second time Hill was still in the lead and pulling away. With two laps to go, it seemed he had the race in the bag and that the Arrows' reliability problems would hold off and let him win. Unfortunately, Damon's hydraulic pump failed, giving him an intermittent throttle and allowing Villeneuve to make up 34 seconds to pass him. Damon crossed the line second. Herbert was third, Michael Schumacher fourth, Ralf Schumacher fifth and Nakano sixth.

Jordan's Ralf Schumacher was called up for national service at a Luftwaffe training base near Cologne.

Alesi and Villeneuve traded blows for pole position, with Villeneuve coming out on top spot at the **Belgian Grand Prix**. A check on Hakkinen's McLaren after qualifying showed irregularities in its fuel. The FIA fined McLaren $25,000 and ordered Hakkinen to start from the rear of the grid.

The race started under the pace car and, in an effort to disperse standing water, it stayed out for the first three laps. It was clear that double World Champion Michael Schumacher had made all the right decisions as he quickly got past Alesi and Villeneuve on the same lap, pulled out a huge gap and never looked back. Other teams struggled to find the right tyres. Hill gambled on more rain and put on intermediate tyres while the rest of the field was changing to slicks, and it cost him. Williams had trouble in the rain again, although both drivers recovered to earn points. Fisichella enjoyed his highest finish in second and Hakkinen followed closely in third.

Mika Hakkinen, who had appealed before the start of the race and was allowed to start from his qualifying positions, was then given a one-race ban, suspended for two races, for overtaking under a yellow flag. He subsequently walked away from a high-speed crash while testing at Monza.

Bernie Ecclestone continued talking about hosting grands prix in the US and South Africa as well as Asian venues.

The rumours of new teams, and the return of some old ones, began circulating as the circus started to look ahead to the 1998 season. BMW announced that it would re-enter Formula One in the year 2000 and supply engines for Williams.

The FIA ruled that Mika Hakkinen be stripped of his third-place finish at Spa and McLaren be fined for fuel irregularities. The FIA accepted that the mistake was not intentional and that Mobil and McLaren had acted in good faith. Villeneuve benefited by an important single point.

Australia apparently rejected a ban on tobacco advertising at international sports events in a bid to keep key events like the grand prix. TWR Arrows announced that Mika Salo would drive for the team in 1998 and 1999.

In the **Italian Grand Prix**, Alesi watched Coulthard win the race through better pit stops, giving up the lead that he had held since the start. Alesi held on to his second place and Frentzen came home in third. Fisichella finished fourth, Villeneuve fifth and Michael Schumacher sixth. Herbert walked away from a high-speed crash after a coming together with Ralf Schumacher. The gap between Michael Schumacher and Villeneuve eased to ten points and Williams came to within one point of Ferrari in the Constructors' Championship.

David Coulthard dedicated his Italian win to the late Diana, Princess of Wales. Coulthard met Diana at Silverstone in 1995 and still has pictures of her and her children up at home. David said he felt very emotional when the national anthem was playing after his win.

Villeneuve and Coulthard received suspended one-race bans for failing to slow down when a yellow flag was shown in the warm-up.

The Tyrrell Formula One team received a multi-million pound boost with the confirmation of a major joint venture with team sponsor European Aviation, to build a new state-of-the-art wind tunnel facility in the airline's base at Bournemouth International Airport.

The **Austrian Grand Prix** – the first in that country since 1987 – was the beginning of the Villeneuve fightback. The Prost team led a grand prix for the first time, through Jarno Trulli, but Villeneuve took nine points more than Michael Schumacher. Hakkinen was second on the grid, but his engine didn't last the first lap. Alesi and Irvine knocked each other out.

Benetton won a High Court action disputing the services of driver Giancarlo Fisichella. Mr Justice Jacob ordered the Jordan team to write to the FIA saying that Fisichella would no longer be driving for the team next year, thus opening a spot for Hill, whose talks with Prost had broken down. Damon Hill subsequently signed a two-year contract with Jordan, but it was revealed that this had been Damon's first choice and that he and Eddie Jordan had settled the deal just after the Italian GP.

Jean Alesi signed a two-year contract with Sauber, moving Herbert to the number two seat with the team.

Hakkinen grabbed pole and held on to it despite the barrage from the rest of the field at the **Luxembourg Grand Prix**. After starting from his first Formula One pole, he promptly set the pace and proved that no one could match him on the day. As bad luck would have it, a mechanical failure robbed him of the win he deserved. Hakkinen's manager Keke Rosberg said, "It's hard to believe, both engines going like that."

Villeneuve nicked ten valuable points, every one of which counted as the other championship contender Michael Schumacher retired on lap 2 after a coming together with his little brother on the first lap. Alesi finished second, and Frentzen third. Patrick Head said that he felt Williams were "on a bit of a roll" and that "the championship could change complexion in just eight days."

David Richards, head of the Subaru rally team, took over from Flavio Briatore as managing director of Benetton. Richards won two world rally championships with Subaru and was a major force with Honda in touring car racing.

At Williams, the A team was officially renewed for 1998. "We are delighted both Jacques and Heinz-Harald will continue Williams' championship attack next season," said Williams. "We are confident that the combination of technical expertise and driver continuity will put us in a strong position."

## October

Jackie Stewart announced that he would be keeping the same line-up for 1998 while Ukyo Katayama announced that he was retiring at the end of the season. After much speculation, Damon Hill announced he would be racing for Jordan in 1998 after Benetton won the legal battle to invoke an option they had on Giancarlo Fisichella.

Jacques Villeneuve was disqualified from the **Japanese Grand Prix** for failing to slow down in a caution area during qualifying. Williams filed an appeal to allow the Canadian to take part, but not necessarily to collect any points. With Villeneuve leading Schumacher, Eddie Irvine made one of the best passing manoeuvres of the year to overtake Hakkinen and Schumacher through the S-Bend corner section and then passed Villeneuve a lap later. He then set out to blitz everyone and pulled out a nice cushion which, in the end, would decide the race. After pit stops, Irvine was leading, second was Michael Schumacher and third Villeneuve. Irvine then slowed down six seconds a lap to allow Michael to catch and pass him, and then he held up Villeneuve behind him.

The Ferrari drivers congratulated themselves, but Frentzen's second gave Williams their ninth constructors' title (a record). Williams withdrew its appeal, so as not to further jeopardise Villeneuve's chances, and so Schumacher went into the final race with a one point lead.

"The man who goes into the last race in the lead is in a position where he can, as we have seen a number of times in previous years, be very aggressive to the person behind him," said Patrick Head, reflecting the sport's desire for a clean fight. Gerhard Berger announced this would be his last season in Formula One, but added "for now".

As if to emphasise the highly competitive nature of the 1997 season, Villeneuve, Michael Schumacher and Frentzen all posted the same lap time (1m 21.072s) in qualifying for the **European Grand Prix** in Jerez.

It all came down to this one race, and Michael Schumacher set out early to stamp his authority on it by taking the lead with a faultless start. It looked as if the Ferrari 50th anniversary year was to have its fairytale ending. However, on lap 48 Villeneuve outbraked Michael Schumacher going into a corner. Schumacher not only tried to close the door, but tried to ram Villeneuve out of the race. The move backfired and Schumacher was left stranded in the sand. Villeneuve was left with a small problem that caused overheating in his rear tyres, which in turn caused spasmodic lap times. In the last lap, he slowed into the chicane to give Hakkinen the lead and his first well-deserved and much-anticipated win. Coulthard also slipped by to leave Villeneuve third and World Champion in his second season of Formula One racing.

The FIA issued a statement saying: "Following a report from the FIA Race Director, the FIA has summoned Michael Schumacher to appear before an extraordinary meeting of the World Motor Sport Council".

## Post-Season

The Labour government did an election policy U-turn by announcing that Formula One would be exempted from an immediate tobacco advertising ban in sport, citing the 50,000 jobs which depend on the industry. It was alleged that one of the ministers concerned had inside knowledge of the industry because her husband was an ex-director and legal advisor to Benetton. The Labour Party decided to return a £1 million donation from Bernie Ecclestone.

Michael Schumacher acknowledged that he had tried to knock Villeneuve out of the last grand prix and the FIA deleted his second place in the championship from the record books, although the individual race results stand. Many observers felt that this was no punishment, but Schumacher's pride was dented and the point was strongly made that any potential champion using foul tactics to secure a victory in the future would find himself disqualified.

After further machinations in the Senna trial, the Italian judge declared that all charges were dropped against the defendants. Thus, one of the potentially damaging outcomes for Formula One was seen off during 1997.

The issue of tobacco advertising also seemed to be easing, with governments and Formula One looking to work together to find alternative financing.

As the year drew to a close, Tyrrell called a press conference on 2 December to announce that it had been acquired by British American Racing. BAR stated that the Tyrrell team would be fully operational during the 1998 season, but would be incorporated into the new British American Racing team the following year.

On his decision to sell the team, Ken Tyrrell explained: "This has probably been the most difficult decision I've ever had to take. It was a decision, however, which I believe was the right one. The cost to compete in Formula One has escalated dramatically and the Tyrrell Racing Organisation is not satisfied with being relegated to the back of the grid. Our competitive spirit is too high. This merger will allow us to get back to the front of the grid again.

"My son, Bob, and I have therefore come to the conclusion that it would be preferable to pass the Tyrrell legacy on to a new team which shares our ideals and philosophy about motor sport.

"Uniquely in Formula One, I believe, Tyrrell remains a family team, and my biggest concern in taking this decision was to ensure that the employees are properly looked after. I believe the arrangement we have come to with British American Racing will allow us to do that."

British American Racing's Managing Director, Craig Pollock, commented: "We're mindful of the tremendous contribution the Tyrrell Racing Organisation has made to Formula One over the years, and we are delighted Ken and Bob will be joining with us.

"The opportunity to acquire Tyrrell makes good business sense for us. I would also like to think that the competitive spirit and open attitude of the Tyrrell Racing Organisation will live on in British American Racing."

Backing for BAR will be provided by BAT – British American Tobacco. Welcome to 1998.

# RACE PROCEDURES

There is a strict timetable laid down by the FIA for the build-up and start of each grand prix race. This set of procedures ensures that no team is favoured when it comes to circuit time, qualifying, warm-up and the actual race. Details of these are given below – all times are local. Note that what follows is a general guide only and liable to change.

## Circuit Practice

There are four sessions of free practice. These take place on the Friday and Saturday, except for the Monaco Grand Prix when the Friday practice is held on the Thursday. The two sessions on the Friday last for one hour each and are held from 11.00 to 12.00 and 13.00 to 14.00. The two sessions on the Saturday last for 45 minutes each and are held from 9.00 to 9.45 and 10.15 to 11.00. A change from the 1998 season is that there is no limitation on the number of laps permitted. Prior to this, there had been a limit of thirty laps across the two sessions.

## Qualifying Session

A single one-hour session is held for qualifying (prior to 1996 there used to be two sessions). This takes place on the Saturday from 13.00 to 14.00. Since 1997, each driver hass been limited to a maximum of twelve qualifying laps, and a lap will count towards the qualifying laps provided the driver has started it before the expiry of the 60-minute clock. The twelve laps are normally performed by teams as three- or four-lap sessions. This is at the discretion of teams and drivers – the usual scenario is an 'out' warm-up lap, where the tyres are brought up to race temperature, two flat-out laps, where drivers go all-out for a fast time, and a final 'in-lap' as drivers come back into the pits.

The fastest lap out of those registered will count as the qualifying time. To qualify for a race, all drivers must establish a lap time that is within 107% of the time set by the fastest driver in the qualifying session. Drivers with times outside this limit will not automatically qualify for the race – the FIA have the right to admit a driver to the race. (A rough guide to 107% times can be found on Page 239.)

The driver's grid position is determined by his time. Thus the fastest qualifying time earns the driver the first or pole position on the starting grid. A spare car may be used in the qualifying session in case of accident or mechanical problems. Indeed, some teams (e.g. Ferrari in 1996 and 1997) even use a special qualifying engine.

From the 1998 season, any car that is given assistance, after stopping, to get back to the pits, will have its fastest lap time of the session deleted.

## Warm-up Session

A thirty-minute warm-up session is held on the Sunday of the race, and this normally starts four and a half hours before the start of the race. If, after this, rain occurs then an extra fifteen-minute session may be sanctioned to allow teams to make wet-weather changes.

## The Start

The race follows a set countdown to the start. Thirty minutes prior to the race the pit lane is opened for just fifteen minutes. During this window all cars must leave their paddocks and make their way to the starting grid. A horn is sounded two minutes prior to the pit lane closure and fifteen minutes prior to the start of the race, the pit lane is closed. Any cars not out of the paddocks must now start from the pit lane – this effectively places the car at the back of the grid.

Once all cars are formed on the grid, a series of time boards is used to display the amount of time remaining to the start of the race. These are carried through the grid and personnel must adhere to their significance.

Ten minutes before the start of the race, all personnel, except drivers, team members and officials, must leave the starting grid. Boards are shown at five minutes, three minutes, one minute and thirty seconds before the start of the race. At the one-minute board, engines are started and all technicians and team staff are required to leave the grid. During this period a series of lights is used to signal stages of the starting countdown. There are five banks of lights, each with five lights. Ten minutes prior to the race, the bottom two sets of red lights (ten in all) flash on and off twice. Five minutes prior to the start, the first two (vertical) red lights are extinguished. At this point, all cars must have their wheels fitted – if not, they must start from either the pit lane or the back of the grid. The next two go out with three minutes to go and another two with one minute to go. The penultimate set of red lights is turned off with 30 seconds to go.

When the count reaches zero, a green flag is displayed and the final set of red lights goes out to be replaced by a set of five green lights across the top of the board – this signals that the cars on the starting grid can advance on their single formation lap. Cars must adhere strictly to their grid position and no overtaking is allowed (cars can be disqualified for doing so). The green lights go out twenty seconds after the cars start the formation lap; should the start need to be aborted, they are replaced by a set of five flashing orange lights. Cars return to their grid position and wait for the start.

When all cars are stationary on the grid, a series of red lights (two vertical at a time) comes on, one light after the other, until they are all switched on –

there is approximately a one-second delay between each set of red lights being turned on. There is then a pre-set delay of up to three seconds, at which point all the red lights are extinguished together and the race can commence.

If rain should come after the five-minute mark then the race director has it within his power to allow teams to change their tyres if they wish. In this case abort lights are shown and the race start countdown begins again from the fifteen-minute mark.

## Stopping the Race

The race may be stopped as a result of accidents or adverse weather conditions. If at any time during the final red-light sequence the race needs to be aborted, the lights freeze in their current state and the race is aborted.

If the race has to be stopped once underway it is done by the waving of a red flag. If the race is stopped before two laps are completed, cars return to their original grid positions and the race is restarted. A new time will be given for the race start and this is normally as soon as feasibly possible after the original race was stopped. Cars that might have had to start from the pit lane now have an opportunity to join the starting grid. In the case of an accident, drivers have the opportunity to use their spare car. If this cannot be made ready in time to join the grid, the car will start from the pit lane.

If more than two laps, but less than 75 per cent, of the race is completed, the race re-starts on a dummy grid, according to positions at the time the race was stopped. The distance of the re-started race is that required to make up the full race distance, less three laps (thus, the overall race is shortened by three complete laps).

If the race is stopped with more than 75 per cent completed, the race is deemed to have been run and positions at the point of the race being stopped are the finishing positions.

## Race Distance

A grand prix race must not be shorter than 190 miles (305 km). The number of laps that a race comprises is the smallest number of laps that will exceed this distance. There is also a two-hour time limit on a race. Should this time limit be exceeded (perhaps due to bad weather conditions), the chequered flag will be shown to the leader at the end of the lap in which the two hour mark is passed – even if the scheduled race distance has not been completed.

## Pit Lane

There is a maximum speed assigned to all pit lanes that must not be exceeded. The maximum speed varies from circuit to circuit and is between 50 – 75 mph (80 – 120 kph).

Cars starting from the pit lane can only join the race after the cars on the starting grid have all passed the exit from the pit lane. Cars in the pit lane are not able to take part in the formation lap.

## Penalties

Minor violations of rules – such as pit lane speeding, 'jump' starts, and dangerous driving (to name three) may be penalised by a Stop-Go penalty. The driver is required to return to his paddock and wait for a 10-second count.

Drivers and teams who do not adhere to the rules face other penalties. For example, a driver who drives an extra lap, say in a practice session, is likely to get a fine. This is typically US$5-10,000. A driver who is found to have driven recklessly or created a crash that was avoidable might receive a suspended race ban that would be invoked if he repeated the feat in the time frame specified.

## Over and Understeer

Two terms are often used regularly by drivers and commentators: over-steer and under-steer. In a perfect world the car will be set-up perfectly to ensure it takes the correct racing line around a curve or through a corner. If, when trying to drive the racing line a driver finds himself going towards the corner and therefore having to compensate, the car is suffering from *over-steer*. If, on the other hand, the car goes towards the outside edge of the corner and again the driver has to compensate to maintain the racing line, the car is suffering from *under-steer*.

Over-steer is when there is a lack of grip at the rear of the car. This can result in the driver losing the back of the car and spinning off. Tyre wear also increases. It is normally cured by increasing the amount of rear wing on the car, ie, making it more perpendicular to create drag and therefore downforce. Over-steer can also be corrected by making the suspension softer and reducing the ride height of the car.

Over-steer is a lack of grip at the front of the car which means that it turns two slowly and out towards the outside edge of the corner. It is caused when there is too little front wing or the front suspension is too stiff, or a combination of both. It can therefore be cured by increasing the front wing and softening the suspension.

Cars can suffer under-steer during a race even if they are set up correctly. This happens when they are following behind a car 'on its gearbox'. The lead car has airflow over its front and rear wings to maintain downforce, however the front of the following car is in a 'hole' because the front car is deflecting the air over it – therefore the front of the following car has reduced stability. Unless a car intends to brake late and try an overtaking manoeuvre at a corner, it will normally 'back-off' to ensure stability through the corner. ∎

# Flags and Signals

There are ten flags that can be shown and these are illustrated on the inside back cover of this annual. A flag's significance may be changed depending on whether it is held stationary or waved.

**Red Flag:** This is only shown at the start/finish line and is used to indicate that the race has been stopped.

**White Flag:** When held stationary it indicates the presence of a slower vehicle on the track. When waved it indicates that the driver may be seriously obstructed by a slower vehicle ahead of him on the track.

**Black Flag:** Shown with white number to indicate the driver to whom it applies. The driver indicated must stop at the Pit within one lap and report to the Clerk of the Course. (This will normally be at the driver's pit paddock where a Stop-Go penalty might be indicated or disqualification.)

**Black and White (Diagonal) Flag:** Used only once per driver as a warning for unsportsmanlike behaviour.

**Black with Red Spot Flag:** Shown with white number to indicate the driver to whom it applies. The driver indicated has a mechanical failure and must stop at his pit.

**Blue Flag:** This flag is used to indicate that a faster car is following. When held stationary the driver concerned must give way, when waved the driver must give way urgently. During a race, failure to give way when the Blue flag is waved may result in a penalty. A Blue flag is also used at the exit from the Pit Lane to indicate to the driver exiting that traffic is approaching on the track.

**Yellow and Red Striped Flag:** When held stationary it indicates that there is oil or water on the track, when waved there is a slippery surface immediately ahead.

**Yellow Flag:** This flag indicates a hazard ahead and there should be no overtaking. When held stationary it indicates that there is a hazard on the track and drivers should drive well within their limits. When waved, cars must slow down and be prepared to change direction or follow an unusual line. When double waved, cars must slow down and be prepared to stop as the track is partially or wholly blocked.

**Green Flag:** This is used to signify the end of a danger area that will have been marked by a yellow flag. Effectively it is an all-clear. Also used to signify the start of the warm-up lap.

**Chequered Flag:** Signifies the end of the race.

# GP Results '97

## At a Glance

| GP | Winner | Pole |
|---|---|---|
| Australian | D.Coulthard (McLaren) | J.Villeneuve (Williams) |
| Brazilian | J.Villeneuve (Williams) | J.Villeneuve (Williams) |
| Argentinian | J.Villeneuve (Williams) | J.Villeneuve (Williams) |
| San Marino | H-H.Frentzen (Williams) | J.Villeneuve (Williams) |
| Monaco | M.Schumacher (Ferrari) | H-H.Frentzen (Williams) |
| Spanish | J.Villeneuve (Williams) | J.Villeneuve (Williams) |
| Canadian | M.Schumacher (Ferrari) | M.Schumacher (Ferrari) |
| French | M.Schumacher (Ferrari) | M.Schumacher (Ferrari) |
| British | J.Villeneuve (Williams) | J.Villeneuve (Williams) |
| German | G.Berger (Benetton) | G.Berger (Benetton) |
| Hungarian | J.Villeneuve (Williams) | M.Schumacher (Ferrari) |
| Belgian | M.Schumacher (Ferrari) | J.Villeneuve (Williams) |
| Italian | D.Coulthard (McLaren) | J.Villeneuve (Williams) |
| Austrian | J.Villeneuve (Williams) | J.Villeneuve (Williams) |
| Luxembourg | J.Villeneuve (Williams) | M.Hakkinen (McLaren) |
| Japanese | M.Schumacher (Ferrari) | J.Villeneuve (Williams) |
| European | M.Hakkinen (McLaren) | J.Villeneuve (Williams) |

## Summary

| | | | |
|---|---|---|---|
| J.Villeneuve (Can) | Williams | 7 wins | 11 poles |
| M.Schumacher (Ger) | Ferrari | 5 wins | 3 poles |
| D.Coulthard (GB) | McLaren | 2 wins | 0 poles |
| H-H.Frentzen (Ger) | Williams | 1 win | 1 pole |
| G.Berger (Aust) | Benetton | 1 win | 1 pole |
| M.Hakkinen (Fin) | McLaren | 1 win | 1 pole |

## Key to Results and Tables

r = retired
dq = disqualified
dnq = did not qualify
dnf = did not finish
dns = did not start
f = fastest lap

## Round 1: Australia – Melbourne

Date: 9 March 1997
Track: 3.280 miles                      Distance: 58 laps, 190.240 miles
Conditions: Warm, sunny/cloudy      Fastest Lap: H-H. Frentzen – 1:30.585
Lap Record: H-H.Frentzen – 1:30.585, Lap 36 at 130.935 mph, 9 Mar 1997

| Pos | Driver | Car | Laps | Time/Reason | Fastest | mph |
|-----|--------|-----|------|-------------|---------|-----|
| 1 | Coulthard | McLaren | 58 | 1:30:28.718 | 1:31.412 | 126.719 |
| 2 | Schumacher, M. | Ferrari | 58 | 1:30:48.764 | 1:31.067 | 126.252 |
| 3 | Hakkinen | McLaren | 58 | 1:30:50.895 | 1:31.509 | 126:203 |
| 4 | Berger | Benetton | 58 | 1:30:51.559 | 1:31.624 | 126.188 |
| 5 | Panis | Prost | 58 | 1:31:29.026 | 1:31.762 | 125.327 |
| 6 | Larini | Sauber | 58 | 1:32:04.758 | 1:32.784 | 124.516 |
| 7 | Nakano | Prost | 56 | 1:31:11.547 | 1:34.171 | 121.392 |
| 8 | Frentzen | Williams | 55 | dnf – brakes | 1:30.585 | 126.705 |
| 9 | Trulli | Minardi | 55 | +3 laps down | 1:35.959 | 120.060 |
| 10 | Diniz | Arrows | 54 | +4 laps down | 1:34.465 | 117.066 |
| r | Barrichello | Stewart | 49 | engine | 1:33.386 | 123.382 |
| r | Salo | Tyrrell | 42 | electrics | 1:34.194 | 113.426 |
| r | Magnussen | Stewart | 36 | rear suspension | 1:35.257 | 120.653 |
| r | Katayama | Minardi | 32 | fuel pump | 1:34.918 | 121.597 |
| r | Alesi | Benetton | 24 | out of fuel | 1:31.976 | 126.093 |
| r | Fisichella | Jordan | 14 | accident | 1:34.147 | 123.222 |
| r | Verstappen | Tyrrell | 2 | accident | 1:37.038 | 113.520 |
| r | Schumacher, R. | Jordan | 1 | drive shaft | 1:48.323 | 109.494 |
| r | Irvine | Ferrari | 0 | damage | – | – |
| r | Villeneuve | Williams | 0 | accident | – | – |
| r | Herbert | Sauber | 0 | accident | – | – |
| dns | Hill | Arrows | 0 | throttle sensor | – | – |

**Starting Grid and Qualifying Times**

| 1 | Villeneuve (Can) | 1:29.369 | 2 | Frentzen (Ger) | 1:31.123 |
|---|------------------|----------|---|----------------|----------|
| 3 | Schumacher M. (Ger) | 1:31.472 | 4 | Coulthard (GB) | 1:31.531 |
| 5 | Irvine (GB) | 1:31.881 | 6 | Hakkinen (Fin) | 1:31.971 |
| 7 | Herbert (GB) | 1:32.287 | 8 | Alesi (Fra) | 1:32.593 |
| 9 | Panis (Fra) | 1:32.842 | 10 | Berger (Aut) | 1:32.870 |
| 11 | Barrichello (Bra) | 1:33.075 | 12 | Schumacher R. (Ger) | 1:33.130 |
| 13 | Larini (Ita) | 1:33.327 | 14 | Fisichella (Ita) | 1:33.552 |
| 15 | Katayama (Jap) | 1:33.798 | 16 | Nakano (Jap) | 1:33.989 |
| 17 | Trulli (Ita) | 1:34.120 | 18 | Salo (Fin) | 1:34.229 |
| 19 | Magnussen (Den) | 1:34.623 | 20 | Hill (GB) | 1:34.806 |
| 21 | Verstappen (Hol) | 1:34.943 | 22 | Diniz (Bra) | 1:35.972 |

*Drivers outside 107% rule:*

| Sospiri (Lola) | 1:40.972 | Rosset (Lola) | 1:42.086 |
|----------------|----------|---------------|----------|

28

## Round 2: Brazil – Interlagos

Date: 30 March 1997
Track: 2.660 miles
Conditions: Humid and overcast
Lap Record: J. Villeneuve – 1:18.397, Lap 28 at 122.471 mph, 30 Mar 1997

Distance: 72 laps, 191.520 miles
Fastest Lap: J. Villeneuve – 1:18.397

| Pos | Driver | Car | Laps | Time/Reason | Fastest | mph |
|-----|--------|-----|------|-------------|---------|-----|
| 1 | Villeneuve | Williams | 72 | 1:36:06.990 | 1:18.397 | 119.871 |
| 2 | Berger | Benetton | 72 | 1:36:11.180 | 1:18.509 | 119.784 |
| 3 | Panis | Prost | 72 | 1:36:22.860 | 1:19.094 | 119.542 |
| 4 | Hakkinen | McLaren | 72 | 1:36:40.023 | 1:18.618 | 119.251 |
| 5 | Schumacher, M. | Ferrari | 72 | 1:36:40.721 | 1:18.773 | 119.174 |
| 6 | Alesi | Benetton | 72 | 1:36:41.010 | 1:18.754 | 119.168 |
| 7 | Herbert | Sauber | 72 | 1:36:57.902 | 1:19.008 | 118.822 |
| 8 | Fisichella | Jordan | 72 | 1:37:07.629 | 1:18.611 | 118.624 |
| 9 | Frentzen | Williams | 72 | 1:37:22.392 | 1:18.707 | 118.138 |
| 10 | Coulthard | McLaren | 71 | 1:36:18.800 | 1:18.925 | 118.128 |
| 11 | Larini | Sauber | 71 | 1:36:17.642 | 1:18.730 | 117.988 |
| 12 | Trulli | Minardi | 71 | 1:36:54.101 | 1:20.105 | 117.248 |
| 13 | Salo | Tyrrell | 71 | 1:37:20.538 | 1:20.376 | 116.718 |
| 14 | Nakano | Prost | 71 | 1:37:25.224 | 1:19.657 | 116.624 |
| 15 | Verstappen | Tyrrell | 70 | 1:36:15.893 | 1:20.274 | 116.362 |
| 16 | Irvine | Ferrari | 70 | 1:30:20.550 | 1:19.275 | 116.268 |
| 17 | Hill | Arrows | 68 | 1:32:35.466 | 1:19.910 | 117.522 |
| 18 | Katayama | Minardi | 67 | 1:36:17.303 | 1:19.960 | 111.348 |
| r | Schumacher, R. | Jordan | 52 | electronics | 1:18.441 | 117.588 |
| r | Barrichello | Stewart | 16 | suspension | 1:20.788 | 116.329 |
| r | Diniz | Arrows | 15 | spin | 1:20.406 | 116.835 |
| dns | Magnussen | Stewart | 0 | accident | – | – |

### Starting Grid and Qualifying Times

| | | | | | |
|---|---|---|---|---|---|
| 1 | Villeneuve (Can) | 1:16.004 | 2 | Schumacher M. (Ger) | 1:16.594 |
| 3 | Berger (Aut) | 1:16.644 | 4 | Hakkinen (Fin) | 1:16.692 |
| 5 | Panis (Fra) | 1:16.756 | 6 | Alesi (Fra) | 1:16.757 |
| 7 | Fisichella (Ita) | 1:16.912 | 8 | Frentzen (Ger) | 1:16.971 |
| 9 | Hill (GB) | 1:17.000 | 10 | Schumacher R. (Ger) | 1:17.175 |
| 11 | Barrichello (Bra) | 1:17.259 | 12 | Coulthard (GB) | 1:17.262 |
| 13 | Herbert (GB) | 1:17.409 | 14 | Irvine (GB) | 1:17.527 |
| 15 | Nakano (Jap) | 1:17.999 | 16 | Diniz (Bra) | 1:18.005 |
| 17 | Trulli (Ita) | 1:18.335 | 18 | Katayama (Jap) | 1:18.357 |
| 19 | Larini (Ita) | 1:18.644 | 20 | Magnussen (Den) | 1:18.773 |
| 21 | Verstappen (Hol) | 1:18.885 | 22 | Salo (Fin) | 1:19.274 |

*Drivers outside 107% rule:*
None – all qualified

Date: 13 April 1997
Track: 2.640 miles
Conditions: Warm and sunny
Lap Record: G.Berger – 1:27.981, Lap 63 at 108.290 mph, 13 April 1997

Distance: 72 laps, 190.080 miles
Fastest Lap: G.Berger – 1:27.981

| Pos | Driver | Car | Laps | Time/Reason | Fastest | mph |
|-----|--------|-----|------|-------------|---------|-----|
| 1 | Villeneuve | Williams | 72 | 1:52:01.715 | 1:28.028 | 102.005 |
| 2 | Irvine | Ferrari | 72 | 1:52:02.694 | 1:28.473 | 101.991 |
| 3 | Schumacher, R. | Jordan | 72 | 1:52:13.804 | 1:28.382 | 101.816 |
| 4 | Herbert | Sauber | 72 | 1:52:31.634 | 1:29.296 | 101.554 |
| 5 | Hakkinen | McLaren | 72 | 1:52:32.066 | 1:29.076 | 101.547 |
| 6 | Berger | Benetton | 72 | 1:52:33.108 | 1:27.981 | 101.531 |
| 7 | Alesi | Benetton | 72 | 1:52:48.074 | 1:28.827 | 101.307 |
| 8 | Salo | Tyrrell | 71 | 1:52:58.521 | 1:29.931 | 99.745 |
| 9 | Trulli | Minardi | 71 | 1:53:28.445 | 1:30.593 | 99.307 |
| 10 | Magnussen | Stewart | 66 | 1:44:55.399 | 1:29.834 | 99.771 |
| r | Larini | Sauber | 53 | spin | 1:28.410 | 98.168 |
| r | Diniz | Arrows | 50 | engine | 1:31.111 | 97.354 |
| r | Nakano | Prost | 49 | engine | 1:29.865 | 98.667 |
| r | Verstappen | Tyrrell | 43 | engine | 1:29.541 | 97.269 |
| r | Katayama | Minardi | 37 | spin | 1:31.869 | 96.073 |
| r | Hill | Arrows | 33 | engine | 1:30.649 | 96.621 |
| r | Fisichella | Jordan | 24 | accident | 1:30.278 | 95.694 |
| r | Barrichello | Stewart | 24 | throttle | 1:29.913 | 93.780 |
| r | Panis | Prost | 16 | hydraulics | 1:29.090 | 93.676 |
| r | Frentzen | Williams | 5 | clutch | 1:31.832 | 76.632 |
| r | Schumacher, M. | Ferrari | 0 | accident | – | – |
| r | Coulthard | McLaren | 0 | accident | – | – |

**Starting Grid and Qualifying Times**

| | | | | | |
|--|--|--|--|--|--|
| 1 | Villeneuve (Can) | 1:24.473 | 2 | Frentzen (Ger) | 1:25.271 |
| 3 | Panis (Fra) | 1:25.491 | 4 | Schumacher M. (Ger) | 1:25.773 |
| 5 | Barrichello (Bra) | 1:25.942 | 6 | Schumacher R. (Ger) | 1:26.218 |
| 7 | Irvine (GB) | 1:26.327 | 8 | Herbert (GB) | 1:26.564 |
| 9 | Fisichella (Ita) | 1:26.619 | 10 | Coulthard (GB) | 1:26.799 |
| 11 | Alesi (Fra) | 1:27.076 | 12 | Berger (Aut) | 1:27.259 |
| 13 | Hill (GB) | 1:27.281 | 14 | Larini (Ita) | 1:27.690 |
| 15 | Magnussen (Den) | 1:28.035 | 16 | Verstappen (Hol) | 1:28.094 |
| 17 | Hakkinen (Fin) | 1:28.135 | 18 | Trulli (Ita) | 1:28.160 |
| 19 | Salo (Fin) | 1:28.224 | 20 | Nakano (Jap) | 1:28.366 |
| 21 | Katayama (Jap) | 1:28.413 | 22 | Diniz (Bra) | 1:28.969 |

*Drivers outside 107% rule:*
    None – all qualified

Date: 27 April 1997
Track: 3.063 miles          Distance: 62 laps, 189.906 miles
Conditions: Dry and overcast     Fastest Lap: H-H.Frentzen – 1:25.531
Lap Record: H-H.Frentzen – 1:25.531 at 128.942 mph, 27 April 1997

| Pos | Driver | Car | Laps | Time/Reason | Fastest | mph |
|-----|--------|-----|------|-------------|---------|-----|
| 1 | Frentzen | Williams | 62 | 1:31:00.673 | 1:25.531 | 125.217 |
| 2 | Schumacher, M. | Ferrari | 62 | 1:31:01.910 | 1:25.537 | 125.189 |
| 3 | Irvine | Ferrari | 62 | 1:32:19.016 | 1:26.811 | 123.446 |
| 4 | Fisichella | Jordan | 62 | 1:32:24.061 | 1:26.620 | 123.334 |
| 5 | Alesi | Benetton | 61 | 1:31:18.063 | 1:27.091 | 122.806 |
| 6 | Hakkinen | McLaren | 61 | 1:31:18.536 | 1:26.791 | 122.806 |
| 7 | Larini | Sauber | 61 | 1:31:39.396 | 1:26.753 | 122.796 |
| 8 | Panis | Prost | 61 | 1:31:56.734 | 1:28.064 | 122.330 |
| 9 | Salo | Tyrrell | 60 | 1:31:05.134 | 1:28.189 | 121.946 |
| 10 | Verstappen | Tyrrell | 60 | 1:31:11.741 | 1:28.886 | 121.663 |
| 11 | Katayama | Minardi | 59 | 1:31:53.912 | 1:29.554 | 120.933 |
| r | Diniz | Arrows | 53 | exhaust | 1:27.793 | 118.008 |
| r | Villeneuve | Williams | 40 | gearbox | 1:25.997 | 120.603 |
| r | Coulthard | McLaren | 38 | engine | 1:26.067 | 123.689 |
| r | Barrichello | Stewart | 32 | engine | 1:27.741 | 122.840 |
| r | Herbert | Sauber | 18 | electrics | 1:27.594 | 121.958 |
| r | Schumacher, R. | Jordan | 17 | drive shaft | 1:27.217 | 122.456 |
| r | Nakano | Prost | 11 | accident | 1:30.554 | 122.459 |
| r | Hill | Arrows | 11 | accident | 1:29.237 | 116.571 |
| r | Berger | Benetton | 4 | spin | 1:33.513 | 116.534 |
| r | Magnussen | Stewart | 2 | spin | 1:36.710 | 110.444 |
| r | Trulli | Minardi | 0 | hydraulics | – | 106.233 |

**Starting Grid and Qualifying Times**

| 1 | Villeneuve (Can) | 1:23.303 | 2 | Frentzen (Ger) | 1:23.646 |
|---|---|---|---|---|---|
| 3 | Schumacher M. (Ger) | 1:23.955 | 4 | Panis (Fra) | 1:24.075 |
| 5 | Schumacher R. (Ger) | 1:24.081 | 6 | Fisichella (Ita) | 1:24.598 |
| 7 | Herbert (GB) | 1:24.723 | 8 | Hakkinen (Fin) | 1:24.812 |
| 9 | Irvine (GB) | 1:24.861 | 10 | Coulthard (GB) | 1:25.077 |
| 11 | Berger (Aut) | 1:25.371 | 12 | Larini (Ita) | 1:25.544 |
| 13 | Barrichello (Bra) | 1:25.579 | 14 | Alesi (Fra) | 1:25.729 |
| 15 | Hill (GB) | 1:25.743 | 16 | Magnussen (Den) | 1:26.192 |
| 17 | Diniz (Bra) | 1:26.253 | 18 | Nakano (Jap) | 1:26.712 |
| 19 | Salo (Fin) | 1:26.852 | 20 | Trulli (Ita) | 1:26.960 |
| 21 | Verstappen (Hol) | 1:27.428 | 22 | Katayama (Jap) | 1:28.727 |

*Drivers outside 107% rule:*
    None – all qualified

## Round 5: Monaco – Monte Carlo

Date: 11 May 1997
Track: 2.092 miles
Conditions: Raining
Lap Record: M. Schumacher – 1:53.315 at 66.450 mph, 11 May 1997

Distance: 62 laps, 129.704 miles
Fastest Lap: M. Schumacher – 1:53.315

| Pos | Driver | Car | Laps | Time/Reason | Fastest | mph |
|-----|--------|-----|------|-------------|---------|-----|
| 1 | Schumacher, M. | Ferrari | 62 | 2:00:05.654 | 1:53.315 | 64.789 |
| 2 | Barrichello | Stewart | 62 | 2:00:58.960 | 1:53.495 | 64.313 |
| 3 | Irvine | Ferrari | 62 | 2:01:27.762 | 1:54.202 | 64.059 |
| 4 | Panis | Prost | 62 | 2:01:50.056 | 1:55.309 | 63.864 |
| 5 | Salo | Tyrrell | 61 | 2:00:18.245 | 1:54.968 | 63.663 |
| 6 | Fisichella | Jordan | 61 | 2:00:25.006 | 1:54.806 | 63.571 |
| 7 | Magnussen | Stewart | 61 | 2:01:52.517 | 1:55.303 | 62.812 |
| 8 | Verstappen | Tyrrell | 60 | 2:00:20.197 | 1:55.045 | 62.573 |
| 9 | Berger | Benetton | 60 | 2:00:44.161 | 1:55.841 | 62.366 |
| 10 | Katayama | Minardi | 60 | 2:01:49.612 | 1:56.101 | 61.807 |
| r | Frentzen | Williams | 39 | accident | 1:53.504 | 62.675 |
| r | Nakano | Prost | 36 | accident | 1:56.906 | 62.383 |
| r | Larini | Sauber | 24 | accident | 1:56.940 | 57.296 |
| r | Alesi | Benetton | 16 | spin | 1:55.451 | 62.811 |
| r | Villeneuve | Williams | 16 | damage | 1:55.218 | 61.295 |
| r | Schumacher, R. | Jordan | 10 | accident | 1:53.430 | 63.771 |
| r | Herbert | Sauber | 9 | accident | 1:55.840 | 63.106 |
| r | Trulli | Minardi | 7 | accident | 2:00.038 | 59.046 |
| r | Coulthard | McLaren | 1 | accident | 2:11.201 | 57.391 |
| r | Hakkinen | McLaren | 1 | accident | 2:15.786 | 55.453 |
| r | Hill | Arrows | 1 | accident | 2:17.648 | 54.703 |
| r | Diniz | Arrows | 0 | spin | – | – |

### Starting Grid and Qualifying Times

| 1 | Frentzen (Ger) | 1:18.216 | 2 | Schumacher M. (Ger) | 1:18.943 |
|---|----------------|----------|---|---------------------|----------|
| 3 | Villeneuve (Can) | 1:18.583 | 4 | Fisichella (Ita) | 1:18.665 |
| 5 | Coulthard (GB) | 1:18.779 | 6 | Schumacher R. (Ger) | 1:18.943 |
| 7 | Herbert (GB) | 1:19.105 | 8 | Hakkinen (Fin) | 1:19.119 |
| 9 | Alesi (Fra) | 1:19.263 | 10 | Barrichello (Bra) | 1:19.295 |
| 11 | Larini (Ita) | 1:19.468 | 12 | Panis (Fra) | 1:19.626 |
| 13 | Hill (GB) | 1:19.674 | 14 | Salo (Fin) | 1:19.694 |
| 15 | Irvine (GB) | 1:19.723 | 16 | Diniz (Bra) | 1:19.860 |
| 17 | Berger (Aut) | 1:20.199 | 18 | Trulli (Ita) | 1:20.349 |
| 19 | Magnussen (Den) | 1:20.516 | 20 | Katayama (Jap) | 1:20.606 |
| 21 | Nakano (Jap) | 1:20.961 | 22 | Verstappen (Hol) | 1:21.290 |

*Drivers outside 107% rule:*
    None – all qualified

Date: 25 May 1997
Track: 2.938 miles
Conditions: Dry and overcast
Distance: 64 laps, 188.032 miles
Fastest Lap: G. Fisichella – 1:22.242
Lap Record: G. Fisichella – 1:22.242 at 128.604 mph, 25 May 1997

| Pos | Driver | Car | Laps | Time/Reason | Fastest | mph |
|-----|--------|-----|------|-------------|---------|-----|
| 1 | Villeneuve | Williams | 64 | 1:30:35.896 | 1:22.534 | 124.475 |
| 2 | Panis | Prost | 64 | 1:30:41.700 | 1:22.422 | 124.342 |
| 3 | Alesi | Benetton | 64 | 1:30:48.430 | 1:23.096 | 124.189 |
| 4 | Schumacher, M. | Ferrari | 64 | 1:30:53.975 | 1:22.295 | 124.064 |
| 5 | Herbert | Sauber | 64 | 1:31:03.882 | 1:23.178 | 123.837 |
| 6 | Coulthard | McLaren | 64 | 1:31:05.640 | 1:22.340 | 123.798 |
| 7 | Hakkinen | McLaren | 64 | 1:31:24.681 | 1:23.241 | 123.368 |
| 8 | Frentzen | Williams | 64 | 1:31:40.035 | 1:22.841 | 123.023 |
| 9 | Fisichella | Jordan | 64 | 1:31:40.663 | 1:22.242 | 123.009 |
| 10 | Berger | Benetton | 64 | 1:31:41.568 | 1:23.106 | 122.989 |
| 11 | Verstappen | Tyrrell | 63 | 1:31:03.478 | 1:24.517 | 121.911 |
| 12 | Irvine | Ferrari | 63 | 1:31:25.313 | 1:22.839 | 121.425 |
| 13 | Magnussen | Stewart | 63 | 1:31:58.723 | 1:25.300 | 120.690 |
| 14 | Morbidelli | Sauber | 62 | 1:30:50.087 | 1:24.647 | 120.269 |
| 15 | Trulli | Minardi | 62 | 1:30:59.358 | 1:24.213 | 120.066 |
| r | Diniz | Arrows | 53 | engine | 1:23.716 | 121.586 |
| r | Schumacher, R. | Jordan | 50 | engine | 1:22.784 | 121.682 |
| r | Barrichello | Stewart | 37 | engine | 1:23.564 | 122.056 |
| r | Salo | Tyrrell | 35 | puncture | 1:24.775 | 119.577 |
| r | Nakano | Prost | 34 | gearbox | 1:23.516 | 121.242 |
| r | Hill | Arrows | 18 | engine | 1:23.761 | 119.707 |
| r | Katayama | Minardi | 11 | hydraulic pump | 1:26.273 | 118.003 |

**Starting Grid and Qualifying Times**

| | | | | | |
|---|---|---|---|---|---|
| 1 | Villeneuve (Can) | 1:16.525 | 2 | Frentzen (Ger) | 1:16.791 |
| 3 | Coulthard (GB) | 1:17.521 | 4 | Alesi (Fra) | 1:17.717 |
| 5 | Hakkinen (Fin) | 1:17.737 | 6 | Berger (Aut) | 1:18.041 |
| 7 | Schumacher M. (Ger) | 1:18.313 | 8 | Fisichella (Ita) | 1:18.385 |
| 9 | Schumacher R. (Ger) | 1:18.423 | 10 | Herbert (GB) | 1:18.494 |
| 11 | Irvine (GB) | 1:18.873 | 12 | Panis (Fra) | 1:19.157 |
| 13 | Morbidelli (Ita) | 1:19.323 | 14 | Salo (Fin) | 1:20.079 |
| 15 | Hill (GB) | 1:20.089 | 16 | Nakano (Jap) | 1:20.103 |
| 17 | Barrichello (Bra) | 1:20.255 | 18 | Trulli (Ita) | 1:20.452 |
| 19 | Verstappen (Hol) | 1:20.502 | 20 | Katayama (Jap) | 1:20.672 |
| 21 | Diniz (Bra) | 1:21.029 | 22 | Magnussen (Den) | 1:21.060 |

*Drivers outside 107% rule:*
    None – all qualified

Date: 15 June 1997
Track: 2.747 miles                     Distance: 54 laps, 148.338 miles
Conditions: Sunny                      Fastest Lap: D. Coulthard – 1:19.635
Lap Record: D. Coulthard – 1:19.635 at 124.190 mph, 15 June 1997

| Pos | Driver | Car | Laps | Time/Reason | Fastest | mph |
|-----|--------|-----|------|-------------|---------|-----|
| 1 | Schumacher, M. | Ferrari | 54 | 1:17:40.646 | 1:20.171 | 114.588 |
| 2 | Alesi | Benetton | 54 | 1:17:43.211 | 1:20.679 | 114.525 |
| 3 | Fisichella | Jordan | 54 | 1:17:43.865 | 1:21.013 | 114.509 |
| 4 | Frentzen | Williams | 54 | 1:17:44.414 | 1:19.997 | 114.496 |
| 5 | Herbert | Sauber | 54 | 1:17:45.362 | 1:20.709 | 114.472 |
| 6 | Nakano | Prost | 54 | 1:18:17.347 | 1:22.077 | 113.693 |
| 7 | Coulthard | McLaren | 54 | 1:18:18.399 | 1:19.635 | 113.667 |
| 8 | Diniz | Arrows | 53 | 1:17:41.197 | 1:22.434 | 112.452 |
| 9 | Hill | Arrows | 53 | 1:17:42.581 | 1:22.435 | 112.419 |
| 10 | Morbidelli | Sauber | 53 | 1:17:46.091 | 1:22.659 | 112.335 |
| 11 | Panis | Prost | 51 | 1:13:27.233 | 1:20.945 | 114.445 |
| r | Salo | Tyrrell | 46 | engine | 1:21.622 | 113.594 |
| r | Verstappen | Tyrrell | 42 | gearbox | 1:21.902 | 113.839 |
| r | Wurz | Benetton | 35 | transmission | 1:21.048 | 113.817 |
| r | Barrichello | Stewart | 33 | gearbox | 1:22.366 | 110.951 |
| r | Trulli | Minardi | 32 | engine | 1:22.712 | 112.204 |
| r | Schumacher, R. | Jordan | 14 | accident | 1:22.372 | 106.680 |
| r | Katayama | Minardi | 5 | accident | 1:24.294 | 111.041 |
| r | Villeneuve | Williams | 1 | accident | 1:28.356 | 111.932 |
| r | Irvine | Ferrari | 0 | damage | – | – |
| r | Hakkinen | McLaren | 0 | accident | – | – |
| r | Magnussen | Stewart | 0 | accident | – | – |

**Starting Grid and Qualifying Times**

| | | | | | |
|---|---|---|---|---|---|
| 1 | Schumacher M. (Ger) | 1:18.095 | 2 | Villeneuve (Can) | 1:18.108 |
| 3 | Barrichello (Bra) | 1:18.388 | 4 | Frentzen (Ger) | 1:18.464 |
| 5 | Coulthard (GB) | 1:18.466 | 6 | Fisichella (Ita) | 1:18.750 |
| 7 | Schumacher R. (Ger) | 1:18.869 | 8 | Alesi (Fra) | 1:18.899 |
| 9 | Hakkinen (Fin) | 1:18.916 | 10 | Panis (Fra) | 1:19.034 |
| 11 | Wurz (Aut) | 1:19.268 | 12 | Irvine (GB) | 1:19.503 |
| 13 | Herbert (GB) | 1:19.622 | 14 | Verstappen (Hol) | 1:20.102 |
| 15 | Hill (GB) | 1:20.129 | 16 | Diniz (Bra) | 1:20.175 |
| 17 | Salo (Fin) | 1:20.336 | 18 | Morbidelli (Ita) | 1:20.357 |
| 19 | Nakano (Jap) | 1:20.370 | 20 | Trulli (Ita) | 1:20.370 |
| 21 | Magnussen (Den) | 1:20.491 | 22 | Katayama (Jap) | 1:21.034 |

*Drivers outside 107% rule:*
    None – all qualified

Date: 29 June 1997
Track: 2.640 miles
Conditions: Dry becoming wet
Distance: 72 laps, 190.080 miles
Fastest Lap: M. Schumacher – 1:17.910
Lap Record: M. Schumacher – 1:17.910 at 122.030 mph, 29 June 1997

| Pos | Driver | Car | Laps | Time/Reason | Fastest | mph |
|---|---|---|---|---|---|---|
| 1 | Schumacher, M. | Ferrari | 72 | 1:38:50.492 | 1:17.910 | 115.356 |
| 2 | Frentzen | Williams | 72 | 1:39:14.029 | 1:18.136 | 114.899 |
| 3 | Irvine | Ferrari | 72 | 1:40:05.293 | 1:19.029 | 113.937 |
| 4 | Villeneuve | Williams | 72 | 1:40:12.276 | 1:18.649 | 113.786 |
| 5 | Alesi | Benetton | 72 | 1:40:13.227 | 1:19.055 | 113.768 |
| 6 | Schumacher, R. | Jordan | 72 | 1:40:20.363 | 1:19.225 | 113.633 |
| 7 | Coulthard | McLaren | 71 | 1:38:40.563 | 1:19.317 | 114.254 |
| 8 | Herbert | Sauber | 71 | 1:39:35.888 | 1:20.885 | 112.880 |
| 9 | Fisichella | Jordan | 71 | 1:40:16.244 | 1:19.225 | 112.131 |
| 10 | Trulli | Prost | 70 | 1:39:26.483 | 1:19.417 | 111.472 |
| 11 | Katayama | Minardi | 70 | 1:40:01.973 | 1:20.534 | 110.813 |
| 12 | Hill | Arrows | 69 | 1:39:10.579 | 1:20.434 | 110.172 |
| r | Salo | Tyrrell | 61 | electrics | 1:20.385 | 113.793 |
| r | Wurz | Benetton | 60 | spin | 1:18.684 | 116.571 |
| r | Diniz | Arrows | 58 | spin | 1:20.557 | 112.866 |
| r | Fontana | Sauber | 40 | spin | 1:19.849 | 109.847 |
| r | Barrichello | Stewart | 36 | engine | 1:18.781 | 115.293 |
| r | Magnussen | Stewart | 33 | brake duct | 1:19.912 | 114.273 |
| r | Hakkinen | McLaren | 18 | engine | 1:20.153 | 117.219 |
| r | Verstappen | Tyrrell | 15 | stuck throttle | 1:22.034 | 113.607 |
| r | Nakano | Prost | 7 | spin | 1:20.662 | 113.606 |
| r | Marques | Minardi | 5 | engine | 1:22.325 | 109.880 |

## Starting Grid and Qualifying Times

| | | | | | |
|---|---|---|---|---|---|
| 1 | Schumacher M. (Ger) | 1:14.548 | 2 | Frentzen (Ger) | 1:14.749 |
| 3 | Schumacher R. (Ger) | 1:14.755 | 4 | Villeneuve (Can) | 1:14.800 |
| 5 | Irvine (GB) | 1:14.860 | 6 | Trulli (Ita) | 1:14.957 |
| 7 | Wurz (Aut) | 1:14.986 | 8 | Alesi (Fra) | 1:15.228 |
| 9 | Coulthard (GB) | 1:15.270 | 10 | Hakkinen (Fin) | 1:15.339 |
| 11 | Fisichella (Ita) | 1:15.453 | 12 | Nakano (Jap) | 1:15.857 |
| 13 | Barrichello (Bra) | 1:15.876 | 14 | Herbert (GB) | 1:16.018 |
| 15 | Magnussen (Den) | 1:16.149 | 16 | Diniz (Bra) | 1:16.536 |
| 17 | Hill (GB) | 1:16.729 | 18 | Verstappen (Hol) | 1:16.941 |
| 19 | Salo (Fin) | 1:17.256 | 20 | Fontana (Arg) | 1:17.538 |
| 21 | Katayama (Jap) | 1:17.563 | 22 | Marques (Bra) | 1:18.280 |

*Drivers outside 107% rule:*
None – all qualified

Date: 13 July 1997
Track: 3.194 miles      Distance: 59 laps, 188.446 miles
Conditions: Sunny      Fastest Lap: M. Schumacher – 1:24.475
Lap Record: M. Schumacher – 1:24.475 at 136.115 mph, 13 July 1997

| Pos | Driver | Car | Laps | Time/Reason | Fastest | mph |
|-----|--------|-----|------|-------------|---------|-----|
| 1 | Villeneuve | Williams | 59 | 1:28:01.665 | 1:25.082 | 128.445 |
| 2 | Alesi | Benetton | 59 | 1:28:11.870 | 1:26.260 | 128.197 |
| 3 | Wurz | Benetton | 59 | 1:28:12.961 | 1:26.429 | 128.170 |
| 4 | Coulthard | McLaren | 59 | 1:28:32.894 | 1:26.475 | 127.690 |
| 5 | Schumacher, R. | Jordan | 59 | 1:28:33.545 | 1:25.872 | 127.674 |
| 6 | Hill | Arrows | 59 | 1:29:15.217 | 1:26.471 | 126.681 |
| 7 | Fisichella | Jordan | 58 | 1:28:05.716 | 1:26.119 | 126.170 |
| 8 | Trulli | Prost | 58 | 1:28:14.818 | 1:26.610 | 125.954 |
| 9 | Fontana | Sauber | 58 | 1:28:49.184 | 1:27.783 | 125.141 |
| 10 | Marques | Minardi | 58 | 1:29:28.078 | 1:29.100 | 124.235 |
| 11 | Nakano | Prost | 57 | 1:26:13.219 | 1:26.778 | 126.692 |
| r | Hakkinen | McLaren | 52 | engine | 1:25.988 | 128.060 |
| r | Magnussen | Stewart | 50 | engine | 1:27.586 | 124.478 |
| r | Verstappen | Tyrrell | 45 | engine | 1:29.137 | 123.360 |
| r | Irvine | Ferrari | 44 | transmission | 1:25.236 | 127.537 |
| r | Salo | Tyrrell | 44 | engine | 1:28.053 | 124.223 |
| r | Herbert | Sauber | 42 | electronics | 1:26.232 | 122.530 |
| r | Schumacher, M. | Ferrari | 38 | wheel bearings | 1:24.475 | 125.634 |
| r | Barrichello | Stewart | 37 | engine | 1:27.877 | 124.452 |
| r | Diniz | Arrows | 29 | engine | 1:27.111 | 123.114 |
| r | Frentzen | Williams | 0 | accident | – | – |
| r | Katayama | Minardi | 0 | accident | – | – |

**Starting Grid and Qualifying Times**

| | | | | |
|---|---|---|---|---|
| 1 | Villeneuve (Can) | 1:21.598 | 2 | Frentzen (Ger) | 1:21.732 |
| 3 | Hakkinen (Fin) | 1:21.797 | 4 | Schumacher M. (Ger) | 1:21.977 |
| 5 | Schumacher R. (Ger) | 1:22.277 | 6 | Coulthard (GB) | 1:22.279 |
| 7 | Irvine (GB) | 1:22.342 | 8 | Wurz (Aut) | 1:22.344 |
| 9 | Herbert (GB) | 1:22.368 | 10 | Fisichella (Ita) | 1:22.371 |
| 11 | Alesi (Fra) | 1:22.392 | 12 | Hill (GB) | 1:23.271 |
| 13 | Trulli (Ita) | 1:23.366 | 14 | Nakano (Jap) | 1:23.887 |
| 15 | Magnussen (Den) | 1:24.067 | 16 | Diniz (Bra) | 1:24.239 |
| 17 | Salo (Fin) | 1:24.478 | 18 | Katayama (Jap) | 1:24.553 |
| 19 | Verstappen (Hol) | 1:25.010 | 20 | Marques (Bra) | 1:25.154 |
| 21 | Barrichello (Bra) | 1:25.525 | 22 | Fontana (Arg) Time disallowed |

*Drivers outside 107% rule:*
   None – all qualified

Date: 27 July 1997
Track: 4.239 miles
Conditions: Hot and dry
Distance: 45 laps, 190.755 miles
Fastest Lap: G. Berger – 1:45.747
Lap Record: G. Berger – 1:45.747 at 144.337 mph, 27 July 1997

| Pos | Driver | Car | Laps | Time/Reason | Fastest | mph |
|---|---|---|---|---|---|---|
| 1 | Berger | Benetton | 45 | 1:20:59.046 | 1:45.747 | 141.354 |
| 2 | Schumacher, M. | Ferrari | 45 | 1:21:16.573 | 1:46.603 | 140.846 |
| 3 | Hakkinen | McLaren | 45 | 1:21:23.816 | 1:46.831 | 140.637 |
| 4 | Trulli | Prost | 45 | 1:21:26.211 | 1:46.733 | 139.947 |
| 5 | Schumacher, R. | Jordan | 45 | 1:21:29.041 | 1:46.127 | 140.487 |
| 6 | Alesi | Benetton | 45 | 1:21:33.763 | 1:45.917 | 140.351 |
| 7 | Nakano | Prost | 45 | 1:22:18.768 | 1:47.939 | 139.073 |
| 8 | Hill | Arrows | 44 | 1:21:09.273 | 1:46.560 | 137.922 |
| 9 | Fontana | Sauber | 44 | 1:21:18.849 | 1:47.908 | 137.652 |
| 10 | Verstappen | Tyrrell | 44 | 1:22:05.839 | 1:50.159 | 136.338 |
| 11 | Fisichella | Jordan | 40 | 1:22:51.576 | 1:46.274 | 139.659 |
| r | Villeneuve | Williams | 33 | spin | 1:47.044 | 140.287 |
| r | Barrichello | Stewart | 33 | engine | 1:47.074 | 139.131 |
| r | Salo | Tyrrell | 33 | clutch | 1:49.611 | 136.212 |
| r | Magnussen | Stewart | 27 | engine | 1:48.189 | 137.860 |
| r | Katayama | Minardi | 23 | out of fuel | 1:50.161 | 137.162 |
| r | Herbert | Sauber | 8 | accident | 1:49.184 | 137.372 |
| r | Diniz | Arrows | 8 | accident | 1:48.836 | 137.343 |
| r | Coulthard | McLaren | 1 | accident | 2:22.236 | 107.241 |
| r | Frentzen | Williams | 1 | damage | 3:13.699 | 78.799 |
| r | Irvine | Ferrari | 1 | damage | 3:16.256 | 77.771 |
| r | Marques | Minardi | 0 | transmission | – | – |

## Starting Grid and Qualifying Times

| | | | | | |
|---|---|---|---|---|---|
| 1 | Berger (Aut) | 1:41.873 | 2 | Fisichella (Ita) | 1:41.896 |
| 3 | Hakkinen (Fin) | 1:42.034 | 4 | Schumacher M. (Ger) | 1:42.181 |
| 5 | Frentzen (Ger) | 1:42.421 | 6 | Alesi (Fra) | 1:42.493 |
| 7 | Schumacher R. (Ger) | 1:42.498 | 8 | Coulthard (GB) | 1:42.687 |
| 9 | Villeneuve (Can) | 1:42.967 | 10 | Irvine (GB) | 1:43.209 |
| 11 | Trulli (Ita) | 1:43.226 | 12 | Barrichello (Bra) | 1:43.272 |
| 13 | Hill (GB) | 1:43.361 | 14 | Herbert (GB) | 1:43.660 |
| 15 | Magnussen (Den) | 1:43.927 | 16 | Diniz (Bra) | 1:44.069 |
| 17 | Nakano (Jap) | 1:44.112 | 18 | Fontana (Arg) | 1:44.552 |
| 19 | Salo (Fin) | 1:45.372 | 20 | Verstappen (Hol) | 1:45.811 |
| 21 | Marques (Bra) | 1:45.942 | 22 | Katayama (Jap) | 1:46.499 |

*Drivers outside 107% rule:*
    None – all qualified

Date: 10 August 1997
Track: 2.465 miles
Conditions: Hot and sunny
Distance: 77 laps, 189.805 miles
Fastest Lap: H-H. Frentzen – 1:18.372
Lap Record: H-H. Frentzen – 1:18.372 at 113.261 mph, 10 August 1997

| Pos | Driver | Car | Laps | Time/Reason | Fastest | mph |
|-----|--------|-----|------|-------------|---------|-----|
| 1 | Villeneuve | Williams | 77 | 1:45:47.149 | 1:19.066 | 107.685 |
| 2 | Hill | Arrows | 77 | 1:45:56.228 | 1:19.648 | 107.531 |
| 3 | Herbert | Sauber | 77 | 1:46:07.594 | 1:20.606 | 107.339 |
| 4 | Schumacher, M. | Ferrari | 77 | 1:46:17.650 | 1:19.684 | 107.170 |
| 5 | Schumacher, R. | Jordan | 77 | 1:46:17.864 | 1:19.651 | 107.166 |
| 6 | Nakano | Prost | 77 | 1:46:28.661 | 1:20.003 | 106.985 |
| 7 | Trulli | Prost | 77 | 1:47:02.701 | 1:21.074 | 106.418 |
| 8 | Berger | Benetton | 77 | 1:47:03.558 | 1:19.923 | 106.404 |
| 9 | Irvine | Ferrari | 76 | 1:44:51.833 | 1:19.527 | 107.221 |
| 10 | Katayama | Minardi | 76 | 1:45:48.747 | 1:20.672 | 106.260 |
| 11 | Alesi | Benetton | 76 | 1:45:56.522 | 1:20.573 | 106.130 |
| 12 | Marques | Minardi | 75 | 1:46:19.969 | 1:21.874 | 104.348 |
| 13 | Salo | Tyrrell | 75 | 1:46:20.754 | 1:21.578 | 104.335 |
| r | Coulthard | McLaren | 65 | electrics | 1:20.329 | 107.751 |
| r | Verstappen | Tyrrell | 61 | gearbox | 1:21.676 | 104.422 |
| r | Diniz | Arrows | 53 | electrics | 1:20.317 | 105.870 |
| r | Fisichella | Jordan | 42 | spin | 1:19.366 | 107.351 |
| r | Frentzen | Williams | 29 | fuel filter | 1:18.372 | 109.380 |
| r | Barrichello | Stewart | 29 | engine | 1:21.409 | 106.264 |
| r | Hakkinen | McLaren | 12 | hydraulics | 1:20.161 | 108.030 |
| r | Morbidelli | Sauber | 7 | engine | 1:21.167 | 102.206 |
| r | Magnussen | Stewart | 5 | steering | 1:21.628 | 90.624 |

**Starting Grid and Qualifying Times**

| | | | | | | |
|---|---|---|---|---|---|---|
| 1 | Schumacher M. (Ger) | 1:14.672 | | 2 | Villeneuve (Can) | 1:14.859 |
| 3 | Hill (GB) | 1:15.044 | | 4 | Hakkinen (Fin) | 1:15.140 |
| 5 | Irvine (GB) | 1:15.424 | | 6 | Frentzen (Ger) | 1:15.520 |
| 7 | Berger (Aut) | 1:15.699 | | 8 | Coulthard (GB) | 1:15.705 |
| 9 | Alesi (Fra) | 1:15.905 | | 10 | Herbert (GB) | 1:16.138 |
| 11 | Barrichello (Bra) | 1:16.138 | | 12 | Trulli (Ita) | 1:16.297 |
| 13 | Fisichella (Ita) | 1:16.300 | | 14 | Schumacher R. (Ger) | 1:16.686 |
| 15 | Morbidelli (Ita) | 1:16.766 | | 16 | Nakano (Jap) | 1:16.784 |
| 17 | Magnussen (Den) | 1:16.858 | | 18 | Verstappen (Hol) | 1:17.095 |
| 19 | Diniz (Bra) | 1:17.118 | | 20 | Katayama (Jap) | 1:17.232 |
| 21 | Salo (Fin) | 1:17.482 | | 22 | Marques (Bra) | 1.18.020 |

*Drivers outside 107% rule:*
    None – all qualified

Date: 24 August 1997
Track: 4.330 miles
Conditions: Wet but drying
Distance: 44 laps, 190.520 miles
Fastest Lap: J. Villeneuve – 1:52.692
Lap Record: J. Villeneuve – 1:52.692 at 138.321 mph, 24 August 1997

| Pos | Driver | Car | Laps | Time/Reason | Fastest | mph |
|---|---|---|---|---|---|---|
| 1 | Schumacher, M. | Ferrari | 44 | 1:33:46.717 | 1:55.340 | 121.886 |
| 2 | Fisichella | Jordan | 44 | 1:34:13.470 | 1:54.688 | 121.310 |
| 3 | Frentzen | Williams | 44 | 1:34:18.864 | 1:53.674 | 121.194 |
| 4 | Herbert | Sauber | 44 | 1:34:25.742 | 1:53.615 | 121.047 |
| 5 | Villeneuve | Williams | 44 | 1:34:28.820 | 1:52.692 | 120.981 |
| 6 | Berger | Benetton | 44 | 1:34:50.458 | 1:53.649 | 120.521 |
| 7 | Diniz | Arrows | 44 | 1:35:12.648 | 1:53.652 | 120.053 |
| 8 | Alesi | Benetton | 44 | 1:35:28.725 | 1:55.348 | 119.716 |
| 9 | Morbidelli | Sauber | 44 | 1.35:29.299 | 1:54.818 | 119.704 |
| 10 | Irvine | Ferrari | 43 | 1:33:07.860 | 1:55.290 | 119.945 |
| 11 | Salo | Tyrrell | 43 | 1:33:47.540 | 1:56.919 | 119.099 |
| 12 | Magnussen | Stewart | 43 | 1:33:58.760 | 1:55.726 | 118.862 |
| 13 | Hill | Arrows | 42 | 1:32:22.015 | 1:54.074 | 118.124 |
| 14 | Katayama | Minardi | 42 | 1:33:10.021 | 1:55.413 | 117.110 |
| 15 | Trulli | Prost | 42 | 1:35:02.667 | 1:55.152 | 114.796 |
| r | Verstappen | Tyrrell | 25 | spin | 1:59.409 | 112.240 |
| r | Schumacher, R. | Jordan | 21 | spin | 1:57.784 | 188.371 |
| r | Coulthard | McLaren | 19 | spin | 1:59.169 | 108.856 |
| r | Marques | Minardi | 18 | spin | 2:02.753 | 105.713 |
| r | Barrichello | Stewart | 8 | steering arm | 2:16.804 | 93.988 |
| r | Nakano | Prost | 5 | electronics | 2:19.161 | 85.413 |
| dq | Hakkinen * | McLaren | 44 | 1:34:17.573 | 1:54.175 | 121.222 |

## Starting Grid and Qualifying Times

| | | | | | | |
|---|---|---|---|---|---|---|
| 1 | Villeneuve (Can) | 1:49.450 | | 2 | Alesi (Fra) | 1:49.759 |
| 3 | Schumacher M. (Ger) | 1:50.293 | | 4 | Fisichella (Ita) | 1:50.470 |
| 5 | Hakkinen (Fin) * | 1:50.503 | | 6 | Schumacher R. (Ger) | 1:50.520 |
| 7 | Frentzen (Ger) | 1:50.656 | | 8 | Diniz (Bra) | 1:50.853 |
| 9 | Hill (GB) | 1:50.970 | | 10 | Coulthard (GB) | 1:51.410 |
| 11 | Herbert (GB) | 1:51.725 | | 12 | Barrichello (Bra) | 1:51.916 |
| 13 | Morbidelli (Ita) | 1:52.094 | | 14 | Trulli (Ita) | 1:52.274 |
| 15 | Berger (Aut) | 1:52.391 | | 16 | Nakano (Jap) | 1:52.749 |
| 17 | Irvine (GB) | 1:52.793 | | 18 | Magnussen (Den) | 1:52.886 |
| 19 | Salo (Fin) | 1:52.897 | | 20 | Katayama (Jap) | 1:53.544 |
| 21 | Verstappen (Hol) | 1:53.725 | | 22 | Marques (Bra) | 1:54.505 |

*Drivers outside 107% rule:* None – all qualified

*Hakkinen disqualified from 3rd and started from back of grid – illegal fuel*

Date: 7 September 1997
Track: 3.585 miles          Distance: 53 laps, 190.005 miles
Conditions: Warm and dry          Fastest Lap: M. Hakkinen – 1:24.808
Lap Record: M. Hakkinen – 1:24.808 at 152.198 mph, 7 September 1997

| Pos | Driver | Car | Laps | Time/Reason | Fastest | mph |
|---|---|---|---|---|---|---|
| 1 | Coulthard | McLaren | 53 | 1:17:04.609 | 1:25.976 | 147.915 |
| 2 | Alesi | Benetton | 53 | 1:17:06.546 | 1:26.067 | 147.853 |
| 3 | Frentzen | Williams | 53 | 1:17:08.952 | 1:25.600 | 147.776 |
| 4 | Fisichella | Jordan | 53 | 1:17:10.480 | 1:25.960 | 147.727 |
| 5 | Villeneuve | Williams | 53 | 1:17:11.025 | 1:25.715 | 147.710 |
| 6 | Schumacher, M. | Ferrari | 53 | 1:17:16.090 | 1:25.863 | 147.549 |
| 7 | Berger | Benetton | 53 | 1:17:17.080 | 1:25.653 | 147.517 |
| 8 | Irvine | Ferrari | 53 | 1:17:22.248 | 1:24.655 | 147.353 |
| 9 | Hakkinen | McLaren | 53 | 1:17:53.982 | 1:24.808 | 146.353 |
| 10 | Trulli | Prost | 53 | 1:18:07.315 | 1:26.718 | 145.937 |
| 11 | Nakano | Prost | 53 | 1:18:07.936 | 1:26.383 | 145.917 |
| 12 | Morbidelli | Sauber | 52 | 1:17:14.938 | 1:27.257 | 144.801 |
| 13 | Barrichello | Stewart | 52 | 1:17:55.672 | 1:27.571 | 143.539 |
| 14 | Marques | Minardi | 50 | 1:17:35.247 | 1:29.116 | 138.623 |
| r | Hill | Arrows | 46 | engine | 1:27.081 | 145.726 |
| r | Schumacher, R. | Jordan | 39 | damage | 1:25.909 | 141.778 |
| r | Herbert | Sauber | 38 | accident | 1:26.572 | 145.953 |
| r | Salo | Tyrrell | 33 | engine | 1:28.004 | 143.928 |
| r | Magnussen | Stewart | 31 | transmission | 1:27.447 | 144.600 |
| r | Verstappen | Tyrrell | 12 | hydraulics | 1:28.227 | 142.198 |
| r | Katayama | Minardi | 8 | puncture | 1:29.133 | 139.649 |
| r | Diniz | Arrows | 4 | suspension | 1:28.569 | 137.354 |

**Starting Grid and Qualifying Times**

| | | | | | |
|---|---|---|---|---|---|
| 1 | Alesi (Fra) | 1:22.990 | 2 | Frentzen (Ger) | 1:23.042 |
| 3 | Fisichella (Ita) | 1:23.066 | 4 | Villeneuve (Can) | 1:23.231 |
| 5 | Hakkinen (Fin) | 1:23.340 | 6 | Coulthard (GB) | 1:23.347 |
| 7 | Berger (Aut) | 1:23.443 | 8 | Schumacher R. (Ger) | 1:23.603 |
| 9 | Schumacher M. (Ger) | 1:23.624 | 10 | Irvine (GB) | 1:23.891 |
| 11 | Barrichello (Bra) | 1:24.177 | 12 | Herbert (GB) | 1:24.242 |
| 13 | Magnussen (Den) | 1:24.394 | 14 | Hill (GB) | 1:24.462 |
| 15 | Nakano (Jap) | 1:24.553 | 16 | Trulli (Ita) | 1:24.567 |
| 17 | Diniz (Bra) | 1:24.639 | 18 | Morbidelli (Ita) | 1:24.735 |
| 19 | Salo (Fin) | 1:25.693 | 20 | Verstappen (Hol) | 1:25.845 |
| 21 | Katayama (Jap) | 1:26.555 | 22 | Marques (Bra) | 1:27.677 |

*Drivers outside 107% rule:*
    None – all qualified

Date: 21 September 1997
Track: 2.670 miles
Conditions: Warm and dry
Distance: 71 laps, 189.570 miles
Fastest Lap: J. Villeneuve – 1:11.814
Lap Record: J. Villeneuve – 1:11.814 at 135.443 mph, 21 September 1997

| Pos | Driver | Car | Laps | Time/Reason | Fastest | mph |
|-----|--------|-----|------|-------------|---------|-----|
| 1 | Villeneuve | Williams | 71 | 1:27:35.999 | 1:11.814 | 131.392 |
| 2 | Coulthard | McLaren | 71 | 1:27:38.908 | 1:12.207 | 131.319 |
| 3 | Frentzen | Williams | 71 | 1:27:39.961 | 1:12.223 | 131.293 |
| 4 | Fisichella | Jordan | 71 | 1:27:48.126 | 1:12.375 | 131.090 |
| 5 | Schumacher, R. | Jordan | 71 | 1:28:07.858 | 1:12.862 | 130.600 |
| 6 | Schumacher, M. | Ferrari | 71 | 1:28:09.409 | 1:12.169 | 130.562 |
| 7 | Hill | Arrows | 71 | 1:28:13.206 | 1:12.903 | 130.468 |
| 8 | Herbert | Sauber | 71 | 1:28:25.056 | 1:12.574 | 130.177 |
| 9 | Morbidelli | Sauber | 71 | 1:28:42.454 | 1:12.826 | 129.751 |
| 10 | Berger | Benetton | 70 | 1:27:46.834 | 1:12.624 | 129.275 |
| 11 | Katayama | Minardi | 69 | 1:27:45.710 | 1:14.394 | 127.455 |
| 12 | Verstappen | Tyrrell | 69 | 1:28:19.144 | 1:13.708 | 126.651 |
| 13 | Diniz | Arrows | 64 | shock absorber | 1:13.074 | 128.730 |
| 14 | Barrichello | Stewart | 67 | accident | 1:12.535 | 130.277 |
| r | Trulli | Prost | 58 | engine | 1:12.598 | 130.870 |
| r | Magnussen | Stewart | 58 | engine | 1:12.605 | 129.985 |
| r | Nakano | Prost | 57 | engine | 1:13.010 | 128.919 |
| r | Salo | Tyrrell | 48 | gearbox | 1:13.862 | 126.983 |
| r | Irvine | Ferrari | 38 | accident | 1:12.704 | 127.941 |
| r | Alesi | Benetton | 37 | accident | 1:12.953 | 129.207 |
| r | Hakkinen | McLaren | 24 | engine | 1:31.574 | 106.216 |
| dq | Marques* | Minardi | 0 | dnq | – | – |

**Starting Grid and Qualifying Times**

| | | | | | |
|---|---|---|---|---|---|
| 1 | Villeneuve (Can) | 1:10.304 | 2 | Hakkinen (Fin) | 1:10.398 |
| 3 | Trulli (Ita) | 1:10.511 | 4 | Frentzen (Ger) | 1:10.670 |
| 5 | Barrichello (Bra) | 1:10.700 | 6 | Magnussen (Den) | 1:11.893 |
| 7 | Hill (GB) | 1:11.025 | 8 | Irvine (GB) | 1:11.051 |
| 9 | Schumacher M. (Ger) | 1:11.056 | 10 | Coulthard (GB) | 1:11.076 |
| 11 | Schumacher R. (Ger) | 1:11.186 | 12 | Herbert (GB) | 1:11.210 |
| 13 | Morbidelli (Ita) | 1:11.261 | 14 | Fisichella (Ita) | 1:11.299 |
| 15 | Alesi (Fra) | 1:11.392 | 16 | Nakano (Jap) | 1:11.596 |
| 17 | Diniz (Bra) | 1:11.615 | 18 | Berger (Aut) | 1:11.620 |
| 19 | Katayama (Jap) | 1:12.036 | 20 | Verstappen (Hol) | 1:12.230 |
| 21 | Salo (Fin) | 1:14.246 | | | |

*Drivers outside 107% rule:* None – all qualified
*\*Tarso Marques disqualified from qualifying – car found to be underweight.*

Date: 28 September 1997
Track: 2.822 miles                    Distance: 67 laps, 189.074 miles
Conditions: Warm and dry             Fastest Lap: H-H. Frentzen – 1:18.805
Lap Record: H-H. Frentzen – 1:18.805 at 129.309 mph, 28 September 1997

| Pos | Driver | Car | Laps | Time/Reason | Fastest | mph |
|---|---|---|---|---|---|---|
| 1 | Villeneuve | Williams | 67 | 1:31:27.843 | 1:19.838 | 125.145 |
| 2 | Alesi | Benetton | 67 | 1:31:39.613 | 1:19.716 | 124.877 |
| 3 | Frentzen | Williams | 67 | 1:31:41.323 | 1:18.805 | 124.838 |
| 4 | Berger | Benetton | 67 | 1:31:44.259 | 1:19.996 | 124.771 |
| 5 | Diniz | Arrows | 67 | 1:32:10.990 | 1:21.262 | 124.168 |
| 6 | Panis | Prost | 67 | 1:32:11.593 | 1:21.086 | 124.155 |
| 7 | Herbert | Sauber | 67 | 1:32:12.197 | 1:20.518 | 124.141 |
| 8 | Hill | Arrows | 67 | 1:32:12.620 | 1:20.407 | 124.132 |
| 9 | Morbidelli | Sauber | 66 | 1:31:51.462 | 1:20.865 | 122.748 |
| 10 | Salo | Tyrrell | 66 | 1:32:18.927 | 1:21.996 | 122.140 |
| r | Verstappen | Tyrrell | 50 | engine | 1:22.455 | 121.431 |
| r | Hakkinen | McLaren | 43 | engine | 1:19.576 | 126.402 |
| r | Barrichello | Stewart | 43 | hydraulics | 1:20.737 | 124.504 |
| r | Coulthard | McLaren | 42 | engine | 1:19.920 | 125.971 |
| r | Magnussen | Stewart | 40 | driveshaft | 1:21.448 | 122.229 |
| r | Irvine | Ferrari | 22 | engine | 1:21.793 | 123.310 |
| r | Nakano | Prost | 16 | engine | 1:21.969 | 122.629 |
| r | Schumacher, M. | Ferrari | 2 | suspension | 1:29.314 | 111.129 |
| r | Marques | Minardi | 1 | engine | 1:36.826 | 105.870 |
| r | Katayama | Minardi | 1 | damage | 3:00.630 | 56.751 |
| r | Schumacher, R. | Jordan | 0 | accident | – | – |
| r | Fisichella | Jordan | 0 | accident | – | – |

**Starting Grid and Qualifying Times**

| 1 | Hakkinen (Fin) | 1:16.602 | 2 | Villeneuve (Can) | 1:16.691 |
|---|---|---|---|---|---|
| 3 | Frentzen (Ger) | 1:16.741 | 4 | Fisichella (Ita) | 1:17.289 |
| 5 | Schumacher M. (Ger) | 1:17.385 | 6 | Coulthard (GB) | 1:17.387 |
| 7 | Berger (Aut) | 1:17.587 | 8 | Schumacher R. (Ger) | 1:17.595 |
| 9 | Barrichello (Bra) | 1:17.614 | 10 | Alesi (Fra) | 1:17.620 |
| 11 | Panis (Fra) | 1:17.650 | 12 | Magnussen (Den) | 1:17.722 |
| 13 | Hill (GB) | 1:17.795 | 14 | Irvine (GB) | 1:17.855 |
| 15 | Diniz (Bra) | 1:18.128 | 16 | Herbert (GB) | 1:18.303 |
| 17 | Nakano (Jap) | 1:18.699 | 18 | Marques (Bra) | 1:19.347 |
| 19 | Morbidelli (Ita) | 1:19.490 | 20 | Salo (Fin) | 1:19.526 |
| 21 | Verstappen (Hol) | 1:19.531 | 22 | Katayama (Jap) | 1:20.615 |

*Drivers outside 107% rule:*
    None – all qualified

## Round 16: Japan – Suzuka

Date: 12 October 1997
Track: 3.642 miles
Conditions: Hot and sunny
Lap Record: H-H. Frentzen – 1:38.942 at 130.662 mph, 12 October 1997

Distance: 53 laps, 193.026 miles
Fastest Lap: H-H. Frentzen – 1:38.942

| Pos | Driver | Car | Laps | Time/Reason | Fastest | mph |
|---|---|---|---|---|---|---|
| 1 | Schumacher, R. | Ferrari | 53 | 1:29:48.446 | 1:39.268 | 128.990 |
| 2 | Frentzen | Williams | 53 | 1:29:49.824 | 1:38.942 | 128.911 |
| 3 | Irvine | Ferrari | 53 | 1:30:14.830 | 1:39.935 | 128.316 |
| 4 | Hakkinen | McLaren | 53 | 1:30:15.575 | 1:40.151 | 128.299 |
| 5 | Alesi | Benetton | 53 | 1:30.28.849 | 1:39.381 | 127.985 |
| 6 | Herbert | Sauber | 53 | 1:30:30.076 | 1:40.266 | 127.956 |
| 7 | Fisichella | Jordan | 53 | 1:30:45.271 | 1:40.217 | 127.599 |
| 8 | Berger | Benetton | 53 | 1:30.48.875 | 1:39.998 | 127.515 |
| 9 | Schumacher, R. | Jordan | 53 | 1:31:10.482 | 1:39.737 | 127.011 |
| 10 | Coulthard | McLaren | 52 | 1:28:51.086 | 1:39.771 | 127.871 |
| 11 | Hill | Arrows | 52 | 1:29:59.070 | 1:41.419 | 126.261 |
| 12 | Diniz | Arrows | 52 | 1:30:43.622 | 1:41.611 | 125.228 |
| 13 | Verstappen | Tyrrell | 52 | 1:31:13.951 | 1:43.051 | 124.534 |
| r | Marques | Minardi | 46 | gearbox | 1:42.699 | 124.572 |
| r | Salo | Tyrrell | 46 | engine | 1:42.996 | 124.384 |
| r | Panis | Prost | 36 | engine | 1:40.430 | 126.431 |
| r | Nakano | Prost | 22 | wheel bearing | 1:41.608 | 120.107 |
| r | Katayama | Minardi | 8 | engine | 1:44.403 | 122.620 |
| r | Barrichello | Stewart | 6 | spin | 1:43.883 | 123.399 |
| r | Magnussen | Stewart | 3 | spin | 1:44.089 | 121.170 |
| dns | Morbidelli | Sauber | 0 | qualifying acc | – | – |
| dq | Villeneuve * | Williams | 53 | 1:30:28.222 | 1:40.163 | 128.000 |

### Starting Grid and Qualifying Times

| | | | | | | |
|---|---|---|---|---|---|---|
| 1 | Villeneuve (Can) | 1:36.071 | | 2 | Schumacher M. (Ger) | 1:36.133 |
| 3 | Irvine (GB) | 1:36.466 | | 4 | Hakkinen (Fin) | 1:36.469 |
| 5 | Berger (Aut) | 1:36.561 | | 6 | Frentzen (Ger) | 1:36.628 |
| 7 | Alesi (Fra) | 1:36.682 | | 8 | Herbert (GB) | 1:36.906 |
| 9 | Fisichella (Ita) | 1:36.917 | | 10 | Panis (Fra) | 1:37.073 |
| 11 | Coulthard (GB) | 1:37.095 | | 12 | Barrichello (Bra) | 1:37.343 |
| 13 | Schumacher R. (Ger) | 1:37.443 | | 14 | Magnussen (Den) | 1:37.480 |
| 15 | Nakano (Jap) | 1:37.588 | | 16 | Diniz (Bra) | 1:37.853 |
| 17 | Hill (GB) | 1:38.022 | | 18 | Morbidelli | 1:38.556 |
| 19 | Katayama (Jap) | 1:38.983 | | 20 | Marques (Bra) | 1:39.678 |
| 21 | Verstappen (Hol) | 1:40.259 | | 22 | Salo (Fin) | 1:40.529 |

*Drivers outside 107% rule:* None – all qualified
* *Villeneuve disqualified from 5th position*

## Round 17: European – Jerez

Date: 26 October 1997
Track: 2.748 miles
Conditions: Hot and sunny
Distance: 69 laps, 189.612 miles
Fastest Lap: H-H. Frentzen – 1:23.135
Lap Record: H-H. Frentzen – 1:23.135 at 118.997 mph, 26 October 1997

| Pos | Driver | Car | Laps | Time/Reason | Fastest | mph |
|---|---|---|---|---|---|---|
| 1 | Hakkinen | McLaren | 69 | 1:38:57.771 | 1:24.072 | 115.108 |
| 2 | Coulthard | McLaren | 69 | 1:38:59.425 | 1:24.006 | 115.075 |
| 3 | Villeneuve | Williams | 69 | 1:38:59.574 | 1:23.906 | 115.073 |
| 4 | Berger | Benetton | 69 | 1:38:59.690 | 1:23.361 | 115.070 |
| 5 | Irvine | Ferrari | 69 | 1:39:01.560 | 1:24.266 | 115.034 |
| 6 | Frentzen | Williams | 69 | 1:39:02.308 | 1:23.135 | 115.020 |
| 7 | Panis | Prost | 69 | 1:40:04.916 | 1:23.941 | 113.821 |
| 8 | Herbert | Sauber | 69 | 1:40:10.732 | 1:25.159 | 113.710 |
| 9 | Magnussen | Stewart | 69 | 1:40:15.258 | 1:25.370 | 113.625 |
| 10 | Nakano | Prost | 69 | 1:40:15.986 | 1:24.679 | 113.611 |
| 11 | Fisichella | Jordan | 68 | 1:39:05.717 | 1:25.434 | 113.288 |
| 12 | Salo | Tyrrell | 68 | 1:39:15.015 | 1:25.237 | 113.111 |
| 13 | Alesi | Benetton | 68 | 1:39:15.717 | 1:23.975 | 113.097 |
| 14 | Fontana | Sauber | 68 | 1:39:45.614 | 1:25.154 | 112.533 |
| 15 | Marques | Minardi | 68 | 1:39:56.704 | 1:25.947 | 112.324 |
| 16 | Verstappen | Tyrrell | 68 | 1:40:06.201 | 1:26.369 | 112.147 |
| 17 | Katayama | Minardi | 68 | 1:40:06.893 | 1:26.215 | 112.134 |
| r | Schumacher, M. | Ferrari | 47 | accident | 1:23.692 | 115.521 |
| r | Hill | Arrows | 47 | gearbox | 1:24.274 | 114.357 |
| r | Schumacher, R. | Jordan | 44 | water leak | 1:25.895 | 112.413 |
| r | Barrichello | Stewart | 30 | gearbox | 1:26.169 | 113.142 |
| r | Diniz | Arrows | 11 | spin | 1:26.434 | 112.553 |

### Starting Grid and Qualifying Times

| 1 | Villeneuve (Can) | 1:21.072 | 2 | Schumacher M. (Ger) | 1:21.072 |
|---|---|---|---|---|---|
| 3 | Frentzen (Ger) | 1:21.072 | 4 | Hill (GB) | 1:21.130 |
| 5 | Hakkinen (Fin) | 1:21.369 | 6 | Coulthard (GB) | 1:21.476 |
| 7 | Irvine (GB) | 1:21.610 | 8 | Berger (Aut) | 1:21.656 |
| 9 | Panis (Fra) | 1:21.735 | 10 | Alesi (Fra) | 1:22.011 |
| 11 | Magnussen (Den) | 1:22.167 | 12 | Barrichello (Bra) | 1:22.222 |
| 13 | Diniz (Bra) | 1:22.234 | 14 | Herbert (GB) | 1:22.263 |
| 15 | Nakano (Jap) | 1:22.351 | 16 | Schumacher R. (Ger) | 1:22.740 |
| 17 | Fisichella (Ita) | 1:22.804 | 18 | Fontana (Arg) | 1:23.281 |
| 19 | Katayama (Jap) | 1:23.409 | 20 | Marques (Bra) | 1:23.854 |
| 21 | Salo (Fin) | 1:24.222 | 22 | Verstappen (Hol) | 1:24.301 |

*Drivers outside 107% rule:*
    None – all qualified

## Winning Margins

Biggest win margin: Belgian, M.Schumacher by 26.753s
Narrowest win margin: Argentinian, Villeneuve by 0.979s

| GP | 1st Place | 2nd Place | Margin |
|---|---|---|---|
| Australian | D. Coulthard (McLaren) | M.Schumacher (Ferrari) | 20.046s |
| Brazilian | J.Villeneuve (Williams) | G.Berger (Benetton) | 4.190s |
| Argentinian | J.Villeneuve (Williams) | E.Irvine (Ferrari) | 0.979s |
| San Marino | H-H.Frentzen (Williams) | M.Schumacher (Ferrari) | 1.237s |
| Monaco | M.Schumacher (Ferrari) | R.Barrichello (Stewart) | 53.306s |
| Spanish | J.Villeneuve (Williams) | O.Panis (Prost) | 5.804s |
| Canadian | M.Schumacher (Ferrari) | J.Alesi (Benetton) | 2.565s |
| French | M.Schumacher (Ferrari) | H-H.Frentzen (Williams) | 23.537s |
| British | J.Villeneuve (Williams) | J.Alesi (Benetton) | 10.205s |
| German | G.Berger (Benetton) | M.Schumacher (Ferrari) | 17.527s |
| Hungarian | J.Villeneuve (Williams) | D.Hill (Arrows) | 9.079s |
| Belgian | M.Schumacher (Ferrari) | G.Fisichella (Jordan) | 26.753s |
| Italian | D. Coulthard (McLaren) | J.Alesi (Benetton) | 1.937s |
| Austrian | J.Villeneuve (Williams) | D. Coulthard (McLaren) | 2.909s |
| Luxembourg | J.Villeneuve (Williams) | J.Alesi (Benetton) | 11.770s |
| Japanese | M.Schumacher (Ferrari) | H-H.Frentzen (Williams) | 1.378s |
| European | M.Hakkinen (McLaren) | D.Coulthard (McLaren) | 1.654s |

## Team Finishes

| Team | Driver | | Driver | |
|---|---|---|---|---|
| Arrows | Hill | 7 | Diniz | 4 |
| Benetton | Alesi | 6 | Berger | 8 |
| | Alesi | 3 | Wurz | 0 |
| Ferrari | Schumacher, M. | 12 | Irvine | 3 |
| Jordan | Schumacher, R. | 5 | Fisichella | 10 |
| Lola | Sospiri | 0 | Rosset | 0 |
| McLaren | Hakkinen | 6 | Coulthard | 7 |
| Minardi | Katayama | 2 | Trulli | 5 |
| | Katayama | 3 | Marques | 3 |
| Prost | Panis | 7 | Nakano | 1 |
| | Trulli | 4 | Nakano | 1 |
| Sauber | Herbert | 2 | Larini | 2 |
| | Herbert | 7 | Morbidelli | 1 |
| | Herbert | 2 | Fontana | 2 |
| Stewart | Barrichello | 3 | Magnussen | 4 |
| Tyrrell | Verstappen | 3 | Salo | 6 |
| Williams | Villeneuve | 8 | Frentzen | 7 |

# Records, Facts and Figures

# FIA DRIVERS' CHAMPIONSHIP PLACINGS 1997

| Pos | Driver | Team | Points |
|-----|--------|------|--------|
| 1 | Jacques Villeneuve (Can) | Williams Renault | 81 |
| 2 | Heinz-Harald Frentzen (Ger) | Williams Renault | 42 |
| 3 | David Coulthard (GB) | McLaren Mercedes | 36 |
|   | Jean Alesi (Fra) | Benetton Renault | 36 |
| 5 | Gerhard Berger (Aut) | Benetton Renault | 27 |
|   | Mika Hakkinen (Fin) | McLaren Mercedes | 27 |
| 7 | Eddie Irvine (GB) | Ferrari | 24 |
| 8 | Giancarlo Fisichella (Ita) | Jordan Peugeot | 20 |
| 9 | Olivier Panis (Fra) | Prost Mugen Honda | 16 |
| 10 | Johnny Herbert (GB) | Sauber Petronas | 15 |
| 11 | Ralf Schumacher (Ger) | Jordan Peugeot | 13 |
| 12 | Damon Hill (GB) | Arrows Yamaha | 7 |
| 13 | Rubens Barrichello (Bra) | Stewart Ford | 6 |
| 14 | Alexander Wurz (Aut) | Benetton Renault | 4 |
| 15 | Jarno Trulli (Ita) | Prost Mugen Honda | 3 |
| 16 | Mika Salo (Fin) | Tyrrell Ford | 2 |
|   | Pedro Diniz (Bra) | Arrows Yamaha | 2 |
|   | Shinji Nakano (Jap) | Prost Mugen Honda | 2 |
| 19 | Nicola Larini (Ita) | Sauber Petronas | 1 |
| – | Michael Schumacher (Ger) | Ferrari | (78) |

*M. Schumacher excluded by FIA from Drivers' Championship.*

# CONSTRUCTORS' CHAMPIONSHIP PLACINGS 1997

| Pos | Team | Tyres | Drivers | Points |
|-----|------|-------|---------|--------|
| 1 | Williams Renault | Goodyear | Villeneuve, Frentzen | 123 |
| 2 | Ferrari | Goodyear | M.Schumacher, Irvine | 102 |
| 3 | Benetton Renault | Goodyear | Alesi, Berger, Wurz | 67 |
| 4 | McLaren Mercedes | Goodyear | Coulthard, Hakkinen | 63 |
| 5 | Jordan Peugeot | Goodyear | Fisichella, R.Schumacher | 33 |
| 6 | Prost Mugen Honda | Bridgestone | Panis, Trulli, Nakano | 21 |
| 7 | Sauber Petronas | Goodyear | Herbert, Larini | 16 |
| 8 | Arrows Yamaha | Bridgestone | Hill, Diniz | 9 |
| 9 | Stewart Ford | Bridgestone | Barrichello, Magnussen | 6 |
| 10 | Tyrrell Ford | Goodyear | Salo, Verstappen | 2 |
| 11 | Minardi Hart | Bridgestone | Katayama, Trulli, Marques | 0 |

| Driver | Team | Au | Br | Ar | SM | Mo | Sp | Ca | Fr | GB | Ge | Hu | Be | It | Au | Lu | Ja | Eu | Pts |
|---|---|---|---|---|---|---|---|---|---|---|---|---|---|---|---|---|---|---|---|
| Alesi | Benetton | r | 6 | 7 | 5 | r | 3 | 2 | 5 | 2 | 6 | 11 | 8 | 2 | r | 2 | 5 | 13 | 36 |
| Barrichello | Stewart | r | r | r | r | 2 | r | r | r | r | r | r | r | r | 14 | r | r | 4 | 6 |
| Berger | Benetton | 4 | 2 | 6f | r | 9 | 10 | – | – | – | 1f | 8 | 6 | 7 | 10 | 4 | 8 | 4 | 27 |
| Coulthard | McLaren | 1 | 10 | r | r | r | 6 | 7 | r | r | r | r | r | 1 | 2 | r | 10 | 2 | 36 |
| Diniz | Arrows | 10 | r | r | 4 | r | 9f | 8 | 9 | 7 | 11 | r | 7 | r | 13 | 5 | 12 | r | 2 |
| Fisichella | Jordan | r | 8 | r | 4 | 6 | 3 | 3 | 9 | 9 | r | 2 | 2 | 4 | 4 | r | 7 | 11 | 20 |
| Fontana | Sauber | – | – | – | – | – | – | – | r | r | r | rf | r | – | – | – | – | – | |
| Frentzen | Williams | 8f | 9 | r | 1f | r | 8 | 4 | 2 | r | 3 | r | 3 | 3 | r | 4 | 2f | 6f | 42 |
| Hakkinen | McLaren | 3 | 4 | 5 | 6 | r | 7 | 5 | r | r | r | 3 | dq | 3 | 8 | 7 | 4 | 1 | 27 |
| Herbert | Sauber | 4 | 7 | 4 | r | 5 | 5 | r | 8 | 6 | 3 | 4 | 4 | 9f | 7 | 8 | 6 | 5 | 15 |
| Hill | Arrows | ds | 17 | r | r | 12 | r | 9 | r | r | 8 | 2 | 13 | r | r | r | 3 | 17 | 7 |
| Irvine | Ferrari | r | 16 | 2 | 3 | 10 | 12 | r | 11 | 10 | r | r | r | 8 | 11 | 3 | 3 | 5 | 24 |
| Katayama | Minardi | r | 18 | r | 11 | r | r | r | r | r | r | r | r | r | r | r | 17 | r | 0 |
| Larini | Sauber | 6 | 11 | 10 | 7 | r | r | – | – | – | – | – | – | – | – | – | – | – | 1 |
| Magnussen | Stewart | r | ds | r | r | 7 | r | r | 10 | r | 7 | r | 12 | 14 | 12 | 9 | r | r | 0 |
| Marques | Minardi | – | – | – | – | – | – | – | r | r | r | r | r | r | r | 14 | 9 | 15 | 0 |
| Morbidelli | Sauber | 7 | – | – | – | – | 14 | – | r | 11 | r | 12 | 9 | 12 | 9 | 9 | dns | 10 | 0 |
| Nakano | Prost | 7 | 14 | r | 9 | 8 | r | 6 | r | r | 7 | 6 | 11 | 11 | r | r | dns | 7 | 2 |
| Panis | Prost | 5 | 3 | 8 | 8 | 4 | 2 | r | – | – | – | – | – | – | – | 6 | r | 12 | 16 |
| Salo | Tyrrell | 5 | 13 | r | 9f | 5 | 11 | r | r | r | r | 13 | r | 6 | r | r | r | r | 2 |
| Schumacher, M. | Ferrari | 2 | 5 | r | 2 | 1f | 4 | 1 | 1 | r | 2 | 4 | 1 | 6 | 6 | r | 1 | r | (78) |
| Schumacher, R. | Jordan | r | r | 3 | r | r | r | r | 6 | 5 | 5 | r | r | r | 3 | 9 | r | r | 13 |
| Trulli | Min/Prost | 9 | 12 | 9 | r | 15 | r | 10 | r | 8 | 4 | 7 | 5 | 10 | 12 | r | 13 | r | 3 |
| Verstappen | Tyrrell | r | 15 | r | 10 | 11 | r | r | r | r | r | r | 15 | r | r | r | dq | 16 | 3 |
| Villeneuve | Williams | 1f | 1 | 1 | r | r | 1 | 4 | 4 | 1 | r | 1 | 5f | 5 | 1f | 1 | dq | 3 | 81 |
| Wurz | Benetton | – | – | – | – | – | – | r | r | 3 | – | – | – | – | – | – | – | – | 4 |

| Driver | Team | Au | Br | Ar | SM | Mo | Sp | Ca | Fr | GB | Ge | Hu | Be | It | Au | Lu | Ja | Eu | Pts |
|---|---|---|---|---|---|---|---|---|---|---|---|---|---|---|---|---|---|---|---|
| Alesi | Benetton | 8 | 6 | 11 | 14 | 9 | 4 | 8 | 13 | 11 | 6 | 9 | 2 | 11 | 15 | 10 | 7 | 10 | 36 |
| Barrichello | Stewart | 11 | 11 | 5 | 13 | 10 | 17 | 3 | 13 | 21 | 12 | 7 | 1 | 6 | 5 | 7 | 12 | 12 | 6 |
| Berger | Benetton | 10 | 3 | 12 | 11 | 17 | 6 | – | – | – | 1 | 7 | 15 | 17 | 18 | 8 | 5 | 8 | 27 |
| Coulthard | McLaren | 4 | 12 | 10 | 10 | 5 | 3 | 9 | 16 | 9 | 5 | 5 | 8 | 6 | 10 | 7 | 5 | 6 | 36 |
| Diniz | Arrows | 22 | 16 | 22 | 17 | 16 | 21 | 16 | 11 | 10 | 16 | 19 | 10 | 17 | 17 | 15 | 16 | 13 | 2 |
| Fisichella | Jordan | 14 | 7 | 9 | 6 | 4 | 8 | 6 | 11 | 10 | 2 | 8 | 4 | 3 | 14 | 4 | 9 | 17 | 20 |
| Fontana | Sauber | – | – | – | – | – | – | – | 20 | 22 | 18 | 13 | 7 | – | – | – | – | 18 | 0 |
| Frentzen | Williams | 2 | 8 | 2 | 2 | 1 | 2 | 4 | – | 3 | 3 | 4 | 6 | 2 | 4 | 3 | 6 | 3 | 42 |
| Hakkinen | McLaren | 6 | 4 | 17 | 8 | 8 | 5 | 9 | 10 | 3 | 5 | 5 | 11 | 5 | 2 | 1 | 4 | 5 | 27 |
| Herbert | Sauber | – | 7 | 8 | 7 | 7 | 10 | 15 | 14 | 4 | 14 | 10 | 12 | 12 | 12 | 16 | 9 | 14 | 15 |
| Hill | Arrows | 20 | 9 | 7 | 15 | 13 | 11 | 13 | 17 | 12 | 13 | 4 | 11 | 14 | 8 | 14 | 3 | 7 | 7 |
| Irvine | Ferrari | 5 | 14 | 21 | 9 | 15 | 12 | 22 | 21 | 7 | 10 | 5 | 17 | 10 | 19 | 22 | 19 | 4 | 24 |
| Katayama | Minardi | 15 | 18 | 14 | 12 | 20 | 22 | – | – | 18 | 22 | 17 | 20 | 21 | – | – | – | – | 0 |
| Larini | Sauber | 13 | 19 | 15 | 11 | 11 | – | – | – | – | – | – | – | – | – | – | – | – | 1 |
| Magnussen | Stewart | 19 | 20 | 16 | 16 | 19 | – | 21 | 15 | 15 | – | 17 | 18 | 13 | 6 | 12 | 14 | 11 | 0 |
| Marques | Minardi | – | – | – | – | – | – | – | 22 | 20 | 21 | 22 | 22 | 22 | – | 18 | 20 | 20 | 0 |
| Morbidelli | Sauber | – | – | – | – | – | 13 | – | – | – | – | 15 | 13 | 18 | 13 | 18 | 18 | – | 0 |
| Nakano | Prost | 16 | 15 | 20 | 18 | 21 | 16 | 19 | 12 | 14 | 17 | 18 | 16 | 15 | 16 | 17 | 15 | 15 | 2 |
| Panis | Prost | 9 | 5 | 3 | 4 | 12 | 12 | 10 | – | – | – | – | – | – | – | 11 | 10 | 9 | 16 |
| Salo | Tyrrell | 18 | 22 | 4 | 19 | 14 | 7 | 17 | 19 | 17 | 21 | 1 | 19 | 19 | 9 | 20 | 22 | 21 | 2 |
| Schumacher, M. | Ferrari | 3 | 2 | 4 | 2 | 2 | 7 | 1 | 1 | 4 | 4 | 3 | 3 | 9 | 2 | 2 | 2 | 2 | (78) |
| Schumacher, R. | Jordan | 12 | 10 | 6 | 5 | 6 | 9 | 7 | 18 | 5 | 20 | 14 | 6 | 8 | 11 | 8 | 13 | 16 | 13 |
| Trulli | Min/Prost | 17 | 17 | 18 | 20 | 18 | 18 | 20 | 6 | 13 | 11 | 12 | 14 | 16 | 3 | 8 | 21 | 3 | 3 |
| Verstappen | Tyrrell | 21 | 21 | 16 | 22 | 22 | 19 | 14 | 4 | 19 | 18 | 18 | 21 | 20 | 4 | 21 | 1 | 22 | 0 |
| Villeneuve | Williams | 1 | 1 | 1 | 1 | 3 | 1 | 2 | 4 | 8 | 20 | 1 | 2 | 6 | 1 | 1 | 1 | 1 | 81 |
| Wurz | Benetton | – | – | – | – | – | – | 11 | 7 | 8 | – | – | – | – | – | – | – | – | 4 |

# DRIVERS – POINTS TALLY – RACE BY RACE '97

| Driver | Team | Au | Br | Ar | SM | Mo | Sp | Ca | Fr | GB | Ge | Hu | Be | It | Au | Lu | Ja | Eu | Total |
|---|---|---|---|---|---|---|---|---|---|---|---|---|---|---|---|---|---|---|---|
| Alesi | Benetton | 0 | 1 | 0 | 2 | 0 | 4 | 6 | 2 | 6 | 1 | 0 | 0 | 6 | 0 | 6 | 2 | 0 | 36 |
| Barrichello | Stewart | 0 | 0 | 0 | 0 | 6 | 0 | 0 | 0 | 0 | 0 | 0 | 0 | 0 | 0 | 0 | 0 | 0 | 6 |
| Berger | Benetton | 3 | 6 | 1 | 0 | 0 | – | – | – | 0 | 10 | 0 | 1 | 0 | 0 | 3 | 0 | 3 | 27 |
| Coulthard | McLaren | 10 | 0 | 0 | 0 | 1 | 0 | 0 | 3 | 0 | 0 | 0 | 0 | 10 | 6 | 0 | 0 | 6 | 36 |
| Diniz | Arrows | 0 | 0 | 0 | 0 | 0 | 0 | 0 | 0 | 0 | 0 | 0 | 0 | 0 | 0 | 0 | 0 | 2 | 2 |
| Fisichella | Jordan | 0 | 3 | 0 | 0 | 0 | 1 | 4 | 0 | 3 | 3 | 0 | 6 | 0 | 0 | 0 | 0 | 0 | 20 |
| Fontana | Sauber | – | – | – | – | – | – | – | – | – | – | – | – | 0 | 0 | – | – | – | 0 |
| Frentzen | Williams | 0 | 0 | 0 | 10 | 0 | 0 | 4 | 6 | 0 | 1 | 4 | 3 | 4 | 4 | 0 | 6 | 0 | 42 |
| Hakkinen | McLaren | 4 | 3 | 0 | 0 | 2 | 0 | 0 | 0 | 0 | 0 | 0 | 0 | 4 | 4 | 0 | 0 | 10 | 27 |
| Herbert | Sauber | 0 | 0 | 3 | 3 | 0 | 1 | 2 | 0 | 0 | 3 | 0 | 2 | 0 | 0 | 1 | 0 | 0 | 15 |
| Hill | Arrows | 0 | 0 | 0 | 0 | 0 | 0 | 0 | 0 | 0 | 1 | 6 | 0 | 0 | 0 | 0 | 0 | 0 | 7 |
| Irvine | Ferrari | 0 | 0 | 6 | 4 | 4 | 0 | 0 | 4 | 0 | 0 | 0 | 0 | 0 | 0 | 0 | 4 | 2 | 24 |
| Katayama | Minardi | 0 | 0 | 0 | 0 | 0 | 0 | 0 | 0 | 0 | 0 | 0 | 0 | 0 | 0 | 0 | 0 | 0 | 0 |
| Larini | Sauber | 0 | 0 | 0 | 1 | 0 | – | – | – | – | – | – | – | – | – | – | – | – | 1 |
| Magnussen | Stewart | 0 | 0 | 0 | 0 | 0 | 0 | 0 | 0 | 0 | 0 | – | – | – | – | – | – | – | 0 |
| Marques | Minardi | – | – | – | – | – | – | – | – | – | – | 0 | 0 | 0 | 0 | 0 | 0 | 0 | 0 |
| Morbidelli | Sauber | 0 | 0 | 0 | 0 | 0 | 0 | 0 | 0 | 0 | 0 | 0 | 0 | – | – | – | – | – | 0 |
| Nakano | Prost | 0 | 0 | 0 | 0 | 0 | 0 | 0 | 0 | 0 | 0 | 2 | 0 | 0 | 0 | 0 | 0 | 0 | 2 |
| Panis | Prost | 2 | 4 | 2 | 0 | 0 | 6 | – | – | – | – | – | – | – | – | 2 | 0 | 0 | 16 |
| Salo | Tyrrell | 0 | 0 | 0 | 0 | 2 | 0 | 0 | 0 | 0 | 0 | 0 | 0 | 0 | 0 | 0 | 0 | 0 | 2 |
| Schumacher, M. | Ferrari | 6 | 2 | 0 | 6 | 10 | 3 | 10 | 10 | 0 | 6 | 3 | 10 | 1 | 1 | 0 | 10 | 0 | (78) |
| Schumacher, R. | Jordan | 0 | 0 | 4 | 0 | 0 | 0 | 0 | 0 | 0 | 0 | 0 | 4 | 0 | 2 | 0 | 3 | 0 | 13 |
| Trulli | Min/Prost | 0 | 0 | 0 | 0 | 0 | 0 | 0 | 0 | 0 | 3 | 0 | 0 | 0 | 0 | 0 | 0 | 0 | 3 |
| Verstappen | Tyrrell | 0 | 0 | 0 | 0 | 0 | 0 | 0 | 0 | 0 | 0 | 0 | 0 | 0 | 0 | 0 | 0 | 0 | 0 |
| Villeneuve | Williams | 0 | 10 | 10 | 0 | 0 | 10 | 0 | 3 | 10 | 0 | 10 | 2 | 2 | 10 | 10 | 0 | 4 | 81 |
| Wurz | Benetton | – | – | – | – | – | – | 0 | 0 | 4 | – | – | – | – | – | – | – | – | 4 |

# CONSTRUCTORS POINTS WON – RACE BY RACE '97

| Team | Pos | Au | Br | Ar | SM | Mo | Sp | Ca | Fr | GB | Ge | Hu | Be | It | Au | Lu | Ja | Eu | Tot | Tyres |
|---|---|---|---|---|---|---|---|---|---|---|---|---|---|---|---|---|---|---|---|---|
| Arrows | 8 | 0 | 0 | 0 | 0 | 0 | 0 | 0 | 0 | 0 | 0 | 6 | 0 | 0 | 0 | 3 | 0 | 0 | 9 | Bridgestone |
| Benetton | 3 | 3 | 6 | 1 | 0 | 0 | 4 | 6 | 0 | 12 | 12 | 0 | 2 | 8 | 0 | 10 | 0 | 3 | 67 | Goodyear |
| Ferrari | 2 | 6 | 2 | 6 | 10 | 14 | 1 | 10 | 14 | 0 | 6 | 2 | 10 | 3 | 2 | 0 | 14 | 2 | 102 | Goodyear |
| Jordan | 5 | 0 | 3 | 6 | 3 | 0 | 2 | 4 | 1 | 2 | 3 | 0 | 6 | 0 | 3 | 0 | 0 | 0 | 33 | Goodyear |
| McLaren | 4 | 14 | 0 | 0 | 2 | 0 | 0 | 0 | 2 | 1 | 4 | 0 | 4 | 11 | 6 | 0 | 3 | 16 | 63 | Goodyear |
| Minardi | 11 | 0 | 0 | 0 | 0 | 0 | 0 | 0 | 0 | 0 | 0 | 0 | 0 | 0 | 0 | 0 | 0 | 0 | 0 | Bridgestone |
| Prost | 6 | 2 | 4 | 0 | 0 | 1 | 6 | 1 | 0 | 1 | 1 | 1 | 0 | 0 | 1 | 2 | 1 | 0 | 21 | Bridgestone |
| Sauber | 7 | 1 | 1 | 3 | 1 | 3 | 0 | 2 | 0 | 0 | 0 | 4 | 0 | 0 | 0 | 1 | 0 | 0 | 16 | Goodyear |
| Stewart | 9 | 0 | 0 | 0 | 0 | 6 | 0 | 0 | 0 | 0 | 0 | 0 | 0 | 0 | 0 | 0 | 0 | 0 | 6 | Bridgestone |
| Tyrrell | 10 | 0 | 0 | 0 | 0 | 2 | 0 | 0 | 0 | 0 | 0 | 0 | 0 | 0 | 0 | 0 | 0 | 0 | 2 | Goodyear |
| Williams | 1 | 0 | 10 | 10 | 10 | 0 | 13 | 3 | 9 | 10 | 0 | 13 | 4 | 4 | 14 | 10 | 8 | 5 | 123 | Goodyear |

# CONSTRUCTORS TOTAL LAPS – RACE BY RACE '97

| Team | Au | Br | Ar | SM | Mo | Sp | Ca | Fr | GB | Ge | Hu | Be | It | Au | Lu | Ja | Eu | Total | % |
|---|---|---|---|---|---|---|---|---|---|---|---|---|---|---|---|---|---|---|---|
| Arrows | 54 | 83 | 83 | 64 | 1 | 71 | 106 | 127 | 88 | 52 | 130 | 86 | 50 | 135 | 134 | 104 | 58 | 1426 | 67.65 |
| Benetton | 92 | 144 | 144 | 65 | 76 | 128 | 132 | 118 | 89 | 90 | 153 | 88 | 106 | 107 | 134 | 106 | 137 | 1909 | 90.56 |
| Ferrari | 58 | 142 | 72 | 124 | 124 | 127 | 54 | 144 | 82 | 46 | 153 | 87 | 106 | 109 | 24 | 106 | 116 | 1674 | 79.41 |
| Jordan | 15 | 124 | 96 | 79 | 71 | 114 | 68 | 143 | 117 | 85 | 119 | 65 | 92 | 142 | 0 | 106 | 112 | 1548 | 73.43 |
| McLaren | 116 | 143 | 72 | 99 | 2 | 128 | 54 | 89 | 111 | 46 | 77 | 63 | 106 | 72 | 85 | 105 | 138 | 1506 | 71.44 |
| Minardi | 87 | 138 | 108 | 59 | 67 | 73 | 54 | 75 | 58 | 23 | 151 | 43 | 58 | 69 | 2 | 54 | 136 | 1255 | 59.54 |
| Prost | 114 | 143 | 65 | 72 | 98 | 98 | 105 | 77 | 115 | 90 | 154 | 47 | 106 | 115 | 83 | 58 | 138 | 1678 | 79.60 |
| Sauber | 58 | 143 | 125 | 79 | 33 | 126 | 107 | 111 | 100 | 52 | 84 | 88 | 90 | 142 | 133 | 53 | 137 | 1661 | 78.80 |
| Stewart | 85 | 16 | 90 | 34 | 123 | 100 | 33 | 69 | 87 | 60 | 34 | 51 | 83 | 125 | 83 | 9 | 99 | 1181 | 56.02 |
| Tyrrell | 44 | 141 | 114 | 120 | 121 | 98 | 88 | 76 | 89 | 77 | 136 | 68 | 45 | 117 | 116 | 98 | 136 | 1684 | 79.89 |
| Williams | 55 | 144 | 77 | 102 | 55 | 128 | 55 | 144 | 59 | 34 | 106 | 88 | 106 | 142 | 134 | 106 | 138 | 1673 | 79.36 |

# DRIVERS – LAPS COMPLETED – RACE BY RACE '97

| Driver | Team | Au | Br | Ar | SM | Mo | Sp | Ca | Fr | GB | Ge | Hu | Be | It | Au | Lu | Ja | Eu | Total |
|---|---|---|---|---|---|---|---|---|---|---|---|---|---|---|---|---|---|---|---|
| Alesi | Benetton | 34 | 72 | 72 | 61 | 16 | 64 | 72 | 72 | 37 | 45 | 76 | 44 | 53 | 37 | 67 | 53 | 68 | 947 |
| Barrichello | Stewart | 49 | 16 | 24 | 32 | 62 | 37 | 33 | 36 | 37 | 33 | 29 | 8 | 52 | 67 | 43 | 6 | 30 | 594 |
| Berger | Benetton | 58 | 72 | 72 | 4 | 60 | 64 | 54 | 71 | 59 | 45 | 77 | 44 | 53 | 70 | 67 | 53 | 69 | 808 |
| Coulthard | McLaren | 58 | 71 | 0 | 38 | 1 | – | 54 | 58 | 29 | 8 | 65 | 19 | 53 | 71 | 42 | 52 | 11 | 788 |
| Diniz | Arrows | 54 | 15 | 50 | 3 | 0 | 53 | 54 | 58 | 58 | 40 | 53 | 44 | 53 | 64 | 0 | 52 | 68 | 668 |
| Fisichella | Jordan | 14 | 72 | 24 | 62 | 61 | 64 | 54 | 71 | 58 | 44 | 42 | 44 | 53 | 71 | – | 53 | 68 | 851 |
| Fontana | Sauber | – | – | – | – | – | – | 40 | 40 | 58 | 44 | – | – | – | – | – | – | – | 210 |
| Frentzen | Williams | 55 | 72 | 5 | 62 | 39 | 64 | 54 | 72 | 52 | 33 | 29 | 44 | 53 | 71 | 67 | 53 | 69 | 810 |
| Hakkinen | McLaren | 58 | 72 | 72 | 61 | 1 | 64 | 0 | 18 | 0 | 45 | 12 | 44 | 1 | 1 | 43 | 53 | 69 | 718 |
| Herbert | Sauber | 0 | 72 | 72 | 18 | 9 | 64 | 54 | 71 | 42 | 8 | 77 | 42 | 38 | 71 | 67 | 52 | 69 | 829 |
| Hill | Arrows | 0 | 68 | 33 | 11 | 1 | 18 | 53 | 69 | 44 | 4 | 77 | 46 | 46 | 71 | 22 | 53 | 47 | 758 |
| Irvine | Ferrari | 32 | 70 | 72 | 62 | 62 | 63 | 5 | 72 | 0 | 1 | 76 | 43 | 53 | 38 | 1 | 8 | 69 | 800 |
| Katayama | Minardi | 58 | 67 | 37 | 59 | 60 | 11 | 5 | 70 | 50 | 23 | 76 | 42 | 8 | 69 | 67 | – | 68 | 636 |
| Larini | Sauber | 36 | 0 | 66 | 61 | 24 | – | – | – | – | – | – | – | – | – | – | – | – | 267 |
| Magnussen | Stewart | – | 71 | 53 | 2 | 61 | 63 | 0 | 5 | 58 | 27 | 75 | 18 | 31 | 58 | 40 | 3 | 69 | 587 |
| Marques | Minardi | – | – | – | – | – | – | – | – | – | – | 7 | 44 | 50 | 71 | – | 46 | – | 321 |
| Morbidelli | Sauber | – | – | – | – | – | 62 | 53 | 54 | 57 | 45 | – | 5 | 52 | 57 | 16 | 22 | – | 355 |
| Nakano | Prost | 56 | 71 | 49 | 11 | 36 | 34 | 54 | 7 | 57 | 45 | 77 | 5 | 53 | 57 | 16 | 36 | 69 | 719 |
| Panis | Prost | 58 | 72 | 16 | 61 | 62 | 64 | 51 | – | – | – | – | – | 35 | 48 | 67 | 46 | 69 | 556 |
| Salo | Tyrrell | 42 | 71 | 0 | 61 | 61 | 35 | 46 | 61 | 44 | 33 | 75 | 43 | 33 | 71 | 66 | 68 | 47 | 903 |
| Schumacher, M. | Ferrari | 58 | 72 | 72 | 62 | 62 | 64 | 14 | 72 | 38 | 45 | 77 | 44 | 53 | 71 | 2 | 53 | 44 | 874 |
| Schumacher, R. | Jordan | 1 | 52 | 72 | 17 | 10 | 50 | 14 | 72 | 59 | 45 | 77 | 21 | 39 | 71 | 0 | 53 | 44 | 697 |
| Trulli | Minardi | 55 | 2 | 71 | 71 | 0 | 62 | 70 | 32 | 70 | 45 | 77 | 12 | 69 | 69 | 50 | 52 | – | 701 |
| Verstappen | Tyrrell | 2 | 70 | 43 | 60 | 60 | 63 | 15 | 45 | 45 | 44 | 61 | 25 | 12 | 69 | 50 | 52 | 68 | 781 |
| Villeneuve | Williams | 0 | 72 | 72 | 72 | 16 | 64 | 1 | 72 | 59 | 33 | 77 | 44 | 53 | 71 | 67 | 53 | 69 | 863 |
| Wurz | Benetton | – | – | – | – | – | – | 35 | 60 | 59 | – | – | – | – | – | – | – | – | 154 |
| Laps in Race | | 58 | 72 | 72 | 62 | 62 | 64 | 54 | 72 | 59 | 45 | 77 | 44 | 53 | 71 | 67 | 53 | 69 | 1054 |

# DRIVERS' WORLD CHAMPIONSHIP WINNERS 1950-1997

R=Races; W=Wins; P=Poles; F=Fastest laps

| Year | Driver | Age | Country | Car | R | W | P | F |
|------|--------|-----|---------|-----|---|---|---|---|
| 1950 | Giuseppe Farina | 44 | Italy | Alfa Romeo | 7 | 3 | 2 | 3 |
| 1951 | Juan-Manuel Fangio | 40 | Argentina | Alfa Romeo | 8 | 3 | 4 | 5 |
| 1952 | Alberto Ascari | 34 | Italy | Ferrari | 8 | 6 | 5 | 5 |
| 1953 | Alberto Ascari | 35 | Italy | Ferrari | 9 | 5 | 6 | 4 |
| 1954 | Juan-Manuel Fangio | 43 | Argentina | Merc/Maserati | 9 | 6 | 5 | 3 |
| 1955 | Juan-Manuel Fangio | 44 | Argentina | Mercedes | 7 | 4 | 3 | 3 |
| 1956 | Juan-Manuel Fangio | 45 | Argentina | Lancia/Ferrari | 8 | 3 | 5 | 3 |
| 1957 | Juan-Manuel Fangio | 46 | Argentina | Maserati | 8 | 4 | 4 | 2 |
| 1958 | Mike Hawthorn | 29 | G. Britain | Ferrari | 11 | 1 | 4 | 5 |
| 1959 | Jack Brabham | 33 | Australia | Cooper | 9 | 2 | 1 | 1 |
| 1960 | Jack Brabham | 34 | Australia | Cooper | 10 | 5 | 3 | 3 |
| 1961 | Phil Hill | 34 | USA | Ferrari | 8 | 2 | 5 | 2 |
| 1962 | Graham Hill | 33 | G. Britain | BRM | 9 | 4 | 1 | 3 |
| 1963 | Jim Clark | 27 | G. Britain | Lotus | 10 | 7 | 7 | 6 |
| 1964 | John Surtees | 30 | G. Britain | Ferrari | 10 | 2 | 2 | 2 |
| 1965 | Jim Clark | 29 | G. Britain | Lotus | 10 | 6 | 6 | 6 |
| 1966 | Jack Brabham | 40 | Australia | Brabham | 9 | 4 | 3 | 1 |
| 1967 | Denis Hulme | 31 | N. Zealand | Brabham | 11 | 2 | 0 | 2 |
| 1968 | Graham Hill | 39 | G. Britain | Lotus | 12 | 3 | 2 | 0 |
| 1969 | Jackie Stewart | 30 | G. Britain | Matra | 11 | 6 | 2 | 5 |
| 1970 | Jochen Rindt | 28 | Austria | Lotus | 13 | 5 | 3 | 1 |
| 1971 | Jackie Stewart | 32 | G. Britain | Tyrrell | 11 | 6 | 6 | 3 |
| 1972 | Emerson Fittipaldi | 26 | Brazil | Lotus | 12 | 5 | 3 | 1 |
| 1973 | Jackie Stewart | 34 | Brazil | Tyrrell | 15 | 5 | 3 | 1 |
| 1974 | Emerson Fittipaldi | 28 | Brazil | McLaren | 15 | 3 | 2 | 0 |
| 1975 | Niki Lauda | 26 | Austria | Ferrari | 14 | 5 | 9 | 2 |
| 1976 | James Hunt | 29 | G. Britain | McLaren | 16 | 6 | 8 | 2 |
| 1977 | Niki Lauda | 28 | Austria | Ferrari | 17 | 3 | 2 | 3 |
| 1978 | Mario Andretti | 38 | USA | Lotus | 16 | 6 | 8 | 3 |
| 1979 | Jody Scheckter | 29 | USA | Ferrari | 15 | 3 | 1 | 1 |
| 1980 | Alan Jones | 34 | Australia | Williams | 14 | 5 | 3 | 5 |
| 1981 | Nelson Piquet | 29 | Brazil | Brabham | 15 | 3 | 4 | 1 |
| 1982 | Keke Rosberg | 34 | Finland | Williams | 16 | 1 | 1 | 0 |
| 1983 | Nelson Piquet | 31 | Brazil | Brabham | 15 | 3 | 1 | 4 |
| 1984 | Niki Lauda | 35 | Austria | McLaren | 16 | 5 | 0 | 5 |
| 1985 | Alain Prost | 30 | France | McLaren | 16 | 5 | 2 | 5 |
| 1986 | Alain Prost | 31 | France | McLaren | 16 | 4 | 1 | 2 |
| 1987 | Nelson Piquet | 35 | Brazil | Williams | 16 | 3 | 4 | 4 |
| 1988 | Ayrton Senna | 28 | Brazil | McLaren | 16 | 8 | 13 | 3 |

| Year | Driver | Age | Country | Car | R | W | P | F |
|------|--------|-----|---------|-----|---|---|---|---|
| | | | | R=Races; W=Wins; P=Poles; F=Fastest laps | | | | |
| 1989 | Alain Prost | 34 | France | McLaren | 16 | 4 | 2 | 5 |
| 1990 | Ayrton Senna | 30 | Brazil | McLaren | 16 | 6 | 10 | 2 |
| 1991 | Ayrton Senna | 31 | Brazil | McLaren | 16 | 7 | 8 | 2 |
| 1992 | Nigel Mansell | 39 | G. Britain | Williams | 16 | 9 | 14 | 8 |
| 1993 | Alain Prost | 38 | France | Williams | 16 | 7 | 13 | 6 |
| 1994 | Michael Schumacher | 25 | Germany | Benetton | 16 | 8 | 6 | 8 |
| 1995 | Michael Schumacher | 26 | Germany | Benetton | 17 | 9 | 4 | 8 |
| 1996 | Damon Hill | 36 | G. Britain | Williams | 16 | 8 | 9 | 5 |
| 1997 | Jacques Villeneuve | 26 | Canada | Williams | 17 | 7 | 11 | 3 |

# DRIVERS' WORLD CHAMPIONSHIP WINS BY NUMBER 1950-97

| Titles | Driver | Country | Year |
|--------|--------|---------|------|
| 5 | Juan-Manuel Fangio | Argentina | 1951, 1954, 1955, 1956, 1957 |
| 4 | Alain Prost | France | 1985, 1986, 1989, 1993 |
| 3 | Jack Brabham | Australia | 1959, 1960, 1966 |
| 3 | Jackie Stewart | Great Britain | 1969, 1971, 1973 |
| 3 | Niki Lauda | Austria | 1975, 1977, 1984 |
| 3 | Nelson Piquet | Brazil | 1981, 1983, 1987 |
| 3 | Ayrton Senna | Brazil | 1988, 1990, 1991 |
| 2 | Alberto Ascari | Italy | 1952, 1953 |
| 2 | Graham Hill | Great Britain | 1962, 1968 |
| 2 | Jim Clark | Great Britain | 1963, 1965 |
| 2 | Emerson Fittipaldi | Brazil | 1972, 1974 |
| 2 | Michael Schumacher | Germany | 1994, 1995 |
| 1 | Giuseppe Farina | Italy | 1950 |
| 1 | Mike Hawthorn | Great Britain | 1958 |
| 1 | Phil Hill | USA | 1961 |
| 1 | John Surtees | Great Britain | 1964 |
| 1 | Denis Hulme | New Zealand | 1967 |
| 1 | Jochen Rindt | Austria | 1970 |
| 1 | James Hunt | Great Britain | 1976 |
| 1 | Mario Andretti | USA | 1978 |
| 1 | Jody Scheckter | USA | 1979 |
| 1 | Alan Jones | Australia | 1980 |
| 1 | Keke Rosberg | Finland | 1982 |
| 1 | Nigel Mansell | Great Britain | 1992 |
| 1 | Damon Hill | Great Britain | 1996 |
| 1 | Jacques Villeneuve | Canada | 1997 |

# 1997 DRIVERS' ALL-TIME RECORDS

| Driver | No | WC | 1st | 2nd | 3rd | 4th | 5th | 6th | P | FL | TP | B |
|---|---|---|---|---|---|---|---|---|---|---|---|---|
| ALESI, Jean | 135 | 0 | 1 | 16 | 14 | 11 | 12 | 6 | 2 | 4 | 225 | 1 |
| BARRICHELLO, Rubens | 81 | 0 | 0 | 1 | 1 | 8 | 4 | 4 | 1 | 1 | 54 | 2 |
| BERGER, Gerhard | 210 | 0 | 10 | 17 | 21 | 26 | 8 | 12 | 12 | 20 | 385 | 1 |
| COULTHARD, David | 58 | 0 | 3 | 8 | 4 | 4 | 3 | 4 | 5 | 5 | 117 | 1 |
| DINIZ, Pedro | 50 | 0 | 0 | 0 | 0 | 0 | 1 | 2 | 0 | 0 | 4 | 5 |
| FISICHELLA, Giancarlo | 25 | 0 | 0 | 1 | 1 | 3 | 0 | 1 | 0 | 0 | 20 | 2 |
| FONTANA, Norberto | 4 | 0 | 0 | 0 | 0 | 0 | 0 | 0 | 0 | 0 | 0 | 9 |
| FRENTZEN, Heinz-Harald | 65 | 0 | 1 | 2 | 5 | 5 | 3 | 8 | 1 | 6 | 71 | 1 |
| HAKKINEN, Mika | 96 | 0 | 1 | 3 | 11 | 7 | 8 | 5 | 1 | 1 | 117 | 1 |
| HERBERT, Johnny | 113 | 0 | 2 | 1 | 3 | 10 | 5 | 4 | 0 | 1 | 82 | 1 |
| HILL, Damon | 84 | 1 | 21 | 15 | 5 | 3 | 1 | 2 | 20 | 19 | 333 | 1 |
| IRVINE, Eddie | 65 | 0 | 0 | 1 | 6 | 3 | 5 | 3 | 0 | 0 | 52 | 2 |
| KATAYAMA, Ukyo | 95 | 0 | 0 | 0 | 0 | 0 | 2 | 1 | 0 | 0 | 5 | 5 |
| LARINI, Nicola | 49 | 0 | 0 | 1 | 0 | 0 | 0 | 1 | 0 | 0 | 7 | 2 |
| MAGNUSSEN, Jan | 18 | 0 | 0 | 0 | 0 | 0 | 0 | 0 | 0 | 0 | 0 | 7 |
| MARQUES, Tarso | 9 | 0 | 0 | 0 | 0 | 0 | 0 | 0 | 0 | 0 | 0 | 10 |
| MORBIDELLI, Gianni | 67 | 0 | 0 | 0 | 1 | 0 | 1 | 3 | 0 | 0 | 9 | 3 |
| NAKANO, Shinji | 17 | 0 | 0 | 0 | 0 | 0 | 0 | 2 | 0 | 0 | 2 | 6 |
| PANIS, Olivier | 59 | 0 | 1 | 3 | 1 | 3 | 4 | 5 | 0 | 0 | 54 | 1 |
| ROSSET, Ricardo | 16 | 0 | 0 | 0 | 0 | 0 | 0 | 0 | 0 | 0 | 0 | 8 |
| SALO, Mika | 52 | 0 | 0 | 0 | 0 | 0 | 5 | 2 | 0 | 0 | 12 | 5 |
| SCHUMACHER, Michael | 102 | 2 | 27 | 17 | 10 | 6 | 3 | 4 | 17 | 29 | 440 | 1 |
| SCHUMACHER, Ralf | 17 | 0 | 0 | 0 | 1 | 0 | 4 | 1 | 0 | 0 | 13 | 3 |
| SOSPIRI, Vincenzo | 0 | 0 | 0 | 0 | 0 | 0 | 0 | 0 | 0 | 0 | 0 | 0 |
| TRULLI, Jarno | 14 | 0 | 0 | 0 | 0 | 1 | 0 | 0 | 0 | 0 | 3 | 4 |
| VERSTAPPEN, Jos | 48 | 0 | 0 | 0 | 2 | 0 | 1 | 1 | 0 | 0 | 11 | 3 |
| VILLENEUVE, Jacques | 33 | 1 | 11 | 5 | 3 | 1 | 2 | 0 | 13 | 9 | 159 | 1 |
| WURZ, Alexander | 3 | 0 | 0 | 0 | 1 | 0 | 0 | 0 | 0 | 0 | 4 | 3 |

*No=Number of Grands Prix. WC=Number of World Championship titles; 1st, 2nd
etc.=Number of times finished in this position; P=Number of Poles; FL=Number of
Fastest Laps; TP=Total number of World Championship Points won to date;
B=Best position achieved.*

*NB: Gerhard Berger did secure an additional point during the 1989 season but this did
not count towards the championship and is not included here.*

# 1997 DRIVERS BY COMPLETION %

| Driver | Races | Com | Ret | DNQ | HP | Pts | Psn | Comp% |
|---|---|---|---|---|---|---|---|---|
| G. Berger | 14 | 13 | 1 | 0 | 1st | 27 | 6/21 | 92.86% |
| J. Alesi | 17 | 14 | 3 | 0 | 2nd | 36 | 4/21 | 82.35% |
| O. Panis | 10 | 8 | 2 | 0 | 2nd | 16 | 10/21 | 80.00% |
| M. Schumacher | 17 | 13 | 4 | 0 | 1st | 78 | 2/21 | 76.47% |
| G. Fisichella | 17 | 13 | 4 | 0 | 2nd | 20 | 9/21 | 76.47% |
| G. Morbidelli | 8 | 6 | 2 | 0 | 9th | 0 | – | 75.00% |
| N. Fontana | 4 | 3 | 1 | 0 | 9th | 0 | – | 75.00% |
| J. Trulli | 7 | 5 | 2 | 0 | 4th | 3 | 16/21 | 71.43% |
| J. Villeneuve | 17 | 12 | 5 | 0 | 1st | 81 | 1/21 | 70.59% |
| H-H. Frentzen | 17 | 12 | 5 | 0 | 1st | 42 | 3/21 | 70.59% |
| E. Irvine | 17 | 11 | 6 | 0 | 2nd | 24 | 8/21 | 64.71% |
| J. Herbert | 17 | 11 | 6 | 0 | 3rd | 15 | 11/21 | 64.71% |
| J. Trulli | 8 | 5 | 3 | 0 | 9th | 0 | – | 62.50% |
| N. Larini | 5 | 3 | 2 | 0 | 6th | 1 | 21/21 | 60.00% |
| D. Hill | 17 | 10 | 7 | 0 | 2nd | 7 | 13/21 | 58.82% |
| D. Coulthard | 17 | 10 | 7 | 0 | 1st | 36 | 4/21 | 58.82% |
| M. Hakkinen | 17 | 10 | 7 | 0 | 1st | 27 | 6/21 | 58.82% |
| J. Verstappen | 17 | 9 | 8 | 0 | 8th | 0 | – | 52.94% |
| U. Katayama | 17 | 8 | 9 | 0 | 10th | 0 | – | 47.06% |
| S. Nakano | 17 | 8 | 9 | 0 | 6th | 2 | 17/21 | 47.06% |
| M. Salo | 17 | 8 | 9 | 0 | 5th | 2 | 17/21 | 47.06% |
| T. Marques | 9 | 4 | 5 | 0 | 10th | 0 | – | 44.44% |
| R. Schumacher | 17 | 7 | 10 | 0 | 3rd | 12 | 12/21 | 41.12% |
| P. Diniz | 17 | 6 | 11 | 0 | 5th | 2 | 17/21 | 35.29% |
| A. Wurz | 3 | 1 | 2 | 0 | 3rd | 4 | 15/21 | 33.33% |
| J. Magnussen | 17 | 5 | 12 | 0 | 7th | 0 | – | 29.41% |
| R. Barrichello | 17 | 3 | 14 | 0 | 2nd | 6 | 14/21 | 17.65% |

*Com=Races Completed; Ret=Races retired in; DNQ=Races Did Not Qualify in; HP=Highest Position achieved in a race; Pts=Driver World Championship Points; Psn=Position in DWC table; Comp%=Race Completion percentage.*

# 1997 TEAMS BY COMPLETION %

| Team | Races | Com | Ret | Pts | Psn | Comp% |
|------|-------|-----|-----|-----|-----|-------|
| Benetton Renault | 34 | 28 | 6 | 67 | 3/10 | 82.35% |
| Ferrari | 34 | 24 | 10 | 102 | 2/10 | 70.59% |
| Williams Renault | 34 | 24 | 10 | 123 | 1/10 | 70.59% |
| Prost Mugen Honda | 34 | 21 | 13 | 21 | 6/10 | 67.74% |
| Sauber Petronas | 34 | 23 | 11 | 16 | 7/10 | 67.65% |
| Jordan Peugeot | 34 | 20 | 14 | 33 | 5/10 | 58.82% |
| McLaren Mercedes | 34 | 20 | 14 | 63 | 4/10 | 58.82% |
| Minardi Hart | 34 | 17 | 17 | 0 | – | 50.00% |
| Tyrrell Ford | 34 | 17 | 17 | 2 | 10/10 | 50.00% |
| Arrows Yamaha | 34 | 16 | 18 | 9 | 8/10 | 47.06% |
| Stewart Ford | 34 | 8 | 26 | 6 | 9/10 | 23.53% |

*Com=Races Completed; Ret=Races Retired in; Pts=Constructors' World Championship Points; Psn=Position in CWC table; Comp%=Race Completion percentage.*

# THREE-YEAR DRIVER POINTS RECORDS 1995-1997

| Driver | 1995 | 1996 | 1997 | Driver | 1995 | 1996 | 1997 |
|--------|------|------|------|--------|------|------|------|
| Alesi | 42 | 47 | 36 | Magnussen | 0 | – | 0 |
| Barrichello | 11 | 14 | 6 | Marques | – | 0 | 0 |
| Berger | 31 | 21 | 27 | Montermini | 0 | 0 | – |
| Boullion | 3 | – | – | Morbidelli | 5 | – | 0 |
| Coulthard | 49 | 18 | 36 | Nakano | – | – | 2 |
| Diniz | 0 | 0 | 2 | Panis | 16 | 13 | 16 |
| Fisichella | – | 0 | 20 | Rosset | – | 0 | 0 |
| Frentzen | 15 | 0 | 42 | Salo | 5 | 0 | 2 |
| Fontana | – | – | 0 | Schumacher, M. | 102 | 59 | 78 |
| Hakkinen | 17 | 31 | 27 | Schumacher, R. | – | – | 13 |
| Herbert | 45 | 0 | 15 | Sospiri | – | – | 0 |
| Hill | 69 | 97 | 7 | Trulli | – | – | 3 |
| Irvine | 10 | 11 | 24 | Verstappen | – | 1 | 0 |
| Katayama | 0 | 0 | 0 | Villeneuve | – | 78 | 81 |
| Lamy | 1 | 0 | – | Wurz | – | – | 4 |
| Larini | – | – | 1 | | | | |

*17 Grands Prix in 1995 and 1997; 16 Grands Prix in 1996. – indicates no races. Number indicates points achieved during the season.*

# WORLD CHAMPIONSHIP DRIVERS WITH 100 POINTS OR MORE

| Driver | Points | Driver | Points | Driver | Points |
|---|---|---|---|---|---|
| Prost | 768.5 | Hulme | 248 | Rosberg | 159.5 |
| Senna | 610 | Fangio | 245 | J. Villeneuve | 159 |
| Piquet | 481.5 | Laffite | 228 | Depailler | 139 |
| Mansell | 480 | Alesi | 225 | Gurney | 133 |
| M. Schumacher | 440 | Regazzoni | 209 | Boutsen | 132 |
| Lauda | 420.5 | Peterson | 206 | De Angelis | 122 |
| Berger | 385 | Jones | 199 | Coulthard | 117 |
| Stewart | 359 | McLaren | 188.5 | Hakkinen | 117 |
| D. Hill | 333 | Moss | 186.5 | Farina | 116.3 |
| Reutemann | 298 | Alboreto | 185.5 | Hawthorn | 112.5 |
| E. Fittipaldi | 281 | Arnoux | 181 | Ascari | 107.5 |
| Patrese | 281 | Ickx | 181 | Rindt | 107 |
| G. Hill | 270 | Andretti | 180 | Ginther | 107 |
| Clark | 255 | Surtees | 180 | Tambay | 103 |
| J. Brabham | 253 | Hunt | 179 | G. Villeneuve | 101 |
| Scheckter | 246 | Watson | 169 | Pironi | 101 |

# WORLD CHAMPIONSHIP LAST RACE DECIDERS

| Year | Grand Prix | Circuit | Drivers |
|---|---|---|---|
| 1950 | Italian | Monza | Farina (30), Fangio (27), Fagioli (24) |
| 1951 | Spanish | Pedralbes | Fangio (31), Ascari (25) |
| 1956 | Italian | Monza | Fangio (30), Collins (25)* |
| 1958 | Morocco | Casablanca | Hawthorn (42), Moss (41) |
| 1959 | USA | Sebring | Brabham (31), Brooks (27), Moss (25.5) |
| 1962 | S. African | E. London | G. Hill (42), Clark (30) |
| 1964 | Mexican | Mexico City | Surtees (40), G. Hill (39), Clark (32) |
| 1967 | Mexican | Mexico City | Hulme (51), Brabham (46) |
| 1968 | Mexican | Mexico City | G. Hill (48), Stewart (36), Hulme (33) |
| 1974 | USA | Watkins Glen | E. Fittipaldi (55), Regazzoni (52), Scheckter (45) |
| 1976 | Japanese | Mount Fuji | Hunt (69), Lauda (68) |
| 1981 | USA | Las Vegas | Piquet (50), Reutemann (49), Laffite (46) |
| 1982 | USA | Las Vegas | Rosberg (44), Watson (39)† |
| 1983 | S. African | Kyalami | Piquet (59), Prost (57), Arnoux (49) |

| Year | Grand Prix | Circuit | Drivers |
|------|------------|---------|---------|
| 1984 | Portuguese | Estoril | Lauda (72), Prost (71.5) |
| 1986 | Australian | Adelaide | Prost (72), Mansell (70), Piquet (69) |
| 1994 | Australian | Adelaide | M. Schumacher (92), D. Hill (91) |
| 1996 | Japanese | Suzuka | D. Hill (97), J. Villeneuve (78) |
| 1997 | European | Jerez | J. Villeneuve (81), M. Schumacher (78) |

*\* Finished third in championship after Moss.   † Finished joint second with Pironi.
Numbers in brackets are final points total.*

# DRIVERS WITH FIVE OR MORE GRAND PRIX WINS

| Wins | Driver |
|------|--------|
| 51 | Alain Prost (France) |
| 41 | Ayrton Senna (Brazil) |
| 31 | Nigel Mansell (Great Britain) |
| 27 | Jackie Stewart (Great Britain), Michael Schumacher (Germany) |
| 25 | Jim Clark (Great Britain), Niki Lauda (Austria) |
| 24 | Juan-Manuel Fangio (Italy) |
| 23 | Nelson Piquet (Brazil) |
| 21 | Damon Hill (Great Britain) |
| 16 | Stirling Moss (Great Britain) |
| 14 | Jack Brabham (Australia), Emerson Fittipaldi (Brazil), Graham Hill (Great Britain) |
| 13 | Alberto Ascari (Italy) |
| 12 | Mario Andretti (USA), Alan Jones (Australia), Carlos Reutemann (Argentina) |
| 11 | Jacques Villeneuve (Canada) |
| 10 | James Hunt (Great Britain), Ronnie Peterson (Switzerland), Jody Scheckter (USA), Gerhard Berger (Austria) |
| 8 | Denis Hulme (New Zealand), Jacky Ickx (Belgium) |
| 7 | Rene Arnoux (France) |
| 6 | Tony Brooks (Great Britain), Jacques Laffite (France), Riccardo Patrese (Italy), Jochen Rindt (Austria), John Surtees (Great Britain), Gilles Villeneuve (Canada) |
| 5 | Michele Alboreto (Italy), Giuseppe Farina (Italy), Clay Regazzoni (Switzerland), Keke Rosberg (Finland), John Watson (Great Britain) |

# DRIVERS WITH FIVE OR MORE POLE POSITIONS

| Poles | Driver |
|---|---|
| 65 | Ayrton Senna (Brazil) |
| 33 | Jim Clark (Great Britain), Alain Prost (France) |
| 32 | Nigel Mansell (Great Britain) |
| 28 | Juan-Manuel Fangio (Italy) |
| 24 | Niki Lauda (Austria), Nelson Piquet (Brazil) |
| 20 | Damon Hill (Great Britain) |
| 18 | Mario Andretti (USA), Rene Arnoux (France) |
| 17 | Jackie Stewart (Great Britain), Michael Schumacher (Germany) |
| 16 | Stirling Moss (Great Britain) |
| 14 | Giuseppe Farina (Italy), James Hunt (Great Britain), Ronnie Peterson (Switzerland), |
| 13 | Jack Brabham (Australia), Graham Hill (Great Britain), Jacky Ickx (Belgium), Jacques Villeneuve (Canada) |
| 12 | Gerhard Berger (Austria) |
| 10 | Jochen Rindt (Austria) |
| 8 | Riccardo Patrese (Italy), John Surtees (Great Britain) |
| 7 | Jacques Laffite (France) |
| 6 | Emerson Fittipaldi (Brazil), Phil Hill (USA), Jean-Pierre Labouille (France), Alan Jones (Australia), Carlos Reutemann (Argentina) |
| 5 | Chris Amon (New Zealand), Giuseppe Farina (Italy), Clay Regazzoni (Switzerland), Keke Rosberg (Finland), Patrick Tambay (France), David Coulthard (Great Britain) |

# DRIVERS WITH FIVE OR MORE FASTEST LAPS

| No | Driver |
|---|---|
| 41 | Alain Prost (France) |
| 30 | Nigel Mansell (Great Britain) |
| 29 | Michael Schumacher (Germany) |
| 28 | Jim Clark (Great Britain) |
| 25 | Niki Lauda (Austria) |
| 23 | Juan-Manuel Fangio (Italy), Nelson Piquet (Brazil) |
| 20 | Stirling Moss (Great Britain), Gerhard Berger (Austria) |
| 19 | Ayrton Senna (Brazil), Damon Hill (Great Britain) |
| 15 | Clay Regazzoni (Switzerland), Jackie Stewart (Great Britain) |
| 14 | Jacky Ickx (Belgium) |
| 13 | Alan Jones (Australia), Riccardo Patrese (Italy) |

| | |
|---|---|
| 12 | Rene Arnoux (France) |
| 11 | Alberto Ascari (Italy), John Surtees (Great Britain) |
| 10 | Mario Andretti (USA), Jack Brabham (Australia), Graham Hill (Great Britain) |
| 9 | Denis Hulme (New Zealand), Ronnie Peterson (USA), Jacques Villeneuve (Canada) |
| 8 | James Hunt (Great Britain) |
| 7 | Jacques Laffite (France), Gilles Villeneuve (Canada) |
| 6 | Giuseppe Farina (Italy), Jose Gonzalez (Argentina), Dan Gurney (USA), Mike Hawthorn (Great Britain), Phil Hill (USA), Didier Pironi (France), Jody Scheckter (USA), Heinz-Harald Frentzen |
| 5 | Carlos Pace (Brazil), John Watson (Great Britain), David Coulthard (Great Britain) |

# DRIVERS WHO HAVE CONTESTED 100 GRANDS PRIX OR MORE

| No | Driver |
|---|---|
| 256 | Riccardo Patrese (Italy) |
| 210 | Gerhard Berger (Austria) |
| 208 | Andrea de Cesaris (Italy) |
| 204 | Nelson Piquet (Brazil) |
| 199 | Alain Prost (France) |
| 194 | Michele Alboreto (Italy) |
| 187 | Nigel Mansell (GB) |
| 176 | Graham Hill (GB), Jacques Laffite (France) |
| 171 | Niki Lauda (Austria) |
| 163 | Thierry Boutsen (Belgium) |
| 161 | Ayrton Senna (Brazil) |
| 158 | Martin Brundle (GB) |
| 152 | John Watson (GB) |
| 149 | Rene Arnoux (France) |
| 147 | Derek Warwick (GB) |
| 146 | Carlos Reutemann (Argentina) |
| 144 | Emerson Fittipaldi (Brazil) |
| 135 | Jean-Pierre Jarier (France), Jean Alesi (France) |
| 132 | Eddie Cheever (USA), Clay Regazzoni (Switzerland) |

| No | Driver |
|---|---|
| 128 | Mario Andretti (USA) |
| 126 | Jack Brabham (Australia) |
| 123 | Ronnie Peterson (USA) |
| 119 | Pierluigi Martini (Italy) |
| 116 | Jacky Ickx (Belgium), Alan Jones (Australia) |
| 113 | Johnny Herbert (GB) |
| 112 | Denis Hulme (New Zealand), Jody Scheckter (USA) |
| 111 | John Surtees (GB) |
| 109 | Philippe Alliot (France) |
| 108 | Elio de Angelis (Italy) |
| 105 | Jochen Mass (Germany) |
| 102 | Joakim Bonnier (Switzerland), Michael Schumacher (Germany) |
| 101 | Bruce McLaren (New Zealand) |

# DRIVERS WITH MORE THAN 5 POLE POSITIONS IN A SEASON

| Poles | Races | Driver | Year(s) |
|-------|-------|--------|---------|
| 14 | 16 | Mansell | 1992 |
| 13 | 16/16 | Senna | 1988 and 1989 |
| | 16 | Prost | 1993 |
| 10 | 16 | Senna | 1990 |
| | 17 | Villeneuve, J. | 1997 |
| 9 | 15/14 | Lauda | 1974 and 1975 |
| | 15 | Peterson | 1973 |
| | 16 | Piquet | 1984 |
| | 16 | Hill, Damon | 1996 |
| 8 | 16/16 | Senna | 1986 and 1991 |
| | 16 | Hunt | 1976 |
| | 16 | Andretti | 1978 |
| | 16 | Mansell | 1987 |
| 7 | 10 | Clark | 1963 |
| | 17 | Andretti | 1977 |
| | 16 | Senna | 1985 |
| | 17 | Hill, Damon | 1995 |
| 6 | 9/10/11 | Clark | 1962, 1965 and 1967 |
| | 9 | Ascari | 1953 |
| | 11 | Stewart | 1971 |
| | 17 | Hunt | 1977 |
| | 16 | Schumacher, M. | 1994 |

# DRIVERS WITH 3 OR MORE SUCCESSIVE GRAND PRIX WINS

| Wins | Driver | Year | Grand Prix |
|------|--------|------|------------|
| 9 | Ascari | 1952/53 | Bel, Fra, GB, Ger, Hol, Ita, Arg, Hol, Bel |
| 5 | Brabham | 1960 | Hol, Bel, Fra, GB, Por |
| | Clark | 1965 | Bel, Fra, GB, Hol, Ger |
| | Mansell | 1992 | SA, Mex, Bra, Esp, San |
| 4 | Senna | 1988 | GB, Ger, Hon, Bel |
| | | 1991 | USA, Bra, San, Mon |
| | Fangio | 1953/54 | Ita/Arg, Bel, Fra |
| | Clark | 1963 | Bel, Hol, Fra, GB |
| | Brabham | 1966 | Fra, GB, Hol, Ger |
| | Rindt | 1970 | Hol, Fra, GB, Ger |

|   | Prost | 1993 | Can, Fra, GB, Ger |
|---|---|---|---|
|   | Schumacher | 1994 | Bra, Pac, San, Mon |
| 3 | Fangio | 1954 | Ger, Sui, Ita |
|   |   | 1957 | Arg, Mon, Fra |
|   | Stewart | 1969 | Hol, Fra, GB |
|   |   | 1971 | Fra, GB, Ger |
|   | Lauda | 1975 | Mon, Bel, Swe |
|   |   | 1975/76 | USA/Bra, SA |
|   | Jones | 1979 | Ger, Aut, Hol |
|   |   | 1980/81 | Can, USAE/USAW |
|   | Prost | 1984/85 | Eur, Por/Bra |
|   |   | 1990 | Mex, Fra, GB |
|   | Mansell | 1991 | Fra, GB, Ger |
|   |   | 1992 | Fra, GB, Ger |
|   | Moss | 1957/58 | Pes, Ita/Arg |
|   | Clark | 1967/68 | USA, Mex/SA |
|   | Senna | 1989 | San, Mon, Mex |
|   | D. Hill | 1993 | Hun, Bel, Ita |
|   |   | 1994 | Bel, Ita, Por |
|   |   | 1996 | Aus, Bra, Arg |
|   | M. Schumacher | 1995 | Eur, Pac, Jap |

# DRIVERS TO WIN THEIR NATIONAL GRAND PRIX

| Wins | Driver | Nat | Year(s) |
|---|---|---|---|
| 6 | Prost | French | 1981, 1983, 1988, 1989, 1990, 1993 |
| 5 | Clark | British | 1962, 1963, 1964, 1965, 1967 |
| 4 | Fangio | Argentine | 1954, 1955, 1956, 1957 |
|   | Mansell | British | 1986, 1987, 1991, 1992 |
| 2 | Ascari | Italian | 1951, 1952 |
|   | Moss | British | 1955, 1957 |
|   | Stewart | British | 1969, 1971 |
|   | E. Fittipaldi | Brazilian | 1973, 1974 |
|   | Piquet | Brazilian | 1983, 1986 |
|   | Senna | Brazilian | 1991, 1993 |
| 1 | Farina | Italian | 1950 |
|   | Collins | British | 1958 |
|   | Scarfiotti | Italian | 1966 |
|   | Pace | Brazilian | 1975 |
|   | Scheckter | S. African | 1975 |
|   | Andretti | American | 1977 |
|   | Hunt | British | 1977 |
|   | Villeneuve, G. | Canadian | 1978 |

| | | | | |
|---|---|---|---|---|
| Jabouille | French | 1979 | | |
| Watson | British | 1981 | | |
| Arnoux | French | 1982 | | |
| Lauda | Austrian | 1984 | | |
| D. Hill | British | 1994 | | |
| Herbert | British | 1995 | | |
| Schumacher, M. | German | 1995 | | |

# GRANDS PRIX WITH DRIVER FATALITIES

| Year | Grand Prix | Venue | Driver | Car | During |
|---|---|---|---|---|---|
| 1954 | Germany | Nurburgring | O. Marimon | Maserati | Practice |
| 1955 | Indianapolis | Indianapolis | B. Vukovich | | Race |
| 1958 | France | Reims | L. Musso | Ferrari | Race |
| 1958 | Germany | Nurburgring | P. Collins | Ferrari | Race |
| 1958 | Morocco | Casablanca | S. Lewis-Evans | Vanwall | Race |
| 1959 | Indianapolis | Indianapolis | J. Unser | | Race |
| | | | B. Cortner | | Race |
| 1960 | Belgium | Spa-Fran' | C. Bristow | | Race |
| | | | A. Stacey | | Race |
| 1961 | Italy | Monza | Von Trips | Ferrari | Race |
| 1964 | Germany | Nurburgring | C. de Beaufort | | Practice |
| 1966 | Germany | Nurburgring | J. Taylor | Brabham | Race |
| 1967 | Monaco | Monaco | L. Bandini | Ferrari | Inj/Race† |
| 1968 | France | Rouen | J. Schlesser | Honda | Race |
| 1969 | Germany | Nurburgring | G. Mitter | | Practice |
| 1970 | Holland | Zandvoort | P. Courage | De Tomaso | Race |
| 1970 | Italy | Monza | J. Rindt | Lotus | Practice |
| 1973 | Holland | Zandvoort | R. Williamson | March | Race |
| 1973 | USA | Watkins Glen | F. Cevert | Tyrrell | Practice |
| 1974 | USA | Watkins Glen | H. Koinigg | Surtees | Race |
| 1975 | Austria | Osterreichring | M. Donohue | M-Penske | Practice |
| 1977 | South Africa | Kyalami | T. Pryce | Shadow | Race |
| 1978 | Italy | Monza | R. Peterson | Lotus | Inj/Race* |
| 1982 | Belgium | Zolder | G. Villeneuve | Ferrari | Practice |
| 1982 | Canada | Montreal | R. Paletti | Osella Ford | Race |
| 1994 | San Marino | Imola | R. Ratzenberger | Simtek | Practice |
| | | | A. Senna | Williams | Race |

† *Died three days after race from burns.*
\* *Died the next day from injuries received during start of race.*

# CONSTRUCTORS' CUP BY CAR

| Titles | Car | Year(s) |
|---|---|---|
| 9 | Williams | 1980, 1981, 1986, 1987, 1992, 1993, 1994, 1996, 1997 |
| 8 | Ferrari | 1961, 1964, 1975, 1976, 1977, 1979, 1982, 1983 |
| 7 | Lotus | 1963, 1965, 1968, 1970, 1972, 1973, 1978 |
| 7 | McLaren | 1974, 1984, 1985, 1988, 1989, 1990, 1991 |
| 2 | Cooper | 1959, 1960 |
| 2 | Brabham | 1966, 1967 |
| 1 | Vanwall | 1958 |
| 1 | BRM | 1962 |
| 1 | Matra | 1969 |
| 1 | Tyrrell | 1971 |
| 1 | Benetton | 1995 |

# CONSTRUCTORS' CUP WINNERS

| Year | Team | Year | Team | Year | Team |
|---|---|---|---|---|---|
| 1958 | Vanwall | 1971 | Tyrrell | 1984 | McLaren |
| 1959 | Cooper | 1972 | Lotus | 1985 | McLaren |
| 1960 | Cooper | 1973 | Lotus | 1986 | Williams |
| 1961 | Ferrari | 1974 | McLaren | 1987 | Williams |
| 1962 | BRM | 1975 | Ferrari | 1988 | McLaren |
| 1963 | Lotus | 1976 | Ferrari | 1989 | McLaren |
| 1964 | Ferrari | 1977 | Ferrari | 1990 | McLaren |
| 1965 | Lotus | 1978 | Lotus | 1991 | McLaren |
| 1966 | Brabham | 1979 | Ferrari | 1992 | Williams |
| 1967 | Brabham | 1980 | Williams | 1993 | Williams |
| 1968 | Lotus | 1981 | Williams | 1994 | Williams |
| 1969 | Matra | 1982 | Ferrari | 1995 | Benetton |
| 1970 | Lotus | 1983 | Ferrari | 1996 | Williams |
| | | | | 1997 | Williams |

# GRAND PRIX WINS PER CAR TYPE

| Wins | Car Type | | | |
|---|---|---|---|---|
| 113 | Ferrari | 17 | BRM | Ligier |
| 107 | McLaren | 16 | Cooper | 3 March, Wolf |
| 103 | Williams | 15 | Renault | 2 Honda |
| 79 | Lotus | 10 | Alfa Romeo | 1 Eagle, |
| 35 | Brabham | 9 | Maserati, | Hesketh, |
| 27 | Benetton | | Matra, | Penske, |
| 23 | Tyrrell | | Mercedes, | Porsche, |
| | | | Vanwall, | Shadow |

# GP PARTICIPATED PER CAR TYPE

| GP | Car Type | | | | |
|----|----------|----|----|----|----|
| 587 | Ferrari | 117 | Surtees | 34 | Theodore |
| 490 | Lotus | 114 | Jordan | 33 | Porsche |
| 460 | McLaren | 112 | Alfa Romeo | 30 | Penske |
| 402 | Tyrrell | 104 | Fittipaldi, | 28 | Vanwall |
| 394 | Brabham | | Shadow | 25 | Eagle |
| 343 | Prost (Ligier) | 99 | ATS | 22 | Pacific |
| 316 | Williams | 98 | Ensign | 20 | Rial |
| 305 | Arrows | 82 | Sauber | 19 | Lola Haas |
| 251 | Benetton | 78 | Dallara | 17 | Onyx, Forti, |
| 230 | March | 69 | Maserati | | Stewart |
| 205 | Minardi | 61 | Matra | 16 | Simtek |
| 197 | BRM | 54 | Zakspeed | 15 | Parnelli |
| 139 | Lola | 48 | AGS, | 12 | Mercedes |
| 132 | Osella | | Larousse, | 11 | Forti |
| 129 | Cooper | | Wolf | 10 | Merzario |
| 123 | Renault | 40 | Gordini | 4 | Lancia |
| | | 35 | Honda | | |

# POLE POSITIONS PER CAR TYPE

| Poles | Car Type | | | | |
|-------|----------|----|----|----|----|
| 121 | Ferrari | 14 | Tyrrell | 4 | Matra |
| 108 | Williams | 12 | Alfa Romeo | 3 | Shadow |
| 107 | Lotus | 11 | BRM, Cooper | 2 | Lancia |
| 80 | McLaren | 10 | Maserati | 1 | Arrows, |
| 39 | Brabham | 9 | Ligier | | Honda, Jordan, |
| 31 | Renault | 8 | Mercedes | | Lola, Porsche, |
| 15 | Benetton | 7 | Vanwall | | Wolf |
| | | 5 | March | | |

# FASTEST LAPS PER CAR TYPE

| Laps | Car Type | | | | |
|------|----------|----|----|----|----|
| 124 | Ferrari | 14 | Alfa Romeo | 2 | Eagle, Honda, |
| 109 | Williams | 13 | Cooper | | Shadow, Wolf, |
| 71 | Lotus, McLaren | 12 | Matra | | Jordan |
| 40 | Brabham | 11 | Ligier | 1 | Ensign, |
| 38 | Benetton | 9 | Mercedes | | Gordini, |
| 20 | Tyrrell | 7 | March | | Hesketh, |
| 18 | Renault | 6 | Vanwall | | Lancia, Parnelli |
| 15 | BRM, Maserati | 4 | Surtees | | |

Drivers 1998

## Introduction

These pages contain an A-Z of drivers who have been named as teams' major drivers for the 1998 Grand Prix season plus all the drivers who featured in the 1997 Grand Prix season. In addition to this, where possible we have also included teams' test drivers and any other drivers who might possibly feature during 1998 and who were known at the time of going to press. While every attempt has been made to ensure that this list is as accurate as possible, new drivers may have come to light after this book went to press. Each entry lists a brief resumé of each driver's F1 career to date and then provides a summary of GP details. This is followed by a list of each of the Grand Prix races he has competed in. Numbers in brackets after named Grands Prix signify the number of points scored in the race in question.

## Team and Driver Number Allocation 1998

Listed below are the numbers allocated to the teams for the 1998 season and the drivers allocated to the numbers by their team at the time of going to press. Although the team numbers will remain consistent, the numbers allocated to drivers may change, especially when teams are using more than two drivers during the season.

| No. | Driver | Country | Team | Car |
|---|---|---|---|---|
| 1 | Jacques Villeneuve | Can | Williams | Williams FW20 |
| 2 | Heinz-Harald Frentzen | Ger | Williams | Williams FW20 |
| 3 | Michael Schumacher | Ger | Ferrari | Ferrari F300 |
| 4 | Eddie Irvine | GB | Ferrari | Ferrari F300 |
| 5 | Giancarlo Fisichella | Ita | Benetton | Benetton B198 |
| 6 | Alexander Wurz | Aut | Benetton | Benetton B198 |
| 7 | David Coulthard | GB | McLaren | McLaren Mercedes MP4-13 |
| 8 | Mika Hakkinen | Fin | McLaren | McLaren Mercedes MP4-13 |
| 9 | Damon Hill | GB | Jordan | Jordan Mugen-Honda 198 |
| 10 | Ralf Schumacher | Ger | Jordan | Jordan Mugen-Honda 198 |
| 11 | Olivier Panis | Fra | Prost | Prost Peugeot AP01 |
| 12 | Jarno Trulli | Ita | Prost | Prost Peugeot AP01 |
| 14 | Jean Alesi | Fra | Sauber | Sauber Petronas C17 |
| 15 | Johnny Herbert | GB | Sauber | Sauber Petronas C17 |
| 16 | Pedro Diniz | Bra | Arrows | Arrows A19 |
| 17 | Mika Salo | Fin | Arrows | Arrows A19 |
| 18 | Rubens Barrichello | Bra | Stewart | Stewart Ford SF2 |
| 19 | Jan Magnussen | Den | Stewart | Stewart Ford SF2 |
| 20 | Toranosuke Takagi | Jap | Tyrrell | Tyrrell Ford 026 |
| 21 | | | Tyrrell | Tyrrell Ford 026 |
| 22 | Esterban Tuero | Arg | Minardi | Minardi M198 |
| 23 | | | Minardi | Minardi M198 |

## Driver Race Summaries 1998

Total profile summaries of the drivers for the 1998 Championship are listed below.

| No. | Driver | Age | Races | Wins | Poles | FLaps | Pts |
|---|---|---|---|---|---|---|---|
| 1 | Jacques Villeneuve | 27 | 33 | 11 | 13 | 9 | 159 |
| 2 | Heinz-Harald Frentzen | 30 | 65 | 1 | 1 | 6 | 71 |
| 3 | Michael Schumacher | 29 | 102 | 27 | 17 | 29 | 440 |
| 4 | Eddie Irvine | 32 | 65 | 0 | 0 | 0 | 52 |
| 5 | Giancarlo Fisichella | 25 | 25 | 0 | 0 | 0 | 20 |
| 6 | Alexander Wurz | 24 | 3 | 0 | 0 | 0 | 4 |
| 7 | David Coulthard | 27 | 58 | 3 | 5 | 5 | 117 |
| 8 | Mika Hakkinen | 29 | 96 | 1 | 1 | 1 | 117 |
| 9 | Damon Hill | 37 | 84 | 21 | 20 | 19 | 333 |
| 10 | Ralf Schumacher | 22 | 17 | 0 | 0 | 0 | 13 |
| 11 | Olivier Panis | 31 | 59 | 1 | 0 | 0 | 54 |
| 12 | Jarno Trulli | 23 | 14 | 0 | 0 | 0 | 3 |
| 14 | Jean Alesi | 33 | 135 | 1 | 2 | 4 | 225 |
| 15 | Johnny Herbert | 33 | 113 | 2 | 0 | 1 | 82 |
| 16 | Pedro Diniz | 27 | 50 | 0 | 0 | 0 | 4 |
| 17 | Mika Salo | 31 | 52 | 0 | 0 | 0 | 12 |
| 18 | Rubens Barrichello | 25 | 81 | 0 | 1 | 1 | 54 |
| 19 | Jan Magnussen | 24 | 18 | 0 | 0 | 0 | 0 |
| 20 | Toranosuke Takagi | 0 | 0 | 0 | 0 | 0 | 0 |
| 21 | | | | | | | |
| 22 | Esterban Tuero | 0 | 0 | 0 | 0 | 0 | 0 |
| 23 | | | | | | | |

**Happy memories for Gerhard Berger celebrating victory in Hungary**

# ALESI, Jean                                                        France

*1997: Benetton Renault*                              *1998: Sauber Petronas*

For the third year in a row Jean Alesi turned in another consistent performance. The Frenchman only failed to finish three and was in the points in ten of the fifteen Grands Prix that he finished. In fact, his lap completion percentage of 88.9 was the best of any driver. This is perhaps more significant given that Alesi often failed to impress in qualifying – only twice getting onto the front row of the grid and having to settle for an average eighth place.

There are always moments in a season when Alesi does something that will infuriate his team and his Benetton mechanics didn't have to wait long. Having qualified on the fourth row of the grid, his race lasted just 34 laps at Melbourne when he retired simply because he ran out of fuel. He had been scheduled to pit on lap 31 but he seemed to be deaf and blind to radio and pit board messages and ultimately the inevitable happened. Team boss Flavio Briatore was far from happy and for the rest of the season the rumours abounded of disagreements between the two of them. Ultimately, both left the team.

In Brazil, Alesi's sixth place grid position was matched on the track as he earned the first of his 36 points of the season having spent much of the race under the gearbox of Michael Schumacher's Ferrari. The improvement in Brazil wasn't matched in Argentina: having moved up to ninth at the start from his original eleventh position, he suffered gear selection troubles and a finish just outside the points.

Alesi's qualifying performance didn't get any better in San Marino and his fourteenth place was to be his second worst of the season. The race went better though and in the final stages Alesi won a scrape with Mika Hakkinen to take fifth place. At Monaco Alesi did better when securing ninth place on the grid but spun out at Portier on lap 16 after challenging Mika Salo's Tyrrell.

Things then got substantially better for the Frenchman as he went on a run of five races where he finished in the points and notched two second-place finishes. In Spain, everything improved when fourth on the grid was matched by a third-place finish. In Canada, qualifying was blighted by gearbox problems but these were put right for the race and a terrific start moved him up five places to third and ultimately to second place on the circuit which was the scene of his only Grand Prix win back in 1995. His six points in Canada took his all-time points tally through the 200 mark. Back in Europe at his home Grand Prix, he matched his Canadian position on the grid but had to settle for fifth place at the end of the race and was big enough to admit to being at fault for pushing off Coulthard's McLaren on the final lap. At Silverstone, Alesi, on a one-stop strategy, drove his way to another second place despite having to start from eleventh place on the grid.

The German Grand Prix saw a change in qualifying fortunes for Alesi – well, for four races at least. Sixth place on the grid at Hockenheim was equalled in the race and, after a finish well down the field in Hungary, Alesi suddenly found himself on the front row of the grid at Spa. However, first the elements and then his tyres conspired against him. Having started on wet-weather tyres, he had to pit for slicks early on and then had to make another stop after his first scheduled pit stop to change his blistering tyres. His performance was also hampered when the rear part of the plank under the car broke, thus creating loss of downforce.

Monza and the Italian Grand Prix proved to be the highlight of his season. Given a rousing welcome by the tifosi, the ex-Ferrari driver took only his second-ever pole position – ironically the other was also at Monza. Alesi held his line from the start but couldn't pull away a lead and lost the initiative to Coulthard when the two pitted together on lap 32. The Scot stayed in front and Alesi had to settle for his third second-place finish of the season.

If the Italian Grand Prix was the high of the year then the Austrian was the low. Alesi's worst qualifying position – 15th – preceded a premature end to the race when Eddie Irvine tried to pass him on the outside. Things didn't look to be going any better at the Luxembourg Grand Prix, although tenth position on the grid was better and couldn't have pointed to the fact that a second place finish was on the cards. He was aided by another great start which saw him catapult up to fifth place before his pit-stop strategy paid dividends and ensured a fourth second place for the third successive season.

Two points at Suzuka in the penultimate race of the season were the last scored by Alesi and in the final meeting of the season, at Jerez, he finished an unlucky thirteenth after a manoeuvre to pass Jan Magnussen sent him off the track and back onto it behind the majority of the field.

Despite the departure of Briatore, Alesi was not retained by Benetton and is driving alongside Johnny Herbert at Sauber during the 1998 season. Alesi's knowledge of the Ferrari-sourced engines that power the Swiss-based team should be beneficial to both parties but a realistic target will be to emulate the fifteen points achieved by Herbert in the 1997 Sauber. Given a full season, Alesi should also make his 150th Grand Prix start in the final couple of races.

**Born:** 11/6/64, Avignon, France. Single, one daughter.

# Grand Prix 1997 Record

| Grand Prix | Grid | Qual Time | Fin | Laps | Race Time | Reason |
|---|---|---|---|---|---|---|
| Australian | 8 | 1:32.593 | – | 34 | | out of fuel |
| Brazilian | 6 | 1:16.757 | 6 | 72 | 1:36:41.010 | |
| Argentinian | 11 | 1:27.076 | 7 | 72 | 1:52:48.074 | |
| San Marino | 14 | 1:25.729 | 5 | 61 | 1:31:18.063 | |
| Monaco | 9 | 1:19.263 | – | 16 | | spin |
| Spanish | 4 | 1:17.717 | 3 | 64 | 1:30:48.430 | |
| Canadian | 8 | 1:18.899 | 2 | 54 | 1:17:43.211 | |
| French | 8 | 1:15.228 | 5 | 72 | 1:40:13.227 | |
| British | 11 | 1:22.392 | 2 | 59 | 1:28:11.870 | |
| German | 6 | 1:42.493 | 6 | 45 | 1:21:33.763 | |
| Hungarian | 9 | 1:15.905 | 11 | 76 | 1:45:56.522 | |

| Belgian | 2 | 1:49.759 | 8 | 44 | 1:35:28.725 | |
| Italian | 1 | 1:22.990 | 2 | 53 | 1:17:06.546 | |
| Austrian | 15 | 1:11.392 | – | 37 | | accident |
| Luxembourg | 10 | 1:17.620 | 2 | 67 | 1:31:39.613 | |
| Japanese | 7 | 1:36.682 | 5 | 53 | 1:30.28.849 | |
| European | 10 | 1:22.011 | 13 | 68 | 1:39:15.717 | |

## 1997 Position Summary

| Contested: | 17 | Finished: | 14 |
|---|---|---|---|
| Pole Positions: | 1 | Fastest Laps: | 0 |
| Points: | 36 | | |
| 1st: | 0 | 2nd: | 4 |
| 3rd: | 1 | 4th: | 0 |
| 5th: | 3 | 6th: | 2 |

## Grand Prix Career Record

| Contested: | 135 | (1989-1997) |
|---|---|---|
| Pole Positions: | 2 | 1994 (Ita), 1997 (Ita) |
| Fastest Laps: | 4 | 1991 (USA), 1995 (Mon), 1996 (Arg, Mon) |
| Points: | 225 | 1989 (8), 1990 (13), 1991 (21), 1992 (18), 1993 (16), 1994 (24), 1995 (42), 1996 (47), 1997 (36) |
| 1st: | 1 | 1995 (Can) |
| 2nd: | 16 | 1990 (USA, Mon), 1993 (Ita), 1994 (GB), 1995 (Arg, San, GB, Eur), 1996 (Bra, Esp, Ger, Ita), 1997 (Can, GB, Ita, Lux) |
| 3rd: | 14 | 1991 (Mon, Ger, Por), 1992 (Esp, Can), 1993 (Mon), 1994 (Bra, Can, Jap), 1996 (Arg, Can, Fra, Hun), 1997 (Esp) |
| 4th: | 11 | 1989 (Fra, Esp), 1991 (Fra, Esp), 1992 (Bra, Aus), 1993 (Por, Aus), 1994 (Esp), 1996 (Bel, Por) |
| 5th: | 12 | 1989 (Ita), 1991 (Hun), 1992 (Ger, Jap), 1994 (Mon), 1995 (Bra, Fra, Por, Pac), 1997 (San, Fra, Jap) |
| 6th: | 6 | 1990 (San), 1991 (Bra), 1994 (Aus), 1996 (San), 1997 (Bra, Ger) |

| Year | Team | No. | Grand Prix |
|---|---|---|---|
| 1989 | Tyrrell Ford | 8 | Fra (3), GB, Ger, Hun, Ita (2), Esp (3), Jap, Aus |
| 1990 | Tyrrell Ford | 15 | USA (6), Bra, San (1), Mon (6), Can, Mex, Fra, GB, Ger, Hun, Bel, Ita, Por, Esp, Aus |
| 1991 | Ferrari | 16 | USA, Bra (1), San, Mon (4), Can, Mex, Fra (3), GB, Ger (4), Hun (2), Bel, Ita, Por (4), Esp (3), Jap, Aus |

| 1992 | Ferrari | 16 | SA, Mex, Bra (3), Esp (4), San, Mon, Can (4), Fra, GB, Ger (2), Hun, Bel, Ita, Por, Jap (2), Aus (3) |
| 1993 | Ferrari | 16 | SA, Bra, Eur, San, Esp, Mon (4), Can, Fra, GB, Ger, Hun, Bel, Ita (6), Por (3), Jap, Aus (3) |
| 1994 | Ferrari | 14 | Bra, Mon (2), Esp (3), Can (4), Fra, GB (6), Ger, Hun, Bel, Ita, Por, Eur, Jap (4), Aus |
| 1995 | Ferrari | 17 | Bra (2), Arg (6), San (6), Esp, Mon, Can (10), Fra (2), GB (6), Ger, Hun, Bel, Ita, Por (2), Eur (6), Pac (2), Jap, Aus |
| 1996 | Benetton Renault | 16 | Aus, Bra (6), Arg (4), Eur, San (1), Mon, Esp (6), Can (4), Fra (4), GB, Ger (6), Hun (4), Bel (3), Ita (6), Por (3), Jap |
| 1997 | Benetton Renault | 17 | Aus, Bra (1), Arg, San (2), Mon, Esp (4), Can (6), Fra (2), GB (6), Ger (1), Hun, Bel, Ita (6), Aut, Lux (6), Jap (2), Eur |

# BADOER, Luca                                                    **Italy**

*1997: –*                                               *1998: (Test Driver Ferrari)*

Having got back into F1 racing as part of the Minardi team in 1995, Luca Badoer was always going to struggle to take his career forward with what proved to be a hopelessly under-funded Forti team. The team lasted just ten Grands Prix before the funding ran out and, during that time, Badoer only managed to finish twice.

He had the distinction, along with his Forti teammate, Andrea Montermini, to become the first driver to fail to qualify for a Grand Prix under the 107% qualification rule. He set a happier record though that same season when he became the first Forti driver to out-qualify a driver from another team when he finished ahead of Ricardo Rosset's Arrows car to secure twentieth position on the grid in Canada.

In the run up to the 1998 season, Badoer was testing at Minardi for a possible drive as partner to Estertban Tuero but opted instead for the Marinello post as replacement for Nicola Larini, who is driving touring cars for Alfa Romeo.

**Born:** 25/1/71, Montebelluna, Treviso, Italy.

## Grand Prix Record

Contested:        35       (1993-1996)
Pole Positions:    0
Fastest Laps:      0

| Year | Team | No. | Grand Prix |
|------|------|-----|-----------|
| 1993 | Lola BMS | 12 | SA, Bra, San, Esp, Can, Fra, GB, Ger, Hun, Bel, Ita, Por |
| 1995 | Minardi Ford | 17 | Bra, Arg, San, Esp, Mon, Can, Fra, GB, Ger, Hun, Bel, Ita, Por, Eur, Pac, Jap, Aus |
| 1996 | Forti Ford | 6 | Bra, Arg, San, Mon, Can, Fra |

# BARRICHELLO, Rubens                              **Brazil**

*1997: Stewart Ford*                              *1998: Stewart Ford*

The excitement of being part of a brand new racing team is one thing, the dedication to the job, even in the face of adversity, is another and in this area Rubens Barrichello had a winning season. With little or no pre-season development time, every practice, qualifying and race session was an on-the-fly testing session as the team and engine supplier, Ford, looked to improve their overall package.

Looked at in isolation, Barrichello's stats make less than impressive reading. Out of seventeen starts he managed only three finishes, and just one of those came in the first twelve races. But what a finish it was as the ever-smiling Brazilian notched his team's first ever championship points with a delirious second place on the streets of Monte Carlo.

Engines aside, there were other teething problems. Take the Brazilian Grand Prix for instance, when Barrichello found himself remaining on the grid as the other cars swept away – his engine had been shut down by the on-board computer because the engine had powered to 16000 rpm. Other retirements were perhaps more predictable: suspension in Brazil and hydraulics in Argentina were typical. In fact, in only one race – the Japanese Grand Prix at Suzuka – did Barrichello commit the crime of spinning out.

The second place at Monaco equalled his best-ever finish – matching his performance in Canada two years earlier and taking his personal all-time world championship points tally through the half century mark. But, perhaps more importantly, it reminded those on-lookers that he is still a serious talent. The wet weather certainly helped his Bridgestone tyres and the street circuit of course ensured there was less strain on the ever-developing Ford engine.

After the high of Monaco, Barrichello's best qualifying performance came two races later in Canada where he secured a third place. In many respects this was an even bigger achievement than the finish in Monaco. Montreal, being a power circuit, really should not have suited his vastly under-powered SF-1. His set-up, where he carried virtually no wing at all and a higher than normal ride height, proved to be more than compensatory. The race told a different story though and, after suffering a ten-second Stop-Go penalty for ignoring yellow flags, his gearbox failed on lap 35.

The Italian and Austrian Grands Prix provided what proved to be the only other finishes for Barrichello in 1997, crossing the line in thirteenth and fourteenth positions respectively. The latter though saw another out-of-the-blue qualifying performance, with a fifth place. As with Montreal, low downforce set-ups greatly aided performance and at the Nurburgring this allowed the Brazilian to briefly hit third spot in the race.

With all of the development data gleaned during 1997, and the introduction of new development engines, the Stewart race team should be able to provide Barrichello with a more reliable unit for 1998. While another podium finish might be more wishful thinking, more race finishes are certain and that in itself should enable the Brazilian to secure more than the six points of 1997.

**Born:** 23/5/72, Sao Paulo, Brazil. Single.

## Grand Prix 1997 Record

| Grand Prix | Grid | Qual Time | Fin | Laps | Race Time | Reason |
|---|---|---|---|---|---|---|
| Australian | 11 | 1:33.075 | – | 49 | | engine |
| Brazilian | 11 | 1:17.259 | – | 16 | | suspension |
| Argentinian | 5 | 1:25.942 | – | 24 | | throttle |
| San Marino | 13 | 1:25.579 | – | 32 | | engine |
| Monaco | 10 | 1:19.295 | 2 | 62 | 2:00:58.960 | |
| Spanish | 17 | 1:20.255 | – | 37 | | engine |
| Canadian | 3 | 1:18.388 | – | 33 | | gearbox |
| French | 13 | 1:15.876 | – | 36 | | engine |
| British | 21 | 1:25.525 | – | 37 | | engine |
| German | 12 | 1:43.272 | – | 33 | | engine |
| Hungarian | 11 | 1:16.138 | – | 29 | | engine |
| Belgian | 12 | 1:51.916 | – | 8 | | steering arm |
| Italian | 11 | 1:24.177 | 13 | 52 | 1:17:55.672 | |
| Austrian | 5 | 1:10.700 | 14 | 67 | | accident |
| Luxembourg | 9 | 1:17.614 | – | 43 | | hydraulics |
| Japanese | 12 | 1:37.343 | – | 6 | | spin |
| European | 12 | 1:22.222 | – | 30 | | gearbox |

## 1997 Position Summary

| | | | |
|---|---|---|---|
| Contested: | 17 | Finished: | 3 |
| Pole Positions: | 0 | Fastest Laps: | 0 |
| Points: | 6 | | |
| 1st: | 0 | 2nd: | 1 |
| 3rd: | 0 | 4th: | 0 |
| 5th: | 0 | 6th: | 0 |

## Grand Prix Career Record

| | | | |
|---|---|---|---|
| Contested: | 81 | (1993-1997) | |
| Pole Positions: | 1 | 1994 (Bel) | |
| Fastest Laps: | 1 | | |
| Points: | 54 | 1993 (2), 1994 (19), 1995 (11), 1996 (14), 1997 (6) | |
| 1st: | 0 | | |
| 2nd: | 1 | 1995 (Can), 1997 (Mon) | |
| 3rd: | 1 | 1994 (Aus) | |
| 4th: | 8 | 1994 (Bra, GB, Ita, Por, Aus), 1995 (Eur), 1996 (Arg, GB) | |
| 5th: | 4 | 1993 (Jap), 1996 (Eur, San, Ita) | |
| 6th: | 4 | 1995 (Fra, Bel), 1996 (Ger, Hun) | |

| Year | Team | No. | Grand Prix |
|---|---|---|---|
| 1993 | Jordan Hart | 16 | SA, Bra, Eur, San, Esp, Mon, Can, Fra, GB, Ger, Hun, Bel, Ita, Por, Jap (2), Aus |
| 1994 | Jordan Hart | 15 | Bra (3), Pac (4), Mon, Esp, Can, Fra, GB (3), Ger, Hun, Bel, Ita (3), Por (3), Eur, Jap, Aus (3) |
| 1995 | Jordan Peugeot | 17 | Bra, Arg, San, Esp, Mon, Can (6), Fra (1), GB, Ger, Hun, Bel (1), Ita, Por, Eur (1), Pac, Jap, Aus |
| 1996 | Jordan Peugeot | 16 | Aus, Bra, Arg (3), Eur (2), San (2), Mon, Esp, Can, Fra, GB (3), Ger (1), Hun (1), Bel, Ita (2), Por, Jap |
| 1997 | Stewart Ford | 17 | Aus, Bra, Arg, San, Mon (6), Esp, Can, Fra, GB, Ger, Hun, Bel, Ita, Aut, Lux, Jap, Eur |

# BERGER, Gerhard                              Austria

*1997: Benetton Renault*                                    *1998: –*

At the end of the 1997 season Gerhard Berger announced what was regarded as his retirement from F1. However, what the affable Austrian said was that he was taking six months out and would then make a decision about his future. Could that mean a return to the circuit in 1999? Possibly, but don't be surprised if you see the seventh-highest points scorer of all time back before the end of the season in a covering position. Certainly, should an enforced vacancy occur within any team in the later stages of the season you can expect Berger's name to be linked with it, whatever his ultimate decision.

For the first time in seven years, Berger failed to complete the full season's race schedule. He missed out on the races in Canada, France and Britain following sinus troubles that required two operations and which would ultimately re-occur in the later stages of the season. Then, just prior to his comeback, his father was killed in an air crash. In amongst all this it was being made obvious by his Benetton team that his services would not be required for the 1998 season, not least because of the performances of his three-race replacement, Benetton test driver Alexander Wurz. But Berger has always had the best answers and he returned with a double first at the German Grand Prix – pole position and maximum points.

The Austrian scored 27 world championship points – an improvement on his 1996 tally and his thirteen finishes from fourteen starts was excellent and represented the highest percentage amongst all drivers. Berger also tripped past the 200 Grand Prix mark with his start at Imola, although ironically the San Marino Grand Prix was the one he failed to finish!

Overall, Berger's qualifying performance was his Achilles' heel, although the problem was manifested by the car's lack of grip when running with low fuel loads as is the norm in qualifying. A tenth place on the Melbourne grid in the first race of the season was converted into three points with a fourth-place finish. Things changed in Brazil when Berger was in the thick of the action. Third on the grid, he pushed eventual winner Villeneuve and led for a while before pit stops put the Canadian back in front. The gap at the end though was a fraction over four seconds.

Everything came back to earth in Argentina with a twelfth position on the grid, but that was halved by the finish of the race and another point was secured. San Marino offered Berger the chance to celebrate his 200th GP but 11th on the grid and a spin on his fifth lap put paid to any anticipated podium festivities.

Monaco and Spain were mostly forgettable with Berger off the pace, and eventually his sinus problems took their toll. Berger's return at Hockenheim was greeted sympathetically following the death of his father. His pole and tenth all-time victory was won with skilful application, and he dominated the whole meeting.

The pole and dominating nature of his win were the highlights of Berger's season after which he failed to get near the running. A sixth place in Belgium was bettered only by two fourth placings in Luxembourg and his final race at Jerez. Grid position continued to be a dominating factor and his eighteenth qualifying position at the Nurburgring was one of the worst of his career.

His final four points at the European Grand Prix represented his 94th points finish and his 210th Grand Prix. I think there will be more still to come. Time will, of course, tell.

**Born:** 27/8/59, Worgl, Austria. Married with two daughters.

# Grand Prix 1997 Record

| Grand Prix | Grid | Qual Time | Fin | Laps | Race Time | Reason |
|---|---|---|---|---|---|---|
| Australian | 10 | 1:32.870 | 4 | 58 | 1:30:51.559 | |
| Brazilian | 3 | 1:16.644 | 2 | 72 | 1:36:11.180 | |
| Argentinian | 12 | 1:27.259 | 6 | 72 | 1:52:33.108 | |
| San Marino | 11 | 1:25.371 | – | 4 | | spin |

| Monaco | 17 | 1:20.199 | 9 | 60 | 2:00:44.161 |
|--------|-----|----------|-----|-----|-------------|
| Spanish | 6 | 1:18.041 | 10 | 64 | 1:31:41.568 |
| German | 1 | 1:41.873 | 1 | 45 | 1:20:59.046 |
| Hungarian | 7 | 1:15.699 | 8 | 77 | 1:47:03.558 |
| Belgian | 15 | 1:52.391 | 6 | 44 | 1:34:50.458 |
| Italian | 7 | 1:23.443 | 7 | 53 | 1:17:17.080 |
| Austrian | 18 | 1:11.620 | 10 | 70 | 1:27:46.834 |
| Luxembourg | 7 | 1:17.587 | 4 | 67 | 1:31:44.259 |
| Japanese | 5 | 1:36.561 | 8 | 53 | 1:30.48.875 |
| European | 8 | 1:21.656 | 4 | 69 | 1:38:59.690 |

## 1997 Position Summary

| | | | |
|--------|-----|--------------|-----|
| Contested: | 14 | Finished: | 13 |
| Pole Positions: | 1 | Fastest Laps: | 2 |
| Points: | 27 | | |
| 1st: | 1 | 2nd: | 1 |
| 3rd: | 0 | 4th: | 3 |
| 5th: | 0 | 6th: | 2 |

## Grand Prix Career Record

| | | |
|-------|------|-------|
| Contested: | 210 | (1984-1997) |
| Pole Positions: | 12 | 1987 (Por, Jap, Aus), 1988 (GB), 1990 (USA, Mex), 1991 (Esp, Jap), 1994 (Ger, Por), 1995 (Bel), 1997 (Ger) |
| Fastest Laps: | 20 | 1986 (Ger, Aut), 1987 (Por, Esp, Aus), 1988 (Bra, Bel, Por), 1989 (Por), 1990 (Bra, USA, Can), 1991 (San, Aus), 1992 (Mex, Can), 1995 (San), 1996 (Bel), 1997 (Arg, Ger) |
| Points: | 385† | 1985 (3), 1986 (17), 1987 (36), 1988 (41), 1989 (20), 1990 (43), 1991 (44), 1992 (49), 1993 (12), 1994 (41), 1995 (31), 1996 (21), 1997 (27)<br>*† Also secured one extra point in 1989 which did not count towards the championship.* |
| 1st: | 10 | 1986 (Mex), 1987 (Jap, Aus), 1988 (Ita), 1989 (Por), 1991 (Jap), 1992 (Can, Aus), 1994 (Ger), 1997 (Ger) |
| 2nd: | 17 | 1987 (Por), 1988 (Bra, Mon), 1989 (Ita, Esp), 1990 (Bra, San), 1991 (San, GB, Bel), 1992 (Por, Jap), 1994 (Pac, Ita, Aus), 1996 (GB), 1997 (Ger) |
| 3rd: | 21 | 1986 (Mon, Mex, Ger), 1990 (Mon, Mex, Ger, Bel, Ita), 1991 (Bra, Aus), 1992 (Hun), 1993 (Hun), 1994 (Mon, Fra), 1995 (Bra, San, Esp, Mon, Ger, Hun), 1996 (San) |

| | | |
|---|---|---|
| 4th: | 26 | 1987 (Bra, Mon, USAE, Ita), 1988 (Fra, Hun, Jap), 1990 (Can, Por, Aus), 1991 (Ger, Hun, Ita), 1992 (Mex, Esp, Ita), 1993 (Can), 1994 (Can), 1995 (Por, Pac), 1996 (Aus, Fra, Jap), 1997 (Aus, Lux, Eur) |
| 5th: | 8 | 1985 (SA), 1986 (Ita), 1988 (San), 1990 (Fra), 1992 (SA, GB), 1993 (Aus), 1994 (Eur) |
| 6th: | 12 | 1985 (Aus), 1986 (Bra, Esp), 1988 (Esp), 1993 (SA, Esp, Ger), 1995 (Arg), 1996 (Bel, Por), 1997 (Arg, Bel) |

| Year | Team | No. | Grand Prix |
|---|---|---|---|
| 1984 | ATS BMW Turbo | 4 | Aut, Ita, Eur, Por |
| 1985 | Arrows BMW Turbo | 16 | Bra, Por, San, Mon, Can, USAE, Fra, GB, Ger, Aut, Hol, Ita, Bel, Eur, SA (2), Aus (1) |
| 1986 | Benetton BMW Turbo | 16 | Bra (1), Esp (1), San (4), Mon, Bel, Can, USAE, Fra, GB, Ger, Hun, Aut, Ita (2), Por, Mex (9), Aus |
| 1987 | Ferrari Turbo | 16 | Bra (3), San, Bel, Mon (3), USAE (3), Fra, GB, Ger, Hun, Aut, Ita (3), Por (6), Esp, Mex, Jap (9), Aus (9) |
| 1988 | Ferrari Turbo | 16 | Bra (6), San (2), Mon (6), Mex (4), Can, USAE, Fra (3), GB, Ger (4), Hun (3), Bel, Ita (9), Por, Esp (1), Jap (3), Aus |
| 1989 | Ferrari | 15 | Bra, San, Mex, USA, Can, Fra, GB, Ger, Hun, Bel, Ita (6), Por (9), Esp (6), Jap, Aus |
| 1990 | McLaren Honda | 16 | USA, Bra (6), San (6), Mon (4), Can (3), Mex (4), Fra (2), GB, Ger (4), Hun, Bel (4), Ita (4), Por (3), Esp, Jap, Aus (3) |
| 1991 | McLaren Honda | 16 | USA, Bra (4), San (6), Mon, Can, Mex, Fra, GB (6), Ger (3), Hun (3), Bel (6), Ita (3), Por, Esp, Jap (9), Aus (4) |
| 1992 | McLaren Honda | 16 | SA (2), Mex (3), Bra, Esp (3), San, Mon, Can (10), Fra, GB(2), Ger, Hun (4), Bel, Ita (3), Por (6), Jap (6), Aus (10) |
| 1993 | Ferrari | 16 | SA (1), Bra, Eur, San, Esp (1), Mon, Can (3), Fra, GB, Ger (1), Hun (4), Bel, Ita, Por, Jap, Aus (2) |
| 1994 | Ferrari | 16 | Bra, Pac (6), San, Mon (4), Esp, Can (3), Fra (4), GB, Ger (10), Hun, Bel, Ita (6), Por, Eur (2), Jap, Aus (6) |

| 1995 | Ferrari | 17 | Bra (4), Arg (1), San (4), Esp (4), Mon (4), Can, Fra, GB, Ger (4), Hun (4), Bel, Ita, Por (3), Eur, Pac (3), Jap, Aus |
| 1996 | Benetton Renault | 16 | Aus (3), Bra, Arg, Eur, San (4), Mon, Esp, Can, Fra (3), GB (6), Ger, Hun, Bel (1), Ita, Por (1), Jap (3) |
| 1997 | Benetton Renault | 14 | Aus (3), Bra (6), Arg (1), San, Mon, Esp, Ger (10), Hun, Bel (1), Ita, Aut, Lux (3), Jap, Eur (3) |

## BOULLION, Jean-Christophe                 France

*1997: (Test Driver: Williams Renault)*

Having completed two seasons as test driver for Williams, Jean-Chrisophe Boullion was linked to a number of teams either in a driving or testing capacity prior to the start of the season. His Formula One debut came in 1995 at Monte Carlo, as a replacement for Karl Wendlinger in the Swiss Sauber team. He competed in eleven races and scored points in two. In 1996 he reverted to the single F1 role as the Williams test driver but competed in three rounds of the Renault Spider Trophy racing at Silverstone, Barcelona and Monza.

**Born:** 27/12/69, Saint-Brieuc, France. Married.

## Grand Prix Record

| | | |
|---|---|---|
| Contested: | 11 | (1995) |
| Pole Positions: | 0 | |
| Fastest Laps: | 0 | |
| Points: | 3 | 1995 (3) |
| 1st: | 0 | |
| 2nd: | 0 | |
| 3rd: | 0 | |
| 4th: | 0 | |
| 5th: | 1 | 1995 (Ger) |
| 6th: | 1 | 1995 (Ita) |

| Year | Team | No. | Grand Prix |
|------|------|-----|------------|
| 1995 | Sauber Ford | 11 | Mon, Can, Fra, GB, Ger (2), Hun, Bel, Ita (1), Por, Eur, Pac |

## BRUNDLE, Martin                 Great Britain

*1997: ITV Race Commentator*            *1998: ITV Race Commentator*

As a Formula 1 Grand Prix driver Martin Brundle has amassed 98 championship points in 158 races. He last drove in a competitive race for

Jordan in 1996 and has since scored many more points as a co-commentator for ITV during their 1997 coverage of the FIA Championship. His ability to accurately analyse car problems and team strategies on the fly have added a new dimension to broadcasts and was certainly the jewel in the ITV crown for 1997. In many respects Brundle was the 'find' of 1997.

Although unlikely to feature as even a semi-regular on the circuit this year, his experience and availability might make him a useful substitute proposition for teams suffering a temporary driver loss. This may even be in a testing role as was the case for Benetton prior to the Hungarian Grand Prix in 1997.

In addition to his role as commentator, Brundle is also a non-executive director for the Arrows team.

**Born:** 1/6/59, Kings Lynn, England. Married with one son and one daughter.

## Grand Prix Career Record

| | | |
|---|---|---|
| Contested: | 158 | (1984-1996) |
| Pole Positions: | 0 | |
| Fastest Laps: | 0 | |
| Points: | 98 | 1986 (8), 1987 (2), 1989 (4), 1991 (2), 1992 (38), 1993 (13), 1994 (16), 1995 (7), 1996 (8) |
| 1st: | 0 | |
| 2nd: | 2 | 1992 (Ita), 1994 (Mon) |
| 3rd: | 7 | 1992 (Fra, GB, Jap, Aus), 1993 (San), 1994 (Aus), 1995 (Fra) |
| 4th: | 8 | 1986 (Aus), 1993 (San, Ger, Bel, Por), 1994 (Hun), 1995 (Fra), 1996 (Ita) |
| 5th: | 12 | 1986 (Bra, GB), 1987 (San), 1989 (Jap), 1991 (Jap), 1992 (Mon, Hun), 1993 (Can, Fra, Hun), 1994 (Ita), 1996 (Jap) |
| 6th: | 10 | 1986 (Hun), 1989 (Mon, Ita), 1993 (Mon, Por, Aus), 1994 (Por), 1996 (Eur, Can, GB) |

| Year | Team | No. | Grand Prix |
|---|---|---|---|
| 1984 | Tyrrell Ford | 7 | Bra, SA, Bel, San, Fra, Can, USAE |
| 1985 | Tyrrell Ford | 7 | Bra, Por, San, Mon, Can, USAE, Ger |
| | Tyrrell Renault Turbo | 8 | Fra, GB, Hol, Ita, Bel, Eur, SA, Aus |
| 1986 | Tyrrell Renault Turbo | 16 | Bra (2), Esp, San, Mon, Bel, Can, USAE, Fra, GB (2), Ger, Hun (1), Aut, Ita, Por, Mex, Aus (3) |
| 1987 | Zakspeed Turbo | 16 | Bra, San (2), Bel, Mon, USAE, Fra, GB, Ger, Hun, Aut, Ita, Por, Esp, Mex, Jap, Aus |
| 1988 | Williams Judd | 1 | Bel |
| 1989 | Brabham Judd | 14 | Bra, San, Mon (1), Mex, USA, GB, Ger, Hun, Bel, Ita (1), Por, Esp, Jap (2), Aus |

| 1991 | Brabham Yamaha | 14 | USA, Bra, San, Can, Mex, Fra, GB, Ger, Hun, Bel, Ita, Por, Esp, Jap (2) |
| 1992 | Benetton Ford | 16 | SA, Mex, Bra, Esp, San (3), Mon (2), Can, Fra (4), GB (4), Ger (3), Hun (2), Bel (3), Ita (6), Por (3), Jap (4), Aus (4) |
| 1993 | Ligier Renault | 16 | SA, Bra, Eur, San (4), Esp, Mon (1), Can (2), Fra (2), GB, Ger, Hun (2), Bel, Ita, Por (1), Jap, Aus (1) |
| 1994 | McLaren Peugeot | 16 | Bra, Pac, San, Mon (6), Esp, Can, Fra, GB, Ger, Hun (3), Bel, Ita (2), Por (1), Eur, Jap, Aus (4) |
| 1995 | Ligier Mugen Honda | 11 | Esp, Mon, Can, Fra (3), GB, Hun, Bel (4), Ita, Por, Eur, Aus |
| 1996 | Jordan Peugeot | 16 | Aus, Bra, Arg, Eur (1), San, Mon, Esp, Can (1), Fra, GB (1), Ger, Hun, Bel, Ita (3), Por, Jap (2) |

# COULTHARD, David
**Great Britain**

*1997: McLaren Mercedes*           *1998: McLaren Mercedes*

David Coulthard had his second-most successful season in 1997 and might have eclipsed the 49 points he secured in a 1995 Williams Renault had he managed more than ten finishes from his seventeen races. Two victories went one better than in 1995 and it would probably have been a hat trick of wins had he not given up his final lap lead in favour of teammate Mika Hakkinen.

Coulthard's season got off to a flyer. Fourth on the grid at Melbourne, the Scot got away and, under intense pressure, coasted home to a win after Frentzen went out. It was the first victory for McLaren in 50 Grands Prix and two and half years and served notice that Coulthard and McLaren were back. However, disappointment followed at Interlagos with only a tenth-place finish achieved from an even worse starting position. It didn't get any better from that point – three non-finishes which included accidents in Argentina and Monaco with only one lap completed. The out in Buenos Aires came after he lost a wheel in a clash with a Schumacher of the Ralf kind and in Monaco, opting for slicks, he simply spun out, as did so many others, on a slippery track.

Thankfully, the rain didn't stay in Spain and things took a turn for the better. His third position on the grid was, surprisingly perhaps, the best he achieved all season but only earned him one point for the final sixth-place finish. In Canada and France, Coulthard was just out of the points and might have done better but for being plagued by blistering tyres.

At home for the British Grand Prix, brake problems hampered his progress from his third row grid position and in the end a fourth place was a good achievement. The Grands Prix of Germany, Hungary and Belgium provided non-finishes. An accident after the first lap at the Hockenheimring was followed by electrical problems at the Hungaroring and a spin brought Spa to a premature end.

What followed in the remaining five races though allowed the season to end on a very positive note and with anticipation and confidence high for the 1998 campaign. Imola provided Coulthard with his third Grand Prix victory and it was followed up by a second placing at the next meeting at the A1-Ring, made all the better given that it was achieved despite a starting position of tenth on the grid and included some excellent pit-stop strategy.

The Luxembourg Grand Prix could have brought another top-two position, but continuing oil problems finally caught up with Coulthard's car and forced him to retire while holding on to second place. At Suzuka for the penultimate race of the season, Coulthard could not get to grips with the balance of the car and he finished tenth – improving on his grid position – despite the engine blowing on the final lap.

Winning ways were engineered for the final race of the season at Jerez and, after Villeneuve yielded to both McLarens on the final lap, Coulthard settled for another second place after allowing teammate Mika Hakkinen to sail past him for his first ever victory.

For 1998, Coulthard should continue his winning ways in a car that looks to be a potential winner throughout. A better performance in qualifying could be critical though and may help to keep the Scot out of the sort of accident troubles that plagued part of his 1997 season.

**Born:** 27/3/71, Twynholm, Scotland. Single.

# Grand Prix 1997 Record

| Grand Prix | Grid | Qual Time | Fin | Laps | Race Time | Reason |
|---|---|---|---|---|---|---|
| Australian | 4 | 1:31.531 | 1 | 58 | 1:30:28.718 | |
| Brazilian | 12 | 1:17.262 | 10 | 71 | 1:36:18.800 | |
| Argentinian | 10 | 1:26.799 | – | 0 | | accident |
| San Marino | 10 | 1:25.077 | – | 38 | | engine |
| Monaco | 5 | 1:18.779 | – | 1 | | accident |
| Spanish | 3 | 1:17.521 | 6 | 64 | 1:31:05.640 | |
| Canadian | 5 | 1:18.466 | 7 | 54 | 1:18:18.399 | |
| French | 9 | 1:15.270 | 7 | 71 | 1:38:40.563 | |
| British | 6 | 1:22.279 | 4 | 59 | 1:28:32.894 | |
| German | 8 | 1:42.687 | – | 1 | | accident |
| Hungarian | 8 | 1:15.705 | – | 65 | | electrics |
| Belgian | 10 | 1:51.410 | – | 19 | | spin |
| Italian | 6 | 1:23.347 | 1 | 53 | 1:17:04.609 | |
| Austrian | 10 | 1:11.076 | 2 | 71 | 1:27:38.908 | |
| Luxembourg | 6 | 1:17.387 | – | 42 | | engine |
| Japanese | 11 | 1:37.095 | 10 | 52 | 1:28:51.086 | |
| European | 6 | 1:21.476 | 2 | 69 | 1:38:59.425 | |

## 1997 Position Summary

| | | | |
|---|---|---|---|
| Contested: | 17 | Finished: | 10 |
| Pole Positions: | 0 | Fastest Laps: | 1 |
| Points: | 36 | | |
| 1st: | 2 | 2nd: | 2 |
| 3rd: | 0 | 4th: | 1 |
| 5th: | 0 | 6th: | 1 |

## Grand Prix Career Record

| | | |
|---|---|---|
| Contested: | 58 | (1994-1997) |
| Pole Positions: | 5 | 1995 (Arg, Ita, Por, Eur, Pac) |
| Fastest Laps: | 5 | 1994 (Ger, Por), 1995 (Bel, Por), 1997 (Can) |
| Points: | 117 | 1994 (14), 1995 (49), 1996 (18), 1997 (36) |
| 1st: | 3 | 1995 (Por), 1997 (Aus, Ita) |
| 2nd: | 8 | 1994 (Por), 1995 (Bra, Ger, Hun, Pac), 1996 (Mon), 1997 (Aut, Eur) |
| 3rd: | 4 | 1995 (Fra, GB, Eur), 1996 (Eur) |
| 4th: | 4 | 1994 (Bel), 1995 (San), 1996 (Can), 1997 (GB) |
| 5th: | 3 | 1994 (Can, GB), 1996 (GB, Ger) |
| 6th: | 4 | 1994 (Ita), 1996 (Fra), 1997 (Esp) |

| Year | Team | No. | Grand Prix |
|---|---|---|---|
| 1994 | Williams Renault | 8 | Esp, Can (2), GB (2), Ger, Hun, Bel (3), Ita (1), Por (6) |
| 1995 | Williams Renault | 17 | Bra (6), Arg, San (3), Esp, Mon, Can, Fra (4), GB (4), Ger (6), Hun (6), Bel, Ita, Por (10), Eur (4), Pac (6), Jap, Aus |
| 1996 | McLaren Mercedes | 16 | Aus, Bra, Arg, Eur (4), San, Mon (6), Esp, Can (3), Fra (1), GB (2), Ger (2), Hun, Bel, Ita, Por, Jap |
| 1997 | McLaren Mercedes | 17 | Aus (10), Bra, Arg, San, Mon, Esp (1), Can, Fra, GB (3), Ger, Hun, Bel, Ita (10), Aut (6), Lux, Jap, Eur (6) |

## DINIZ, Pedro                                                    Brazil

*1997: Arrows Yamaha*                                  *1998: Arrows Yamaha*

The 1997 season was very nearly a mirror image of the 1996 season for Pedro Diniz – six finishes and two championship points in both. There was however an improvement in overall qualifying position and his fifth place at the Luxembourg Grand Prix was a career best. There was also a distinct improvement in the Brazilian's driving and for the first time he was not the brunt of criticism for ever holding up traffic or taking out other cars.

The impetuous nature is still there, although his four spins – all of which brought retirements – might have been put down to greater effort on his behalf to be more competitive in a generally un-competitive car.

For any team, and particularly Arrows, Diniz is important. He was once described by the former Benetton boss Flavio Briatore as one of the two most important drivers in the world because he brings vast amounts of sponsorship money with him to pay for his drive – reports of $10 million a year are common.

As the number two driver to Damon Hill, Diniz can point to having out-qualified the then reigning World Champion twice (France and Japan) and of the five times they both finished races, he beat Hill home on three occasions (Canada, Belgium, Luxembourg).

The first of Diniz's six finishes came at Melbourne after he had failed to qualify inside the 107% rule! However, an appeal by team boss Tom Walkinshaw on the grounds of *force majeure* after the gearbox problems had prevented the Brazilian getting a competitive time was successful, and he finished in tenth place. After five failures to finish on the back of some poor qualifying positions, the Canadian Grand Prix saw the Brazilian come home in eighth position just over a second ahead of teammate Damon Hill, despite suffering with brake fade.

Another four races without a completion saw a more consistent performance in qualifying and at Magny-Cours a place ahead of Hill on the grid. The Belgian meeting at Spa was probably the best overall performance by Diniz, having qualified an all-time-best eighth and, having lost time with a wheel nut problem, was placed eighth at the finish after colliding with Eddie Irvine on the final lap. That position was eventually improved to seventh when Mika Hakkinen was subsequently excluded from the results.

Qualifying performance again hindered starting position for the remaining races of the season but three finishes in the last four races showed more consistency from Diniz and the Luxembourg Grand Prix provided the high point with a fifth position from a drive that was notable for his success in holding off the pursuing Olivier Panis.

Before the season had ended Pedro Diniz had committed himself to the Arrows team for a further two years and that should help him to improve some relatively consistent performances to date.

**Born:** 22/5/70, Sao Paulo, Brazil. Single.

# Grand Prix 1997 Record

| Grand Prix | Grid | Qual Time | Fin | Laps | Race Time | Reason |
|---|---|---|---|---|---|---|
| Australian | 22 | 1:35.972 | 10 | 54 | 4 laps down | |
| Brazilian | 16 | 1:18.005 | – | 15 | | spin |
| Argentinian | 22 | 1:28.969 | – | 50 | | engine |
| San Marino | 17 | 1:26.253 | – | 53 | | exhaust |
| Monaco | 16 | 1:19.860 | – | 0 | | spin |
| Spanish | 21 | 1:21.029 | – | 53 | | engine |

| | | | | | | |
|---|---|---|---|---|---|---|
| Canadian | 16 | 1:20.175 | 8 | 53 | 1:17:41.197 | |
| French | 16 | 1:16.536 | – | 58 | | spin |
| British | 16 | 1:24.239 | – | 29 | | engine |
| German | 16 | 1:44.069 | – | 8 | | accident |
| Hungarian | 19 | 1:17.118 | – | 53 | | electrics |
| Belgian | 8 | 1:50.853 | 7 | 44 | 1:35:12.648 | |
| Italian | 17 | 1:24.639 | – | 4 | | suspension |
| Austrian | 17 | 1:11.615 | 13 | 64 | | shock absorber |
| Luxembourg | 15 | 1:18.128 | 5 | 67 | 1:32:10.990 | |
| Japanese | 16 | 1:37.853 | 12 | 52 | 1:30:43.622 | |
| European | 13 | 1:22.234 | – | 11 | | spin |

## 1997 Position Summary

| | | | |
|---|---|---|---|
| Contested: | 17 | Finished: | 6 |
| Pole Positions: | 0 | Fastest Laps: | 0 |
| Points: | 2 | | |
| 1st: | 0 | 2nd: | 0 |
| 3rd: | 0 | 4th: | 0 |
| 5th: | 1 | 6th: | 0 |

## Grand Prix Career Record

| | | |
|---|---|---|
| Contested: | 50 | (1995-97) |
| Pole Positions: | 0 | |
| Fastest Laps: | 0 | |
| Points: | 4 | 1996 (2), 1997 (2) |
| 1st: | 0 | |
| 2nd: | 0 | |
| 3rd: | 0 | |
| 4th: | 0 | |
| 5th: | 1 | 1997 (Lux) |
| 6th: | 2 | 1996 (Esp, Ita) |

| Year | Team | No. | Grand Prix |
|---|---|---|---|
| 1995 | Forti Ford | 17 | Bra, Arg, San, Esp, Mon, Can, Fra, GB, Ger, Hun, Bel, Ita, Por, Eur, Pac, Jap, Aus |
| 1996 | Minardi Ford | 16 | Aus, Bra, Arg, Eur, San, Mon, Esp (1), Can, Fra, GB, Ger, Hun, Bel, Ita (1), Por, Jap |
| 1997 | Arrows Yamaha | 17 | Aus, Bra, Arg, San, Mon, Esp, Can, Fra, GB, Ger, Hun, Bel, Ita, Aut, Lux (2), Jap, Eur |

# FISICHELLA, Giancarlo                                    Italy

*1997: Jordan Peugeot*                          *1998: Benetton Mecachrome*

Giancarlo Fisichella's performance during the 1997 season made him one of the hottest properties in Formula One, and this led to a battle in the courts between Jordan and Benetton to determine who had an option on his services for the 1998 season. The decision came through in the week prior to the German Grand Prix with Benetton winning the day.

The Italian's rise through the Grand Prix ranks has been phenomenal. After just eight races for the Minardi Ford team in 1996 – having started as a test driver – his potential was identified by Eddie Jordan who partnered him with Ralf Schumacher.

The season started with a stutter in Australia where lack of grid hindered qualifying and over-enthusiasm ended in tears when Fisichella crashed out on lap 15 while trying a dubious move to get past Rubens Barrichello. After finishing eighth in Brazil in the T-car, the Italian found himself punted off by no less than his own teammate. Not the best way to end Jordan's 100th Grand Prix.

Imola provided celebration as Fisichella came home fourth to score his first-ever championship points and he might have mounted the podium following a ding-dong battle with Eddie Irvine which was won by the Ferrari driver. Another point was secured at Monaco where he put in an excellent qualifying run to start on the second row of the grid.

Lack of power and heavy tyre wear were the main causes for an indifferent showing in Spain, but Montreal was different when a blistering start saw him move up three places to third place – a position which he maintained to win that first-ever podium finish.

The next four events were largely best forgotten. At Silverstone, Fisichella had looked impressive after a poor qualifying run and was in second place before a tour of the gravel created the need for an extra pit-stop and a drop to seventh place. Qualifying in Germany was a complete contrast where he secured his first front row position – just a few fractions of a second off the pole position of Gerhard Berger. Pit stops had put Fisichella out ahead in the race and it looked very much like a first win for him. But with Berger pushing, the pressure was too much and a mistake by the Italian allowed the Austrian through. Late in the race a puncture proved terminal and put him out of the race right at the end.

The Hungaroring provided the third of his four non-finishes, again coming when Fisichella tried an overtaking manoeuvre that failed. Despite the error, the race had shown a distinct improvement in the Jordan driver's racing form and this carried through into the remaining races. At Spa, Fisichella was again on the second row of the grid and drove excellently to hold off the challenge of Mika Hakkinen to finish second behind the Ferrari of Michael Schumacher. Second row was again the starting point in Monza, albeit improved to a third place on the grid. His start wasn't great and this ultimately forced him back to a fourth place, although just under six seconds behind the race winner.

Fourth place was again achieved at the A1-Ring, but was an altogether better performance after the Italian had lined up fourteenth on the grid. His one-stop race worked perfectly. Qualifying form returned at the Nurburgring but was wasted on the first lap when he again came together with his teammate and crashed out.

The final two races of the season didn't bring any more points and, at both Suzuka and Jerez, lack of grip proved problematic and ultimately made the car and drive uncompetitive in both qualifying and race.

Fisichella's 20-points season at Jordan might have been more successful other than for the impetuous nature of some of his drives. The jovial Italian possesses undoubted talent and the assertion that he is a future world champion is not without foundation. In 1998 he finds himself teamed, for the second year, with an inexperienced and young driver in Alexander Wurz and, it should not be forgotten, a third new team in as many years.

Benetton's investment may be more long term than short term, but could still provide the platform for Fisichella to get off the mark with a victory during 1998.

**Born:** 14/1/73, Roma, Italy. Single.

## Grand Prix 1997 Record

| Grand Prix | Grid | Qual Time | Fin | Laps | Race Time | Reason |
|---|---|---|---|---|---|---|
| Australian | 14 | 1:33.552 | – | 14 | | accident |
| Brazilian | 7 | 1:16.912 | 8 | 72 | 1:37:07.629 | |
| Argentinian | 9 | 1:26.619 | – | 24 | | accident |
| San Marino | 6 | 1:24.598 | 4 | 62 | 1:32:24.061 | |
| Monaco | 4 | 1:18.665 | 6 | 61 | 2:00:25.006 | |
| Spanish | 8 | 1:18.385 | 9 | 64 | 1:31:40.663 | |
| Canadian | 6 | 1:18.750 | 3 | 54 | 1:17:43.865 | |
| French | 11 | 1:15.453 | 9 | 71 | 1:40:16.244 | |
| British | 10 | 1:22.371 | 7 | 58 | 1:28:05.716 | |
| German | 2 | 1:41.896 | 11 | 40 | 1:22:51.576 | |
| Hungarian | 13 | 1:16.300 | – | 42 | | spin |
| Belgian | 4 | 1:50.470 | 2 | 44 | 1:34:13.470 | |
| Italian | 3 | 1:23.066 | 4 | 53 | 1:17:10.480 | |
| Austrian | 14 | 1:11.299 | 4 | 71 | 1:27:48.126 | |
| Luxembourg | 4 | 1:17.289 | – | 0 | | accident |
| Japanese | 9 | 1:16.917 | 7 | 53 | 1:30:45.271 | |
| European | 17 | 1:22.804 | 11 | 68 | 1:39:05.717 | |

## 1997 Position Summary

| | | | |
|---|---|---|---|
| Contested: | 17 | Finished: | 13 |
| Pole Positions: | 0 | Fastest Laps: | 0 |
| Points: | 20 | | |

| | | | |
|------|---|------|---|
| 1st: | 0 | 2nd: | 1 |
| 3rd: | 1 | 4th: | 3 |
| 5th: | 0 | 6th: | 1 |

## Grand Prix Career Record

| | | |
|---|---|---|
| Contested: | 25 | |
| Pole Positions: | 0 | |
| Fastest Laps: | 0 | |
| Points: | 20 | 1997 (20) |
| 1st: | 0 | |
| 2nd: | 1 | 1997 (Bel) |
| 3rd: | 1 | 1997 (Can) |
| 4th: | 3 | 1997 (San, Ita, Aut) |
| 5th: | 0 | |
| 6th: | 1 | 1997 (Mon) |

| Year | Team | No. | Grand Prix |
|------|------|-----|-----------|
| 1996 | Minardi Ford | 8 | Aus, Eur, San, Mon, Esp, Can, Fra, GB |
| 1997 | Jordan Peugeot | 17 | Aus, Bra, Arg, San (3), Mon (1), Esp, Can (4), Fra, GB, Ger, Hun, Bel (6), Ita (3), Aut (3), Lux, Jap, Eur |

# FONTANA, Norberto                                   Argentina

*1997: (Test Driver: Sauber Petronas)*                        *1998: –*

Norberto Fontana took his seat in four races for Sauber after Gianni Morbidelli was forced out through injury. The Sauber test driver matched the best positions achieved by Morbidelli when recording two ninth places and a fourteenth. Qualifying, however, proved more difficult, and at the French Grand Prix the only Argentine driver on the Formula One circuit in 1997 started from near the back of the grid. The race was more curious for the team when they found Fontana pitting when he was not expected to do so and he eventually spun out after 40 laps.

At Silverstone he was forced to start the British Grand Prix from the back of the grid after failing to stop at the official weighbridge during qualifying. He had managed a fourteenth place before his error and in many respects it makes his final ninth position all the more creditable. His first stint of driving came to an end at Hockenheim where he again came home a steady ninth despite taking a spin at the first chicane.

With Morbidelli back in the driver's seat, Fontana got one final stab at the circuit in the last race of the season in Jerez, after an injured wrist had sidelined the Italian. Fontana's form turned out to be unchanged, qualifying eighteenth on the grid and finishing fourteenth.

**Born:** 20/1/73, Arrecifes, Argentina. Single.

## Grand Prix 1997 Record

| Grand Prix | Grid | Qual Time | Fin | Laps | Race Time | Reason |
|---|---|---|---|---|---|---|
| French | 20 | 1:17.538 | – | 40 | | spin |
| British | 22 | disallowed | 9 | 58 | 1:28:49.184 | |
| German | 18 | 1:44.552 | 9 | 44 | 1:21:18.849 | |
| European | 18 | 1:23.281 | 14 | 68 | 1:39:45.614 | |

## 1997 Position Summary

| | | | |
|---|---|---|---|
| Contested: | 4 | Finished: | 3 |
| Pole Positions: | 0 | Fastest Laps: | 0 |
| Points: | 0 | | |
| 1st-6th: | 0 | | |
| Best Position: | 9th – twice (GB, Ger) | | |

## Grand Prix Career Record

| | |
|---|---|
| Contested: | 4 |
| Pole Positions: | 0 |
| Fastest Laps: | 0 |
| 1st-6th: | 0 |
| Best Position: | 9th – 1997 (GB, Ger) |

| Year | Team | No. | Grand Prix |
|---|---|---|---|
| 1997 | Sauber Petronas | 4 | Fra, GB, Ger, Eur |

## FRENTZEN, Heinz-Harald                                    Germany

*1997: Williams Renault*                          *1998: Williams Mecachrome*

In many respects 1997 was a difficult season for Heinz-Harald. He arrived at Williams as a replacement for the then reigning world champion Damon Hill and, having been spoken of as a future world champion himself, he was under immediate pressure. After three races and without a point, it is fair to say that the vultures were out.

Qualifying in Melbourne had provided promise with a second place on the grid, from which he led until his first pit stop. Lost time resulted in a final eighth placing despite crashing out near the end when a disk brake shattered. Brazil increased the pressure, especially as teammate Villeneuve raced to pole and victory. Frentzen started eighth and finished ninth in what was a nightmarish weekend. Things looked better in Argentina where he was back on the front row of the grid, but his luck was lacking when his clutch gave up the ghost after five laps.

By this time there were rumours of discontent but, in retrospect, it seems it was also the point where the German started to impose his own will on the team and his own views on set-up and tyre choice were taken on board. If that was the case, it worked a treat. A second successive front row position on the grid was crowned with not just his first points for Williams but also his first

Grand Prix win. Frentzen looked at ease with his car and his three-stop strategy pulled him out ahead in the ultimate shake-up, having trailed behind Villeneuve and Schumacher in the earlier stages. His upturn in form looked set to continue in Monte Carlo but, having won his first pole position, the hard work was thrown away when one of several spins finally put paid to his Monaco Grand Prix challenge after 39 laps.

The aggressive edge that Frentzen had to his driving was taken a little too far in Canada where he thrashed his tyres so hard that he scored only three points with a fourth place in Montreal. A brief resurgence saw second position won at Magny-Cours. It was a brief respite though, with three consecutive non-finishes following, and in the first two of those races, at Silverstone and Hockenheim, he completed just one lap in total – the most damning error coming at the British Grand Prix where he stalled the car on the front row and was rammed out by Verstappen when he eventually got underway.

The Belgian Grand Prix finally brought consistency to Frentzen's season, and you can't get more consistent than taking four successive podium placings. After four third-place finishes, Frentzen drove a superb race at Suzuka to secure second place, and the points that gave Williams their second successive Constructors' Cup.

In the final race of the season, at Jerez, Frentzen was looking to play team games to help Villeneuve in his championship bid and, although finishing with a final point, might have done better had he not made the mistake of stopping in the McLaren pit during his second stop.

The 1998 season will be an important one for Heinz-Harald. Although he ultimately finished second in the Drivers' Championship after the disqualification of Schumacher, his points tally was only half that of Villeneuve and only then because of a greater consistency in the second half of the season. A better start to the season is an absolute must if he is to be challenging for the title and looking to continue in the Williams seat.

**Born:** 18/5/67, Mönchengladbach, Germany. Single.

# Grand Prix 1997 Record

| Grand Prix | Grid | Qual Time | Fin | Laps | Race Time | Reason |
|---|---|---|---|---|---|---|
| Australian | 2 | 1:31.123 | 8 | 55 | | shattered brakes |
| Brazilian | 8 | 1:16.971 | 9 | 72 | 1:37:22.392 | |
| Argentinian | 2 | 1:25.271 | – | 5 | | clutch |
| San Marino | 2 | 1:23.646 | 1 | 62 | 1:31:00.673 | |
| Monaco | 1 | 1:18.216 | – | 39 | | accident |
| Spanish | 2 | 1:16.791 | 8 | 64 | 1:31:40.035 | |
| Canadian | 4 | 1:18.464 | 4 | 54 | 1:17:44.414 | |
| French | 2 | 1:14.749 | 2 | 72 | 1:39:14.029 | |
| British | 2 | 1:21.732 | – | 0 | | accident |
| German | 5 | 1:42.421 | – | 1 | | damage |
| Hungarian | 6 | 1:15.520 | – | 29 | | fuel filter |

| | | | | | |
|---|---|---|---|---|---|
| Belgian | 7 | 1:50.656 | 3 | 44 | 1:34:18.864 |
| Italian | 2 | 1:23.042 | 3 | 53 | 1:17:08.952 |
| Austrian | 4 | 1:10.670 | 3 | 71 | 1:27:39.961 |
| Luxembourg | 3 | 1:16.741 | 3 | 67 | 1:31:41.323 |
| Japanese | 6 | 1:36.628 | 2 | 53 | 1:29:49.824 |
| European | 3 | 1:21.072 | 6 | 69 | 1:39:02.308 |

## 1997 Position Summary

| | | | |
|---|---|---|---|
| Contested: | 17 | Finished: | 12 |
| Pole Positions: | 1 | Fastest Laps: | 6 |
| Points: | 42 | | |
| 1st: | 1 | 2nd: | 2 |
| 3rd: | 4 | 4th: | 1 |
| 5th: | 0 | 6th: | 1 |

## Grand Prix Career Record

| | | |
|---|---|---|
| Contested: | 65 | (1994-1997) |
| Pole Positions: | 1 | 1997 (Mon) |
| Fastest Laps: | 6 | 1997 (Aus, San, Hun, Lux, Jap, Eur) |
| Points: | 71 | 1994 (7), 1995 (15), 1996 (7), 1997 (42) |
| 1st: | 1 | 1997 (San) |
| 2nd: | 2 | 1997 (Fra, Jap) |
| 3rd: | 5 | 1995 (Ita), 1997 (Bel, Ita, Aus, Lux) |
| 4th: | 5 | 1994 (Fra), 1995 (Bel), 1996 (Mon, Esp), 1997 (Can) |
| 5th: | 3 | 1994 (Pac), 1995 (Arg, Hun) |
| 6th: | 8 | 1994 (Eur, Jap), 1995 (San, Mon, GB, Por), 1996 (Jap), 1997 (Eur) |

| Year | Team | No. | Grand Prix |
|---|---|---|---|
| 1994 | Sauber Mercedes | 15 | Bra, Pac (2), San, Esp, Can, Fra (3), GB, Ger, Hun, Bel, Ita, Por, Eur (1), Jap (1), Aus |
| 1995 | Sauber Ford | 17 | Bra, Arg (2), San (1), Esp, Mon (1), Can, Fra, GB (1), Ger, Hun (2), Bel (3), Ita (4), Por (1), Eur, Pac, Jap, Aus |
| 1996 | Sauber Ford | 16 | Aus, Bra, Arg, Eur, San, Mon (3), Esp (3), Can, Fra, GB, Ger, Hun, Bel, Ita, Por, Jap (1) |
| 1997 | Williams Renault | 17 | Aus, Bra, Arg, San (10), Mon, Esp, Can (3), Fra (6), GB, Ger, Hun, Bel (4), Ita (4), Aut (4), Lux (4), Jap (6), Eur (1) |

*1997: McLaren Mercedes*                      *1998: McLaren Mercedes*

The talk of 1997 regarding Mika Hakkinen came at the final race in Jerez where the Finn secured his first-ever Grand Prix win in what was his 96th race. It was in many respects a just reward for one of Formula One's most consistent performers, and especially as only car failures had seemingly denied him victories at other venues. However, the win did look a little contrived as race leader Jacques Villeneuve let him and his teammate Coulthard through. But it was also apparent that both McLarens were the faster cars and were clearly steering clear of the race for the world championship.

That victory allowed Hakkinen to record his second-best season in Formula One, and it would have equalled his best-ever season had his third place result at Spa been allowed to stand. Those four points were docked after it had been found that the fuel in his car during qualification had not matched the pre-meeting sample supplied to the FIA for approval.

Consistency was very much the basis of Hakkinen's season. Apart from aberrations in Argentina and France, he was consistently in the top four rows and recorded a magnificent first-ever pole position at Luxembourg. His finishing was equally impressive and of his ten race completions only three failed to secure points – including his disqualification from third place at Spa.

The first four races of the 1997 season brought finishes of third, fourth, fifth and sixth respectively, the first three of which had to be won with some exciting battles with other contenders. In Monaco, the Finn fell foul of the conditions and cannoned into the back of Alesi's Benetton after just one lap. While these first five races saw Hakkinen's finish placing improve or equal his qualifying number, San Marino was different. Having qualified fifth he had to settle for seventh after a detour through a gravel trap created the need for an unscheduled pit stop.

The Canadian meeting was the start of three races without a finish. In Montreal, an accident at the first corner proved decisive and the French Grand Prix was a struggle, qualifying just tenth and before engine gave up the ghost after eighteen laps. Despite a third non-finish, the British race showed the potential that existed for both driver and car. Having qualified third, he took control of the race and was holding off second placed Villeneuve until his engine let him down seven laps from the chequered flag.

Hydraulic problems caused retirement after just twelve laps of the Hungaroring after a promising qualification run that earned a place on the second row of the grid. Then, at Spa, came the fuel dispute that meant that Hakkinen had to start the race under threat of disqualification. That threat became reality a couple of weeks after the race in which the Finn produced another exceptional drive to finish third, even though, eventually, it didn't count for anything.

The Italian Grand Prix saw Hakkinen record ninth place – his worst finish of the year – and this was followed by successive engine failures in the Austrian and Luxembourg races. In Japan, grid and finish were locked in fourth place before the ultimate success at Jerez, which will provide Hakkinen with the platform for even greater improvement and the ability to add to his solitary Grand Prix win.

**Born:** 28/9/68, Helsinki, Finland. Single.

## Grand Prix 1997 Record

| Grand Prix | Grid | Qual Time | Fin | Laps | Race Time | Reason |
|---|---|---|---|---|---|---|
| Australian | 6 | 1:31.971 | 3 | 58 | 1:30:50.895 | |
| Brazilian | 4 | 1:16.692 | 4 | 72 | 1:36:40.023 | |
| Argentinian | 17 | 1:28.135 | 5 | 72 | 1:52:32.066 | |
| San Marino | 8 | 1:24.812 | 6 | 61 | 1:31:18.536 | |
| Monaco | 8 | 1:19.119 | – | 1 | | accident |
| Spanish | 5 | 1:17.737 | 7 | 64 | 1:31:24.681 | |
| Canadian | 9 | 1:18.916 | – | 0 | | accident |
| French | 10 | 1:15.339 | – | 18 | | engine |
| British | 3 | 1:21.797 | – | 52 | | engine |
| German | 3 | 1:42.034 | 3 | 45 | 1:21:23.816 | |
| Hungarian | 4 | 1:15.140 | – | 12 | | hydraulics |
| Belgian | 5 | 1:50.503 | dq (3rd) | 44 | 1:34:17.573 | |
| Italian | 5 | 1:23.340 | 9 | 53 | 1:17:53.982 | |
| Austrian | 2 | 1:10.398 | – | 1 | | engine |
| Luxembourg | 1 | 1:16.602 | – | 43 | | engine |
| Japanese | 4 | 1:36.469 | 4 | 53 | 1:30:15.575 | |
| European | 5 | 1:21.369 | 1 | 69 | 1:38:57.771 | |

## 1997 Position Summary

| | | | |
|---|---|---|---|
| Contested: | 17 | Finished: | 10 |
| Pole Positions: | 1 | Fastest Laps: | 1 |
| Points: | 27 | | |
| 1st: | 1 | 2nd: | 0 |
| 3rd: | 2 | 4th: | 2 |
| 5th: | 1 | 6th: | 1 |

## Grand Prix Career Record

| | | |
|---|---|---|
| Contested: | 96 | (1991-1997) |
| Pole Positions: | 1 | 1997 (Lux) |
| Fastest Laps: | 1 | 1997 (Ita) |
| Points: | 117 | 1991 (2), 1992 (11), 1993 (4), 1994 (25), 1995 (17), 1996 (31), 1997 (27) |
| 1st: | 1 | 1997 (Eur) |
| 2nd: | 3 | 1994 (Bel), 1995 (Ita, Jap) |
| 3rd: | 11 | 1993 (Jap), 1994 (San, GB, Bel, Por), 1996 (GB, Bel, Ita, Jap), 1997 (Aus, Ger) |

| | | | |
|---|---|---|---|
| 4th: | 7 | 1992 (Fra, Hun), 1994 (GB), 1996 (Bra, Hun), 1997 (Bra, Jap) |
| 5th: | 8 | 1991 (San), 1992 (Por), 1995 (San), 1996 (Aus, Esp, Can, Fra), 1997 (Arg) |
| 6th: | 5 | 1992 (Mex, GB, Bel), 1996 (Mon), 1997 (San) |

| Year | Team | No. | Grand Prix |
|---|---|---|---|
| 1991 | Lotus Judd | 15 | USA, Bra, San (2), Mon, Can, Mex, GB, Ger, Hun, Bel, Ita, Por, Esp, Jap, Aus |
| 1992 | Lotus Ford | 15 | SA, Mex (1), Bra, Esp, Mon, Can, Fra (3), GB (1), Ger, Hun (3), Bel (1), Ita, Por (2), Jap, Aus |
| 1993 | McLaren Ford | 3 | Por, Jap (4), Aus |
| 1994 | McLaren Peugeot | 15 | Bra, Pac, San (4), Mon, Esp, Can, Fra, GB (3), Ger, Bel (6), Ita (4), Por (4), Eur (4), Jap, Aus |
| 1995 | McLaren Mercedes | 15 | Bra (3), Arg, San (2), Esp, Mon, Can, Fra, GB, Ger, Hun, Bel, Ita (6), Por, Eur, Jap (6) |
| 1996 | McLaren Mercedes | 16 | Aus (2), Bra (3), Arg, Eur, San, Mon (1), Esp (2), Can (2), Fra (2), GB (4), Ger, Hun (3), Bel (4), Ita (4), Por, Jap (4) |
| 1997 | McLaren Mercedes | 17 | Aus (4), Bra(3), Arg (2), San (1), Mon, Esp, Can, Fra, GB, Ger (4), Hun, Bel, Ita, Aut, Lux, Jap (3), Eur (10) |

# HERBERT, Johnny                                    Great Britain

*1997: Sauber Petronas*                              *1998: Sauber Petronas*

Having had a year of bedding in at Sauber, Herbert, no doubt helped by a more competitive and reliable engine, had his second-best season since he started Formula One racing in 1989. Scoring points on a more consistent basis, for the second successive year, Herbert provided the Swiss team with their only podium finish and, remarkably, never finished lower than eighth position in the eight races he completed. Herbert has now provided two of Sauber's third-place finishes.

However, the season didn't get off to the most auspicious of starts. Having qualified a commendable seventh place, the Englishman found himself taken out at the first corner by another Ferrari-powered car driven by Eddie Irvine. The number seven proved more lucky for Herbert in Brazil and marked his final finishing position, achieved from a much lower thirteenth on the grid.

Ironically, Herbert again had a coming together with Irvine at the start in an accident that forced the race to re-start and Herbert into the spare car.

Argentina provided him with his first points of the season. From eighth on the grid, Herbert overcame the not insignificant problem of his engine cutting out every time he ran over a kerb. Brake problems also took their toll so, in retrospect, a final fourth place was a remarkable achievement.

As with many other drivers, the first two races of the European circuit proved too great a barrier. Both San Marino and Monaco provided some success in qualifying runs with seventh positions in both starts, but an electrical problem in San Marino and an accident in the wet of Monaco prevented any further point taking.

In Spain, Herbert snatched fifth place from David Coulthard on the very last lap of the race and in Canada another fifth place might well have been much better had his pit-lane speed limiter not malfunctioned and resulted in him incurring a ten second Stop-Go penalty. Grid position had been disappointing in both these races and didn't improve in France where an eighth place in the race was taken after a fourteenth place qualification.

Silverstone and Hockenheim provided the setting for two more non-finishes – electric problems ultimately causing his Sauber to give up the ghost in Northamptonshire after having run as high as fourth position. At the German race, Pedro Diniz rammed Herbert off the track and out of what was proving to be a pretty good showing.

The Hungarian Grand Prix provided Sauber with their third-ever podium finish when Herbert drove tactfully after a good start, preserving his tyres to get him up through the places from his tenth position on the grid. An equally good drive followed for him at Spa, where well-timed tyre changes took account of changing weather conditions and provided the platform for his second fourth place of the year.

An accident at Monza, not helped by massive under-steer on the car, brought a premature end to the Italian Grand Prix but set the mark for consistent performances in the final four races of the year, although only sixth place in Suzuka provided any points.

Johnny Herbert competed in his 100th Grand Prix at Monaco and, although that was one race he didn't finish, the experience he has gained as a steady and consistent runner has clearly benefited the Sauber team. While with the Benetton team in 1995, he secured both his Grand Prix victories in similar fashion, by driving sensibly and avoiding the sort of rash manoeuvres that often end in grief. Given that Herbert's consistent finishes towards the front of the field have invariably been achieved from the middle to back of the grid, one can only reflect on what might be possible in 1998 should a more competitive qualifying package be available.

**Born:** 27/6/64, Brentwood, Essex, England. Married with two daughters.

# Grand Prix 1997 Record

| Grand Prix | Grid | Qual Time | Fin | Laps | Race Time | Reason |
|---|---|---|---|---|---|---|
| Australian | 7 | 1:32.287 | – | 0 | | accident |
| Brazilian | 13 | 1:17.409 | 7 | 72 | 1:36:57.902 | |
| Argentinian | 8 | 1:26.564 | 4 | 72 | 1:52:31.634 | |
| San Marino | 7 | 1:24.723 | – | 18 | | electrics |
| Monaco | 7 | 1:19.105 | – | 9 | | accident |
| Spanish | 10 | 1:18.494 | 5 | 64 | 1:31:03.882 | |
| Canadian | 13 | 1:19.622 | 5 | 54 | 1:17:45.362 | |
| French | 14 | 1:16.018 | 8 | 71 | 1:39:35.888 | |
| British | 9 | 1:22.368 | – | 42 | | electronics |
| German | 14 | 1:43.660 | – | 8 | | accident |
| Hungarian | 10 | 1:16.138 | 3 | 77 | 1:46:07.594 | |
| Belgian | 11 | 1:51.725 | 4 | 44 | 1:34:25.742 | |
| Italian | 12 | 1:24.242 | – | 38 | | accident |
| Austrian | 12 | 1:11.210 | 8 | 71 | 1:28:25.056 | |
| Luxembourg | 16 | 1:18.303 | 7 | 67 | 1:32:12.197 | |
| Japanese | 8 | 1:36.906 | 6 | 53 | 1:30:30.076 | |
| European | 14 | 1:22.263 | 8 | 69 | 1:40:10.732 | |

# 1997 Position Summary

| | | | |
|---|---|---|---|
| Contested: | 17 | Finished: | 11 |
| Pole Positions: | 0 | Fastest Laps: | 0 |
| Points: | 15 | | |
| 1st: | 0 | 2nd: | 0 |
| 3rd: | 1 | 4th: | 2 |
| 5th: | 2 | 6th: | 1 |

# Grand Prix Career Record

| | | |
|---|---|---|
| Contested: | 113 | (1989-1997) |
| Pole Positions: | 0 | |
| Fastest Laps: | 1 | 1995 (Ita) |
| Points: | 82 | 1989 (5), 1992 (2), 1993 (11), 1995 (45), 1996 (4), 1997 (15) |
| 1st: | 2 | 1995 (GB, Ita) |
| 2nd: | 1 | 1995 (Esp) |
| 3rd: | 3 | 1995 (Jap), 1996 (Mon), 1997 (Hun) |
| 4th: | 10 | 1991 (Bra), 1993 (Bra, Eur, GB) 1995 (Arg, Mon, Ger, Hun), 1997 (Arg, Bel) |
| 5th: | 5 | 1989 (USA), 1993 (Bel), 1995 (Eur), 1997 (Esp, Can) |
| 6th: | 4 | 1992 (SA, Fra), 1995 (Pac), 1997 (Jap) |

| Year | Team | No. | Grand Prix |
|---|---|---|---|
| 1989 | Benetton Ford | 5 | Bra (3), San, Mon, Mex, USA (2) |
| | Tyrrell Ford | 1 | Bel |

| 1990 | Lotus Lamborghini | 2 | Jap, Aus |
|------|-------------------|-----|----------|
| 1991 | Lotus Judd | 7 | Mex, Fra, GB, Bel, Por, Jap, Aus |
| 1992 | Lotus Ford | 16 | SA (1), Mex, Bra, Esp, San, Mon, Can, Fra (1), GB, Ger, Hun, Bel, Ita, Por, Jap, Aus |
| 1993 | Lotus Ford | 16 | SA, Bra (3), Eur (3), San, Esp, Mon, Can, Fra, GB (3), Ger, Hun, Bel (2), Ita, Por, Jap, Aus |
| 1994 | Lotus Mugen Honda | 13 | Bra, Pac, San, Mon, Esp, Can, Fra, GB, Ger, Hun, Bel, Ita, Por |
|      | Ligier Renault | 1 | Eur |
|      | Benetton Ford | 2 | Jap, Aus |
| 1995 | Benetton Renault | 17 | Bra, Arg (3), San, Esp (6), Mon (3), Can, Fra, GB (10), Ger (3), Hun (3), Bel, Ita (10), Por, Eur (2), Pac (1), Jap (4), Aus |
| 1996 | Sauber Ford | 16 | Aus, Bra, Arg, Eur, San, Mon (4), Esp, Can, Fra, GB, Ger, Hun, Bel, Ita, Por, Jap |
| 1997 | Sauber Petronas | 17 | Aus, Bra, Arg (3), San, Mon, Esp (2), Can (2), Fra, GB, Ger, Hun (4), Bel (3), Ita, Aut, Lux, Jap (1), Eur |

## HILL, Damon OBE                                    Great Britain

*1997: Arrows Yamaha*                     *1998: Jordan Mugen Honda*

Hill's decision to opt for the Arrows team for the 1997 season must have come as a shock to even his most dedicated fans. Was it the lure of the task of being able to play a major role in turning one of The Show's smaller teams into a major player or the £4.5 million salary? Maybe it was a bit of both, but there can be little doubt that the un-competitive nature of the car and some lack-lustre performances by the then reigning World Champion led to the parting of the ways. Jordan, one of those who were in the frame for his signature last year, will come up with a much better package for the 1998 season and could well provide Hill with the couple of victories that Arrows boss Tom Walkinshaw had anticipated he would bring to the 1997 Arrows season.

Two wins in an Arrows car without a single Grand Prix victory in its history was always going to be a tall order; indeed, even one win was probably over-optimistic. However, but for the failure of a 50p washer it would have materialised at the Hungaroring where Hill produced what is arguably his greatest-ever performance to date. Having never finished outside of the top two places, Hill maintained his record and showed that his race driving is amongst the best. Having qualified third, he led the race after a fine start. He brilliantly overtook Michael Schumacher on lap 11 and lead the way. It was race 299 for Arrows and there can have been few impartial observers who didn't feel for Hill when, with two laps to go, he started to slow and was eventually pipped on the line by his former Williams teammate Jacques Villeneuve. It must have been a bitter-sweet experience for Hill himself who described his third-place grid run as "the best of my career".

It was, however, largely a season of under-achieving and the only other high point came at Silverstone when he finished sixth at a time when it looked as though he might become the first world champion to end a title reign without scoring a point. That came after a 'clearing of the air' when Arrows team boss Tom Walkinshaw was critical of his number one, and one suspects that may have been the beginning of the end of Hill's time at Leafield.

In truth, the season up until Silverstone had been a disaster, and Melbourne rather set the scene when his car gave up on the formation lap. A seventeenth place at Interlagos at least provided a finish, but four successive failures – two engines and two accidents – fuelled speculation about his future. Frustration also started to set in and was exemplified at Imola when he was given a one-race ban, suspended for one race, for running into the back of Shinji Nakano's Prost early in the race 'causing an avoidable accident'.

Progress started to happen from Montreal, which marked the start of nine finishes from the remaining eleven races, six of which were inside the top ten. Spa might have seen a further two points for Hill, but any chance of holding on to his fifth position was lost when he stalled his car in the pits during a scheduled stop.

By the time of the last race of the season, Hill had already signed for the Jordan team and nearly completed his brief Arrows sojourn with a pole position – with just 0.054 seconds separating him from the number one starting slot. The race was also progressing well until another failure meant that Hill ended the season as he started it – as a spectator.

The 1998 season will bring better things for Hill. He enters a team that, like Arrows, had not won a Grand Prix up until the start of the 1998 season. By the start of the 1999 season Hill may well have changed that, and how ironic if it came at the Hungaroring.

**Born:** 17/9/60, Hampstead, London, England. Married with two daughters and one son.

## Grand Prix 1997 Record

| Grand Prix | Grid | Qual Time | Fin | Laps | Race Time | Reason |
|---|---|---|---|---|---|---|
| Australian | 20 | 1:34.806 | dns | 0 | | throttle sensor |
| Brazilian | 9 | 1:17.090 | 17 | 68 | 1:32:35.466 | |
| Argentinian | 13 | 1:27.281 | – | 33 | | engine |
| San Marino | 15 | 1:25.743 | – | 11 | | accident |
| Monaco | 13 | 1:19.674 | – | 1 | | accident |
| Spanish | 15 | 1:20.089 | – | 18 | | engine |
| Canadian | 15 | 1:20.129 | 9 | 53 | 1:17:42.581 | |

| | | | | | | |
|---|---|---|---|---|---|---|
| French | 17 | 1:16.729 | 12 | 69 | 1:39:10.579 | |
| British | 12 | 1:23.271 | 6 | 59 | 1:29:15.217 | |
| German | 13 | 1:43.361 | 8 | 44 | 1:21:09.273 | |
| Hungarian | 3 | 1:15.044 | 2 | 77 | 1:45:56.228 | |
| Belgian | 9 | 1:50.970 | 13 | 42 | 1:32:22.015 | |
| Italian | 14 | 1:24.462 | – | 46 | | engine |
| Austrian | 7 | 1:11.025 | 7 | 71 | 1:28:13.206 | |
| Luxembourg | 13 | 1:17.795 | 8 | 67 | 1:32:12.620 | |
| Japanese | 17 | 1:38.022 | 11 | 52 | 1:29:59.070 | |
| European | 4 | 1:21.130 | – | 47 | | gearbox |

## 1997 Position Summary

| | | | |
|---|---|---|---|
| Contested: | 17 | Finished: | 10 |
| Pole Positions: | 0 | Fastest Laps: | 0 |
| Points: | 7 | | |
| 1st: | 0 | 2nd: | 1 |
| 3rd: | 0 | 4th: | 0 |
| 5th: | 0 | 6th: | 1 |

## Grand Prix Career Record

| | | |
|---|---|---|
| Contested: | 84 | (1992-1997) |
| Pole Positions: | 20 | 1993 (Fra, Por), 1994 (Fra, GB), 1995 (Bra, Mon, Fra, GB, Ger, Hun, Aus), 1996 (Bra, Arg, Eur, Esp, Can, GB, Ger, Ita, Por) |
| Fastest Laps: | 19 | 1993 (GB, Ita, Por, Aus), 1994 (San, Fra, GB, Bel, Ita, Jap), 1995 (Esp, Hun, GB, Aus), 1996 (Bra, Eur, San, Ger, Hun) |
| Points: | 333 | 1993 (69), 1994 (91), 1995 (69), 1996 (97), 1997 (7) |
| 1st: | 21 | 1993 (Hun, Bel, Ita), 1994 (Esp, GB, Bel, Ita, Por, Jap), 1995 (Arg, San, Hun, Aus), 1996 (Aus, Bra, Arg, San, Can, Fra, Ger, Jap) |
| 2nd: | 15 | 1993 (Bra, Eur, Mon, Fra), 1994 (Bra, Can, Fra, Hun, Eur), 1995 (Mon, Fra, Bel), 1996 (Hun, Por), 1997 (Hun) |
| 3rd: | 5 | 1993 (Can, Por, Aus), 1995 (Por, Pac) |
| 4th: | 3 | 1993 (Jap), 1995 (Esp), 1996 (Eur) |
| 5th: | 1 | 1996 (Bel) |
| 6th: | 2 | 1994 (San), 1997 (GB) |

| Year | Team | No. | Grand Prix |
|---|---|---|---|
| 1992 | Brabham Judd | 2 | GB, Hun |
| 1993 | Williams Renault | 16 | SA, Bra (6), Eur (6), San, Esp, Mon (6), Can (4), Fra (6), GB, Ger, Hun (10), Bel (10, Ita (10, Por (4), Jap (3), Aus (4) |

| 1994 | Williams Renault | 16 | Bra (6), Pac, San (1), Mon, Esp (10), Can (6), Fra (6), GB (10), Ger, Hun (6), Bel (10), Ita (10), Por (10), Eur (6), Jap (10), Aus |
| 1995 | Williams Renault | 17 | Bra, Arg (10), San (10), Esp (3), Mon (6), Can, Fra (6), GB, Ger, Hun (10), Bel (6), Ita, Por (4), Eur, Pac (4), Jap, Aus (10) |
| 1996 | Williams Renault | 16 | Aus (10), Bra (10), Arg (10), Eur (3), San (10), Mon, Esp, Can (10), Fra (10), GB, Ger (10), Hun (6), Bel (2), Ita, Por (6), Jap (10) |
| 1997 | Arrows | 17 | Aus, Bra, Arg, San, Mon, Esp, Can, Fra, GB (1), Ger, Hun (6), Bel, Ita, Aut, Lux, Jap, Eur |

# IRVINE, Eddie                              Great Britain

*1997: Ferrari*                                          *1998: Ferrari*

At the end of the 1997 season, Eddie Irvine asserted that he was getting closer to teammate Michael Schumacher and was, as far as a team driver was concerned at least, 'a damn sight closer than anyone had ever been'. Certainly the facts seem to bear that out. Irvine's 24 points marked his best-ever tally, a tally that has improved in each of his five years in Formula One racing.

Schumacher also appreciated the Ulsterman's work towards his cause, and this was never more evident than in Suzuka where Irvine played no small part in ensuring that Schumacher senior came home with the win that ensured the Drivers' World Championship went down to the final race.

While his German teammate appreciated his contribution, the rest of the F1 drivers didn't always share that view and he courted their wrath for much of the season with a number of dubious moves that sometimes resulted in collisions and retirements. The first of these accusations came at the opening race in Australia where he seemed to make an error that put him out at the first corner, along with Herbert and Villeneuve.

Irvine had started from fifth place on the grid in Melbourne, a position he matched twice more along with a third place in Suzuka but, in general, his season in this respect was rather indifferent. This may have been in no small part because of the team's aims in the direction of Schumacher, but it will undoubtedly need improving if Irvine is to make further headway in 1998.

Although the race at Interlagos was finished, sixteenth place was less than impressive and offered no improvement over the fourteenth place starting position. Buenos Aires was a different matter though, with the Ulsterman recording his highest-ever finish in a Grand Prix. His second place was achieved with some excellent driving and for some ten laps during mid-race he held the lead before Villeneuve's Williams finally took control.

What goes up must come down, but not so in this case as Irvine continued in a rich vein of form that saw him take podium finishes at both Imola and Monte Carlo. Spain and Canada did, however, provide disappointment. Blistering tyres were again the plague in Spain and his position wasn't helped by a ten-second Stop-Go penalty for holding up Panis and Alesi on lap 59, while a tangle with Magnussen at the first corner ended his race in Montreal.

In France, Irvine was quick to start from his fifth place on the grid and quickly moved up to third position – a place he maintained until the chequered flag. Things looked even better at Silverstone and, despite hitting a hare, he managed to run second before having to retire with a damaged transmission on lap 45. Damage caused an even earlier retirement in Germany after he had collided with Heinz-Harald Frentzen's Williams car on the very first lap.

Hungary, Belgium and Italy were disappointing. Although being placed in the first two meetings, neither were finished as he twice found himself the victim of shunts. Nothing improved at either the A1-Ring nor the Nurburgring which were non-finishes, the latter through engine failure.

At Suzuka, Irvine played the ultimate team game to help ensure a victory for teammate Michael Schumacher. On a circuit he knows so well, he leapt out in front for long periods and looked to be in total domination of the race before slowing to allow Schumacher through and hold up Villeneuve. Another good, solid drive, even if some way off the pace, was had in Jerez where he was unsuccessful in holding off Berger in his final race, and thus had to settle for fifth position.

The influence of Michael Schumacher seems to be wearing well on Eddie Irvine. There is no doubt that Irvine worked harder than ever in 1997 and he will also have his ambitions and hopes set high for the 1998 season when he will be looking for a first victory of his own. It may have come in 1997 in Argentina and it had been a real possibility, almost a certainty, at Suzuka. Many F1 supporters hope he will break his duck this time around.

**Born:** 10/11/65, Newtownards, Northern Ireland. Single.

# Grand Prix 1997 Record

| Grand Prix | Grid | Qual Time | Fin | Laps | Race Time | Reason |
|---|---|---|---|---|---|---|
| Australian | 5 | 1:31.881 | – | 0 | | accident damage |
| Brazilian | 14 | 1:17.527 | 16 | 70 | 1:30:20.550 | |
| Argentinian | 7 | 1:26.327 | 2 | 72 | 1:52:02.694 | |
| San Marino | 9 | 1:24.861 | 3 | 62 | 1:32:19.016 | |
| Monaco | 15 | 1:19.723 | 3 | 62 | 2:01:27.762 | |
| Spanish | 11 | 1:18.873 | 12 | 63 | 1:31:25.313 | |
| Canadian | 12 | 1:19.503 | – | 0 | | accident damage |
| French | 5 | 1:14.860 | 3 | 72 | 1:40:05.293 | |
| British | 7 | 1:22.342 | – | 44 | | transmission |
| German | 10 | 1:43.209 | – | 1 | | damage |
| Hungarian | 5 | 1:15.424 | 9 | 76 | 1:44:51.833 | |
| Belgian | 17 | 1:52.793 | 10 | 43 | 1:33:07.860 | |

| | | | | | | | |
|---|---|---|---|---|---|---|---|
| Italian | 10 | 1:23.891 | 8 | 53 | 1:17:22.248 | | |
| Austrian | 8 | 1:11.051 | – | 38 | | accident | |
| Luxembourg | 14 | 1:17.855 | – | 22 | | engine | |
| Japanese | 3 | 1:36.466 | 3 | 53 | 1:30:14.830 | | |
| European | 7 | 1:21.610 | 5 | 69 | 1:39:01.560 | | |

## 1997 Position Summary

| | | | |
|---|---|---|---|
| Contested: | 17 | Finished: | 11 |
| Pole Positions: | 0 | Fastest Laps: | 0 |
| Points: | 24 | | |
| 1st: | 0 | 2nd: | 1 |
| 3rd: | 4 | 4th: | 0 |
| 5th: | 1 | 6th: | 0 |

## Grand Prix Career Record

| | | |
|---|---|---|
| Contested: | 65 | (1993-1997) |
| Pole Positions: | 0 | |
| Fastest Laps: | 0 | |
| Points: | 52 | 1993 (1), 1994 (6), 1995 (10), 1996 (11), 1997 (24) |
| 1st: | 0 | |
| 2nd: | 1 | 1997 (Arg) |
| 3rd: | 6 | 1995 (Can), 1996 (Aus), 1997 (San, Mon, Fra, Jap) |
| 4th: | 3 | 1994 (Eur), 1995 (Esp), 1996 (San) |
| 5th: | 5 | 1994 (Jap), 1995 (Esp), 1996 (Arg, Por), 1997 (Eur) |
| 6th: | 3 | 1993 (Jap), 1994 (Esp), 1995 (Eur) |

| Year | Team | No. | Grand Prix |
|---|---|---|---|
| 1993 | Jordan Hart | 2 | Jap (1), Aus |
| 1994 | Jordan Hart | 13 | Bra, Esp (1), Can, Fra, GB, Ger, Hun, Bel, Ita, Por, Eur (3), Jap (2), Aus |
| 1995 | Jordan Peugeot | 17 | Bra, Arg, San, Esp (2)l, Mon, Can (4), Fra, GB, Ger, Hun, Bel, Ita, Por, Eur (1), Pac, Jap (3), Aus |
| 1996 | Ferrari | 16 | Aus (4), Bra, Arg (2), Eur, San (3), Mon, Esp, Can, Fra, GB, Ger, Hun, Bel, Ita, Por (2), Jap |
| 1997 | Ferrari | 17 | Aus, Bra, Arg (6), San (4), Mon (4), Esp, Can, Fra (4), GB, Ger, Hun, Bel, Ita, Aut, Lux, Jap (4), Eur (2) |

## KATAYAMA, Ukyo                                         Japan

*1997: Minardi Hart*                                        *1998: –*

After six years of racing in the lower reaches of the Formula One field, Ukyo
Katayama decided to call it a day. The 1997 season was the final one for the

jovial Japanese who has often been the brunt of jokes but was also the first to make light of his own achievements whenever the occasion called.

Having been part of the 1992 Larousse Venturi Lamborghini team, Katayama spent four years at Tyrrell where, in 1994, he recorded his total of five championship points with two fifth places and one sixth. For the 1997 season he found himself in Italy, in the Minardi seat, but never offering a serious threat of scoring a point.

In a car sporting the Hart engine, the season's best qualifying came in the calendar opener in Australia where a fifteenth grid position was secured. His race lasted just 33 laps when a collision with former Tyrrell teammate Jos Verstappen caused his faltering fuel-feed system to fail for good.

Beyond Melbourne, grid position never got better than eighteenth with a twentieth place being the norm more often than not. Brazil brought his first finish of the year which would probably have been better than eighteenth had he not stalled his car at the race's second start.

After a spin in Argentina, in no small part due to a sticking throttle, Imola provided a change in fortunes with a respectable eleventh position that was hampered by his selection of wet settings for what proved to be a dry afternoon. Wet settings were the order of the day for Monaco though and with it came his best finish of the year even though he found that his tenth place was the last finishing position.

Problems came to the fore in Spain where a hydraulic pump failure proved terminal, as did a stuck throttle in Canada on lap five. The French meeting proved a temporary respite for Katayama who hurt his back in driving his car to eleventh place. Disappointment continued at Silverstone when he spun on the grid at the start, and at Hockenheim he ran out of fuel after he complained he could not see the pit boards or hear the radio after a collision had made the car jumpy on the straight.

Another season's best performance came in Hungary, where Katayama matched the tenth place he had secured in Monaco. For the Belgian Grand Prix, Katayama had run as high as twelfth but a spin late on relegated him to a final fourteenth position. Accident damage inflicted by one of the gravel run-offs put paid to the Italian race early on but he made amends by running a good race at the Austrian Grand Prix to come home eleventh. Nine completed laps was the sum of the mileage done in the ensuing races of the Luxembourg and Japanese Grands Prix.

Hopes of a good farewell were dashed early on in Jerez for the European Grand Prix where Katayama came home last in his last race.

Although Katayama may have gone from the world stage of Grand Prix driving, his name may still feature in the sporting pages. His ambition now centres on his other great love of mountaineering – to climb Everest without the use of carried oxygen.

**Born:** 29/5/63, Tokyo, Japan. Married with one son and one daughter.

## Grand Prix 1997 Record

| Grand Prix | Grid | Qual Time | Fin | Laps | Race Time | Reason |
|---|---|---|---|---|---|---|
| Australian | 15 | 1:33.798 | – | 32 | | fuel feed |
| Brazilian | 18 | 1:18.357 | 18 | 67 | 1:36:17.303 | |
| Argentinian | 21 | 1:28.413 | – | 37 | | spin |
| San Marino | 22 | 1:28.727 | 11 | 59 | 1:31:53.912 | |
| Monaco | 20 | 1:20.606 | 10 | 60 | 2:01:49.612 | |
| Spanish | 20 | 1:20.672 | – | 11 | | hydraulic pump |
| Canadian | 22 | 1:21.034 | – | 5 | | accident |
| French | 21 | 1:17.563 | 11 | 70 | 1:40:01.973 | |
| British | 18 | 1:24.553 | – | 0 | | accident |
| German | 22 | 1:46.499 | – | 23 | | out of fuel |
| Hungarian | 20 | 1:17.232 | 10 | 76 | 1:45:48.747 | |
| Belgian | 20 | 1:53.544 | 14 | 42 | 1:33:10.021 | |
| Italian | 21 | 1:26.555 | – | 8 | | puncture/accident |
| Austrian | 19 | 1:12.036 | 11 | 69 | 1:27:45.710 | |
| Luxembourg | 22 | 1:20.615 | – | 1 | | damage |
| Japanese | 19 | 1:38.983 | – | 8 | | engine |
| European | 19 | 1:23.409 | 17 | 68 | 1:40:06.893 | |

## 1997 Position Summary

| | | | |
|---|---|---|---|
| Contested: | 17 | Finished: | 8 |
| Pole Positions: | 0 | Fastest Laps: | 0 |
| Points: | 0 | | |
| 1st-6th: | 0 | | |
| Best Position: | 10th – twice (Mon, Hun) | | |

## Grand Prix Career Record

| | | |
|---|---|---|
| Contested: | 95 | (1992-1997) |
| Pole Positions: | 0 | |
| Fastest Laps: | 0 | |
| Points: | 5 | 1994 (5) |
| 1st: | 0 | |
| 2nd: | 0 | |
| 3rd: | 0 | |
| 4th: | 0 | |
| 5th: | 2 | 1994 (Bra, San) |
| 6th: | 1 | 1994 (GB) |

| Year | Team | No. | Grand Prix |
|---|---|---|---|
| 1992 | Larousse Venturi Lamborghini | | |
| | | 14 | SA, Mex, Bra, San, Can, Fra, GB, Ger, Hun, Bel, Ita, Por, Jap, Aus |

| 1993 | Tyrrell Yamaha | 16 | SA, Bra, Eur, San, Esp, Mon, Can, Fra, GB, Ger, Hun, Bel, Ita, Por, Jap, Aus |
| 1994 | Tyrrell Yamaha | 16 | Bra (2), Pac, San (2), Mon, Esp, Can, Fra, GB (1), Ger, Hun, Bel, Ita, Por, Eur, Jap, Aus |
| 1995 | Tyrrell Yamaha | 16 | Bra, Arg, San, Esp, Mon, Can, Fra, GB, Ger, Hun, Bel, Ita, Por, Pac, Jap, Aus |
| 1996 | Tyrrell Yamaha | 16 | Aus, Bra, Arg, Eur, San, Mon, Esp, Can, Fra, GB, Ger, Hun, Bel, Ita, Por, Jap |
| 1997 | Minardi Hart | 17 | Aus, Bra, Arg, San, Mon, Esp, Can, Fra, GB, Ger, Hun, Bel, Ita, Aut, Lux, Jap, Eur |

# KRISTENSEN, Tom                                      Denmark

*1997: –*

Spent the pre-season testing with Minardi with a view to securing their second driver's spot. Kristensen compteded in the 1997 Formula 3000 championship and finished in sixth positional overall as part of the Auto Sport Team. Was part of the winning Joest Team at the Le Mans 24-hour race last year, together with Alboreto and Johansson.

**Born:** 7/7/67. Hobro, Denmark.

# LARINI, Nicola                                        Italy

*1997: Sauber Petronas*                                    *1998: –*

Nicola Larini started the season as the number two driver at Sauber and after his showing in the first race of the year looked as though he was about to make an impression and earn his first full-season's drive since he featured in the Ligier-Ford team of 1990. It soon turned sour though, and he found himself out of the drive despite a reasonable start to his Sauber career.

Larini had arrived at Sauber fresh from the position of test driver at Ferrari and in Melbourne, he put on a good show, having qualified thirteenth and earning the Swiss team their first point of the season. In Brazil, he qualified a disappointing nineteenth but worked his way up to eleventh place and provided his team with their first double finish of the season.

Larini was always off the pace in Argentina and found himself forced even further back when he lost over 30 seconds with a refuelling problem. Amazingly, he recorded the fourth fastest lap, but ultimately spun out when he tried to get past Jan Magnussen's Stewart-Ford

San Marino might have provided Larini with additional points had he not misjudged his braking points into corners during the race. Having qualified

106

twelfth he rose as high as seventh during the race, a position he maintained to the end. It was though, to be his last race completion for the Swiss team. In Monaco he spun off twice and necessitated two calls in at the pit before finally coming to grief on lap 27. Shortly after the race Larini, who had been very critical of the Sauber team in his native Italian press, was shown the door.

**Born:** 19/3/64, Camaiore, Italy. Married with two daughters.

## Grand Prix 1997 Record

| Grand Prix | Grid | Qual Time | Fin | Laps | Race Time | Reason |
|---|---|---|---|---|---|---|
| Australian | 13 | 1:33.327 | 6 | 58 | 1:32:04.758 | |
| Brazilian | 19 | 1:18.644 | 11 | 71 | 1:36:17.642 | |
| Argentinian | 14 | 1:27.690 | – | 53 | | spin |
| San Marino | 12 | 1:25.544 | 7 | 61 | 1:31:39.396 | |
| Monaco | 11 | 1:19.468 | – | 24 | | accident |

## 1997 Position Summary

| | | | |
|---|---|---|---|
| Contested: | 5 | Finished: | 3 |
| Pole Positions: | 0 | Fastest Laps: | 0 |
| Points: | 1 | | |
| 1st: | 0 | 2nd: | 0 |
| 3rd: | 0 | 4th: | 0 |
| 5th: | 0 | 6th: | 1 |

## Grand Prix Career Record

| | | |
|---|---|---|
| Contested: | 49 | (1987-1997) |
| Fastest laps: | 0 | |
| Pole Positions: | 0 | |
| Points: | 7 | 1994 (6), 1997 (1) |
| 1st: | 0 | |
| 2nd: | 1 | 1994 (San) |
| 3rd: | 0 | |
| 4th: | 0 | |
| 5th: | 0 | |
| 6th: | 1 | 1997 (Aus) |

| Year | Team | No. | Grand Prix |
|---|---|---|---|
| 1987 | Coloni | 5 | Por, Esp, Mex, Jap, Aus |
| 1988 | Osella Alpha Romeo Turbo | 10 | Mon, USAE, Fra, GB, Ger, Bel, Ita, Por, Esp, Jap |
| 1989 | Osella Turbo | 9 | Bra, San, Can, GB, Hun, Ita, Esp, Jap, Aus |
| 1990 | Ligier-Ford | 16 | USA, Bra, San, Mon, Can, Mex, Fra, GB, Ger, Hun, Bel, Ita, Por, Esp, Jap, Aus |

| 1992 | Ferrari | 2 | Jap, Aus |
| 1994 | Ferrari | 2 | Pac, San (6) |
| 1997 | Sauber Petronas | 5 | Aus (1), Bra, Arg, San, Mon |

# MAGNUSSEN, Jan                                    Denmark

*1997: Stewart Ford*                                    *1998: Stewart Ford*

Having earned his F1 spurs as a test driver for McLaren in 1996 and substituted for the injured Mika Hakkinen in the last race of the previous season, Magnussen's role was largely as number two driver to Rubens Barrichello in 1997. But although he failed to secure any points in his first full season, the Dane did manage more finishes than his colleague – five from seventeen starts.

Perhaps not surprisingly, given his lack of experience, one can imagine a few dressing-downs for the driver behind the scenes as his sometimes impetuous nature led to a number of early race departures. Five times he failed to reach double lap figures, although he did find himself at the wrong end of several engine failures and his ultimate dedication to the Stewart cause played no small part in the team maintaining his services for the 1998 season.

Attaining a good grid position was invariably a problem for Magnussen and only at the A1-Ring for the Austrian Grand Prix did the Dane manage to break into the first five rows when he recorded a fine sixth position. With that exception, the last few rows were the norm, although there was distinct improvement at the tail end of the calendar.

With virtually no practice, Magnussen started the season in Australia on the last but one row of the grid and managed to get over half way through the race before a buckled rear suspension finally got the better of their debutante car. At Interlagos, things got worse with a multiple tangle at the first corner effectively removing him from the race.

Better was to come though and at Buenos Aires a fifteenth place grid position was complemented by Magnussen's first Stewart completion when he drove home in tenth place – ironically matching the position he achieved for McLaren in that solitary first drive of 1995.

Having spun after only two laps at Imola, Magnussen recorded his highest-ever Grand Prix finish when driving home in seventh place at Monte Carlo, thus helping to record Stewart's first double finish of the season. A second successive finish for Magnussen (the only one to be achieved all season long) came in Spain, but it marked the start of five races without a finish.

Spa saw a fourth finish of the season, but three further mechanical failures and a spin after only three laps followed. At the European Grand Prix, the season ended on a positive note with Magnussen qualifying in eleventh place and performing even better in the race to move up two places to ninth.

**Born:** 4/7/73, Roskilde, Denmark. Single. One son.

## Grand Prix 1997 Record

| Grand Prix | Grid | Qual Time | Fin | Laps | Race Time | Reason |
|---|---|---|---|---|---|---|
| Australian | 19 | 1:34.623 | – | 36 | | suspension |
| Brazilian | 20 | 1:18.773 | – | 0 | dns | accident |
| Argentinian | 15 | 1:28.035 | 10 | 66 | 1:44:55.399 | |
| San Marino | 16 | 1:26.192 | – | 2 | | spin |
| Monaco | 19 | 1:20.516 | 7 | 61 | 2:01:52.517 | |
| Spanish | 22 | 1:21.060 | 13 | 63 | 1:31:58.723 | |
| Canadian | 21 | 1:20.491 | – | 0 | | accident |
| French | 15 | 1:16.149 | – | 33 | | brake duct |
| British | 15 | 1:24.067 | – | 50 | | engine |
| German | 15 | 1:43.927 | – | 27 | | engine |
| Hungarian | 17 | 1:16.858 | – | 5 | | steering |
| Belgian | 18 | 1:52.886 | 12 | 43 | 1:33:58.760 | |
| Italian | 13 | 1:24.394 | – | 31 | | transmission |
| Austrian | 6 | 1:11.893 | – | 58 | | engine |
| Luxembourg | 12 | 1:17.722 | – | 40 | | driveshaft |
| Japanese | 14 | 1:37.480 | – | 3 | | spin |
| European | 11 | 1:22.167 | 9 | 69 | 1:40:15.258 | |

## 1997 Position Summary

| | | | |
|---|---|---|---|
| Contested: | 17 | Finished: | 5 |
| Pole Positions: | 0 | Fastest Laps: | 0 |
| Points: | 0 | | |
| 1st-6th: | 0 | | |
| Best Position: | 7th – Mon | | |

## Grand Prix Career Record

| | | |
|---|---|---|
| Contested: | 18 | (1995-1996) |
| Pole Positions: | 0 | |
| Fastest Laps: | 0 | |
| 1st-6th: | 0 | |
| Best Finish: | 7th | 1997 (Mon) |

| Year | Team | No. | Grand Prix |
|---|---|---|---|
| 1995 | McLaren Mercedes | 1 | Pac |
| 1997 | Stewart Ford | 17 | Aus, Bra, Arg, San, Mon, Esp, Can, Fra, GB, Ger, Hun, Bel, Ita, Aut, Lux, Jap, Eur |

# MARQUES, Tarso                                    Brazil

*1997: (Test Driver: Minardi Hart)*                              *1998: –*

Having filled in twice during the 1996 season, Minardi test driver Tarso
Marques held down a Minardi drive for the second half of the season after

Jarno Trulli had gone to join the Prost team to fill the void left by the injured Panis.

Despite the knowledge gained as test driver for the previous two seasons, Marques was unable to build on the start offered by Trulli and managed just four finishes from nine Grands Prix. In his first race at Silverstone though, he did match the best position achieved by the established Katayama when he came home in tenth place. At the German Grand Prix, Marques made up the back row of the grid with teammate Katayama and remained there when the race got underway, suffering a broken transmission.

In Hungary, having started at the back of the grid, he managed to improve one place before the finish by passing Mika Salo. A spin at Spa after eighteen laps brought an early end to a race during which he had moved up to twelfth place. Then, in Austria, he failed to get onto the grid when he was disqualified after the Brazilian's car was found to be underweight. The Minardi-Hart M197 was found to be 3 kg too light.

The Luxembourg meeting went just one lap when his engine failed as did his gearbox a couple of weeks later in Suzuka. The final race of the season at least produced a fifteenth-place finish for the Brazilian.

**Born:** 19/1/76, Curitiba, Brazil. Single.

## Grand Prix 1997 Record

| Grand Prix | Grid | Qual Time | Fin | Laps | Race Time | Reason |
|---|---|---|---|---|---|---|
| French | 22 | 1:18.280 | – | 5 | | engine |
| British | 20 | 1:25.154 | 10 | 58 | 1:29:28.078 | |
| German | 21 | 1:45.942 | – | 0 | | transmission |
| Hungarian | 22 | 1.18.020 | 12 | 75 | 1:46:19.969 | |
| Belgian | 22 | 1:54.505 | – | 18 | | spin |
| Italian | 22 | 1:27.677 | 14 | 50 | 1:17:35.247 | |
| Austrian * | – | – | – | – | | dq |
| Luxembourg | 18 | 1:19.347 | – | 1 | | engine |
| Japanese | 20 | 1:39.678 | – | 46 | | gearbox |
| European | 20 | 1:23.854 | 15 | 68 | 1:39:56.704 | |

* Disqualified – car underweight in qualifying session.

## 1997 Position Summary

| | | | |
|---|---|---|---|
| Contested: | 9 | Finished: | 4 |
| Pole Positions: | 0 | Fastest Laps: | 0 |
| Points: | 0 | | |
| 1st-6th: | 0 | | |
| Best Position: | 10th – GB | | |

## Grand Prix Career Record

| | |
|---|---|
| Contested: | 11 |
| Pole Positions: | 0 |
| Fastest Laps: | 0 |
| Points: | 0 |

| 1st-6th: | 0 | | |
|---|---|---|---|
| Best Finish: | 10th | 1997 (GB) | |

| Year | Team | No. | Grand Prix |
|---|---|---|---|
| 1996 | Minardi Ford | 2 | Bra, Arg |
| 1997 | Minardi Hart | *9 | Fra, GB, Ger, Hun, Bel, Ita, Lux, Jap, Eur |

*Disqualified after Austrian Grand Prix qualifying session due to underweight car. Was not on grid for race therefore does not count towards Grands Prix contested.*

# MONTERMINI, Andrea                                        Italy

*1997: –*

Andrea Montermini was being linked with several teams prior to the start of the 1998 season. A talented driver, those who look at his recent forays into the F1 world may be put-off not least because his last two F1 teams have collapsed!

In 1995 he drove for Pacific, who collapsed after the season had finished and in 1996 he drove for the Forti team, who didn't even see the season out – the British Grand Prix at Silverstone being their last track excursion.

Of the ten races, he took part in during 1996, he only managed to finish one – that in Argentina when he finished tenth. In three others he started but failed to finish and in five others he fell foul of the 107% rule.

With twenty-seven races behind him, he has yet to secure his first World Championship point.

**Born:** 30/5/64, Sassuolo, Modena, Italy. Single.

## Grand Prix Record

| Contested: | 27 | |
|---|---|---|
| Pole Positions: | 0 | |
| Fastest Laps: | 0 | |
| Points: | 0 | |
| 1st-6th: | 0 | |
| Best Finish: | 8th | 1995 (Ger) |

| Year | Team | No. | Grand Prix |
|---|---|---|---|
| 1995 | Pacific Ford | 17 | Bra, Arg, San, Esp, Mon, Can, Fra, GB, Ger, Hun, Bel, Ita, Por, Eur, Pac, Jap, Aus |
| 1996 | Forti Ford | 10 | Aus, Bra, Arg, Eur, San, Mon, Esp, Can, Fra, GB |

# MONTOYA, Juan Pablo                                Colombia

*1997: –                          1998: (Test Driver: Williams Mecachrome)*
Twenty-two years of age, Colombian Juan Pablo Montoya was selected as
test driver for the Williams team after a series of pre-season trials which
included three other hopefuls – Nicolas Minassian, Soheil Ayari and Max
Wilson. Montoya has no previous F1 experience but finished second in last
year's FIA F3000 Championship, having secured three wins duiring the
season. At the time of going to press, it looks as though he will be continuing
in F3000 alongside his testing duties. He has previously competed in the
British Formula Vauxhall Championship – (third in 1995) and the British F3
Championship (1996) where he secured two wins, one pole position and five
fastest laps.
**Born:** 20/9/75, Bogota, Colombia. Single.

# MORBIDELLI, Gianni                                  Italy

*1997: Sauber Petronas (Test Driver: Ferrari)                          1998: –*
You could be forgiven for thinking that Gianni Morbidelli's season was
scripted a little bit like a comedy soap opera. Having started the season as a
test driver at Ferrari as a replacement for Nicola Larini, he found himself
replacing the same person in the second car at Sauber after Larini's services
had been dispensed with.

With great eagerness to get the season underway in his first race at Spain
he was given a Stop-Go penalty for a jump start. He also had what was
possibly the most bizarre accident of the season at the Spanish Grand Prix
when he accelerated too hard out of the pits and spun across the straight and
into the wall.

Accidents blighted his season and he missed the French, British and
German Grands Prix after he broke his arm in a high-speed testing crash
when he lost control coming out of the Magny-Cours circuit's fast
Nurburgring S-bend. The car spun through 360 degrees sending him crashing
into a concrete wall at 115 mph. He was also forced to miss the Japanese
Grand Prix at Suzuka after injuring his wrist in a heavy crash during
qualifying.

Despite all that, he did manage to get six completions from his eight races,
although his performances were less impressive than the countryman he
replaced. Perhaps his ill-luck could be attributed to his thirteenth position on
the grid in Spain from which there was no improvement. Clutch problems
played their part in a disappointing fourteenth placing. Tyre wear and
blistering was a major reason for lack of performance in Canada after which
Morbidelli found himself out for three races with that broken arm.

His return at the Hungarian Grand Prix lasted only eight laps after he
collided with Jan Magnussen at the start and ultimately retired with associated
engine problems. The race in Belgium provided Morbidelli with his best
finish of the year – a ninth place that he would go on to match twice more

before the season was out. A disappointing performance in qualifying at Monza left him floundering in an eighteenth grid position for his home Grand Prix, only improving marginally to a lapped twelfth finish.

Ninth positions came at the Austrian and Luxembourg races, again from lowly starting positions. Having again struggled in qualifying at Jerez, a wrist injury prevented him from starting the race, thus ending the season on a disappointing note.

**Born:** 13/1/68, Italy. Single.

## Grand Prix 1997 Record

| Grand Prix | Grid | Qual Time | Fin | Laps | Race Time | Reason |
|---|---|---|---|---|---|---|
| Spanish | 13 | 1:19.323 | 14 | 62 | 1:30:50.087 | |
| Canadian | 18 | 1:20.357 | 10 | 53 | 1:17:46.091 | |
| Hungarian | 15 | 1:16.766 | – | 7 | | engine |
| Belgian | 13 | 1:52.094 | 9 | 44 | 1.35:29.299 | |
| Italian | 18 | 1:24.735 | 12 | 52 | 1:17:14.938 | |
| Austrian | 13 | 1:11.261 | 9 | 71 | 1:28:42.454 | |
| Luxembourg | 19 | 1:19.490 | 9 | 66 | 1:31:51.462 | |
| Japanese | 18 | 1:38.556 | dns | – | | qualifying acc |

## 1997 Position Summary

| | | | |
|---|---|---|---|
| Contested: | 7 | Finished: | 6 |
| Pole Positions: | 0 | Fastest Laps: | 0 |
| Points: | 0 | | |
| 1st-6th: | 0 | | |
| Best Position: | 9th – three times (Bel, Aus, Lux) | | |

## Grand Prix Career Record

| | | |
|---|---|---|
| Contested: | 67 | (1990-1997) |
| Pole Positions: | 0 | |
| Fastest Laps: | 0 | |
| Points: | 9 | 1991 (1), 1994 (3), 1995 (5) |
| 1st: | 0 | |
| 2nd: | 0 | |
| 3rd: | 1 | 1995 (Aus) |
| 4th: | 0 | |
| 5th: | 1 | 1994 (Ger) |
| 6th: | 3 | 1991 (Aus), 1994 (Bel), 1995 (Can) |

| Year | Team | No. | Grand Prix |
|---|---|---|---|
| 1990 | Dallara Ford | 1 | Bra |
| | Minardi Ford | 2 | Jap, Aus |
| 1991 | Minardi Ferrari | 15 | USA, Bra, San, Mon, Can, Mex, Fra, GB, Ger, Hun, Bel, Ita, Por, Esp, Jap |
| | Ferrari | 1 | Aus (1) |
| 1992 | Minardi Lamborghini | 15 | SA, Mex, Bra, Esp, San, Mon, Can, |

| 1994 | Footwork Ford | 16 | Fra, GB, Ger, Bel, Ita, Por, Jap, Aus Bra, Pac, San, Mon, Esp, Can, Fra, GB, Ger (2), Hun, Bel (1), Ita, Por, Eur, Jap, Aus |
| 1995 | Arrows Hart | 10 | Bra, Arg, San, Esp, Mon, Can (1), Fra, Pac, Jap, Aus (4) |
| 1997 | Sauber Petronas | 7 | Esp, Can, Hun, Bel, Ita, Aut, Lux |

# MULLER, Jorg                                          Germany

*1997: (Test Driver: Arrows Yamaha)    1998: (Test Driver: Sauber Petronas)*
Muller competed for many years in the German Formula 3 Championship, winning the title in 1994 with eleven wins. In the same year he had his first test in a Formula One car with Ligier. In 1996 he became European Formula 3000 Champion and also won the Spa 24-hour race in a BMW. Following testing with Arrows during 1996, he was appointed as test driver for the 1997 season. In January 1998 he was appointed as test driver for the Sauber team for the 1998 season.
**Born:** 3/9/69, Kerkrade, Holland. Single.

# NAKANO, Shinji                                          Japan

*1997: Prost Mugen Honda                                    1998: –*
Nakano made his debut in the Prost team in 1997 having worked as a test driver for the 1996 outfit under the Ligier banner. His drive came as part of the deal that ensured Prost the contract with their Japanese engine suppliers Mugen Honda. It proved to be a difficult first season for Nakano who managed just two points and eight finishes in what should have been a competitive car. His performances in qualifying were even less impressive with fifteenth being the highest place achieved on the grid.

Having struggled to get to grips with qualifying in Melbourne, Nakano had to settle for sixteenth position in his first race. Nevertheless, he performed admirably in his first drive and, despite making a couple of unscheduled detours, worked his way through the field in a steady drive to finish seventh. Qualifying in Brazil went marginally better, but he could make no such impression on the race and finished fourteenth.

The Argentine Grand Prix marked the start of four successive races without a finish. An engine failed in Argentina where he had qualified a lowly twentieth while accidents took their toll in San Marino and Monaco. Gearbox problems then intervened in Spain. None of these races provided any improvement in qualifying and the grid position 21 in Monaco was the worst for the year.

Montreal rewarded him with his first ever championship point, achieved from another poor grid position and after teammate Panis' crash had stopped the race. Magny-Cours produced a spin on lap nine and, after a steady eleventh at Silverstone, there seemed to be distinct signs of improvement as Nakano finished seventh and then sixth at the German and Hungarian races respectively. His drive at the British Grand Prix was especially impressive as he looked to be delivering his potential.

The season however was to fizzle out with just two more low-order completions coming at Monza and Jerez, although the failures in between were down to reliability problems.

Rumours were rife well before the end of the 1997 season that Prost team manager Alain Prost wanted to replace him for the final few races but was unable to negotiate a suitable deal with Mugen Honda to do so. With Peugeot supplying Prost for 1998, Nakano's contract was not renewed and the Japanese was seeking a new drive.

**Born:** 1/4/71, Osaka, Japan. Single.

## Grand Prix 1997 Record

| Grand Prix | Grid | Qual Time | Fin | Laps | Race Time | Reason |
|---|---|---|---|---|---|---|
| Australian | 16 | 1:33.989 | 7 | 56 | 1:31:11.547 | |
| Brazilian | 15 | 1:17.999 | 14 | 71 | 1:37:25.224 | |
| Argentinian | 20 | 1:28.366 | – | 49 | | engine |
| San Marino | 18 | 1:26.712 | – | 11 | | accident |
| Monaco | 21 | 1:20.961 | – | 36 | | accident |
| Spanish | 16 | 1:20.103 | – | 34 | | gearbox |
| Canadian | 19 | 1:20.370 | 6 | 54 | 1:18:17.347 | |
| French | 12 | 1:15.857 | – | 7 | | spin |
| British | 14 | 1:23.887 | 11 | 57 | 1:26:13.219 | |
| German | 17 | 1:44.112 | 7 | 45 | 1:22:18.768 | |
| Hungarian | 16 | 1:16.784 | 6 | 77 | 1:46:28.661 | |
| Belgian | 16 | 1:52.749 | – | 5 | | electronics |
| Italian | 15 | 1:24.553 | 11 | 53 | 1:18:07.936 | |
| Austrian | 16 | 1:11.596 | – | 57 | | engine |
| Luxembourg | 17 | 1:18.699 | – | 16 | | engine |
| Japanese | 15 | 1:37.588 | – | 22 | | wheel bearing |
| European | 15 | 1:22.351 | 10 | 69 | 1:40:15.986 | |

## 1997 Position Summary

| | | | |
|---|---|---|---|
| Contested: | 17 | Finished: | 8 |
| Pole Positions: | 0 | Fastest Laps: | 0 |
| Points: | 2 | | |
| 1st: | 0 | 2nd: | 0 |
| 3rd: | 0 | 4th: | 0 |
| 5th: | 0 | 6th: | 2 |

## Grand Prix Career Record

| | | |
|---|---|---|
| Contested: | 17 | (1997) |
| Pole Positions: | 0 | |
| Fastest Laps: | 0 | |

| Points: | 2 | 1997 (2) |
|---|---|---|
| 1st: | 0 | |
| 2nd: | 0 | |
| 3rd: | 0 | |
| 4th: | 0 | |
| 5th: | 0 | |
| 6th: | 2 | 1997 (Can, Hun) |

| Year | Team | No. | Grand Prix |
|---|---|---|---|
| 1997 | Prost Mugen Honda | 17 | Aus, Bra, Arg, San, Mon, Esp, Can (2), Fra, GB, Ger, Hun (2), Bel, Ita, Aut, Lux, Jap, Eur |

# PANIS, Olivier                                    France

*1997: Prost Mugen Honda*                    *1998: Prost Peugeot*

Having started to make his name as a driver of some talent during the 1996 season, Olivier Panis had every right to expect further enhancements to his driving record in 1997. Under the guidance of Alain Prost and with the self belief that is central to confidence, Panis was well on the way to establishing himself in the top three drivers when an horrendous crash at the Canadian Grand Prix looked likely to end his season.

Coming through the double bend at Turn Six and Seven and out towards Pont de La Concorde, Panis' Prost clipped a wall and then ploughed into another at 150mph. Thankfully the wall that halted the Frenchman's car almost instantly was a tyre barrier otherwise Panis might have suffered more than his two broken legs. One can only imagine the sort of g-force experienced.

That the Frenchman was back and racing for the final three races of the season is almost miraculous and should not detract from the seriousness of the incident and how close he might have come to an even worse fate had those tyres not been in place.

Up until that point, Panis had been showing some fine form and went into the Montreal race in third place in the Drivers' Championship after several fine race performances that might have brought even greater rewards had his car been more competitive in qualifying.

In Australia Panis lined up ninth on the grid and drove a steady race recording a number of fast laps that helped him finish in fifth place to create a small piece of history by earning Bridgestone's first championship points. At Interlagos qualifying went much better when he qualified a career-best fifth. The race went even better and he moved up to second at one point before Berger took him during a pit stop. Third though provided the first of two podium finishes.

The Argentine Grand Prix had looked to have even greater possibilities for

Panis. A marvellous run in qualifying put him on the second row and, with a one-stop strategy, he was staying in contact with the leaders until a hydraulic failure on lap seventeen forced him out. Panis was on the second row once again in Imola but it was clear his car seemed difficult to handle and tyre wear didn't help the situation and a disappointing eighth was recorded.

In Monaco the situation was reversed. At the venue of the Frenchman's only Grand Prix triumph he qualified only twelfth but in changeable weather conditions he made the most of his opportunities and worked his way as high as third before settling for a fourth place finish.

In Spain things looked to be going much the same way as in Monaco. Another indifferent qualifying performance found him only twelfth on the grid but he drove well and lapped consistently fast enough to allow him to leave the likes of David Coulthard in his wake on the way to second place.

With things on the up the Canadian Grand Prix dawned but, having qualified tenth, Panis was officially recorded in eleventh place after the race was stopped following his accident. Amazingly, just eight races later the Luxembourg Grand Prix saw the return of Panis and the Frenchman celebrated with a point. He qualified in eleventh place and, despite understeer, pushed Pedro Diniz hard in the final stages in an attempt to take fifth.

Suzuka was the venue for his only other non-finish of the year in a weekend where his car was plagued by engine failures. The final race in Jerez proved only slightly better for him with a ninth place on the grid and seventh at the line. At the end of the 1997 season, Panis signed a new two-year contract to stay with Prost although the second year is an option to keep the driver. With the power of Peugeot Panis may find himself with an even better package for 1998 and, provided the Bridgestone tyres can maintain the pace, and fate allowing, Panis may be allowed the sort of season most expected him to produce in 1997.

**Born:** 2/9/66, Lyon, France. Married with one son.

# Grand Prix 1997 Record

| Grand Prix | Grid | Qual Time | Fin | Laps | Race Time | Reason |
|---|---|---|---|---|---|---|
| Australian | 9 | 1:32.842 | 5 | 58 | 1:31:29.026 | |
| Brazilian | 5 | 1:16.756 | 3 | 72 | 1:36:22.860 | |
| Argentinian | 3 | 1:25.491 | – | 16 | | hydraulics |
| San Marino | 4 | 1:24.075 | 8 | 61 | 1:31:56.734 | |
| Monaco | 12 | 1:19.626 | 4 | 62 | 2:01:50.056 | |
| Spanish | 12 | 1:19.157 | 2 | 64 | 1:30:41.700 | |
| Canadian | 10 | 1:19.034 | 11 | 51 | 1:13:27.233 | |
| Luxembourg | 11 | 1:17.650 | 6 | 67 | 1:32:11.593 | |
| Japanese | 10 | 1:37.073 | – | 36 | | engine |
| European | 9 | 1:21.735 | 7 | 69 | 1:40:04.916 | |

# 1997 Position Summary

| Contested: | 10 | Finished: | 8 |
|---|---|---|---|
| Pole Positions: | 0 | Fastest Laps: | 0 |
| Points: | 16 | | |
| 1st: | 0 | 2nd: | 1 |
| 3rd: | 1 | 4th: | 1 |
| 5th: | 1 | 6th: | 1 |

## Grand Prix Career Record

| | | |
|---|---|---|
| Contested: | 59 | (1994-1997) |
| Pole Positions: | 0 | |
| Fastest Laps: | 0 | |
| Points: | 54 | 1994 (9), 1995 (16), 1993 (13), 1997 (16) |
| 1st: | 1 | 1996 (Mon) |
| 2nd: | 3 | 1994 (Ger), 1995 (Aus), 1997 (Esp) |
| 3rd: | 1 | 1997 (Bra) |
| 4th: | 3 | 1995 (Can, GB), 1997 (Mon) |
| 5th: | 4 | 1994 (Aus), 1995 (Jap), 1996 (Hun), 1997 (Aus) |
| 6th: | 5 | 1994 (Hun), 1995 (Esp, Hun), 1996 (Bra), 1997 (Lux) |

| Year | Team | No. | Grand Prix |
|---|---|---|---|
| 1994 | Ligier Renault | 16 | Bra, Pac, San, Mon, Esp, Can, Fra, GB, Ger (6), Hun (1), Bel, Ita, Por, Eur, Jap, Aus (2) |
| 1995 | Ligier Mugen Honda | 17 | Bra, Arg, San, Esp (1), Mon, Can (3), Fra, GB (3), Ger, Hun (1), Bel, Ita, Por, Eur, Pac, Jap (2), Aus (6) |
| 1996 | Ligier Mugen Honda | 16 | Aus, Bra (1), Arg, Eur, San, Mon (10), Esp, Can, Fra, GB, Ger, Hun (2), Bel, Ita, Por, Jap |
| 1997 | Prost Mugen Honda | 10 | Aus (2), Bra (4), Arg, San, Mon (3), Esp (6), Can, Lux (1), Jap, Eur |

# ROSSET, Ricardo                                    Brazil

*1997: Lola Ford*                                         *1998: –*

Ricardo Rosset made his debut on the Formula One scene in 1996 as a driver for the Arrows Hart team. He finished eight of his sixteen races and achieved an all-time high of eighth at the Hungaroring that same year. With new owner Tom Walkinshaw shuffling his pack for 1997, Rosset found himself joining the new, but ultimately ill-fated Lola team.

Qualifying in Melbourne was as far as it went, but some eleven seconds off the pace in an inadequate car proved too much and he was excluded from the start by the 107% qualification rule. There would be no further opportunities

on the big circuit as Lola went into liquidation.
**Born:** 27/7/68, Sao Paulo, Brazil. Single.

## Grand Prix 1997 Record

| Grand Prix | Grid | Qual Time | Fin | Laps | Race Time | Reason |
|---|---|---|---|---|---|---|
| Australian | 24 | 1:42.086 | | | 107% | – did not qualify |

### 1997 Position Summary

| | | | |
|---|---|---|---|
| Contested: | 0 | Finished: | 0 |
| Pole Positions: | 0 | Fastest Laps: | 0 |
| Points: | 0 | | |
| 1st-6th: | 0 | | |

## Grand Prix Career Record

| | | |
|---|---|---|
| Contested: | 16 | |
| Pole Positions: | 0 | |
| Fastest Laps: | 0 | |
| 1st-6th: | 0 | |
| Best Finish: | 8th | 1996 (Hun) |

| Year | Team | No. | Grand Prix |
|---|---|---|---|
| 1996 | Arrows Hart | 16 | Aus, Bra, Arg, Eur, San, Mon, Esp, Can, Fra, GB, Ger, Hun, Bel, Ita, Por, Jap |
| 1997 | Lola Ford | – | *Failed to qualify for Australian GP* |

# SALO, Mika                                    Finland

*1997: Tyrrell Ford*                          *1998: Arrows Yamaha*

It must have been a depressing year for Mika Salo. Having been spoken of as a driver of the future for one of the big four teams, he completed the term of his three-year contract at Tyrrell in what was an under-powered car and spent much of the season in a bid to fight out the final grid positions with the Minardis.

Having scored five points in his two previous seasons, his fifth position at Monaco was to be his only reward of the season and the only points won by his team. The race at Monaco was a gamble taken and won by the Tyrrell team who opted to run him through it without stopping for fuel and tyres. A brave decision that worked.

Having coasted out of the Australian Grand Prix with electrical problems, Salo managed to inject a burst of form that saw him move from thirteenth position at Interlagos through to fifth in Monaco. An eighth in Argentina and ninth in San Marino were equally well won. The Finn's fifth place was matched by what was to be the first of two fourteenth place grid positions – his highest of the season – which marked his average starting point in 1996.

Those four completions were followed by five non-finishes, all but one of

119

which were down to mechanical or electrical problems. Having got back to finishing ways in Hungary and Belgium, engine and gearbox problems added disappointment to the meetings in Italy and Austria. Salo ran home in tenth after starting in twentieth position in Luxembourg and, after an engine failure in Suzuka, the end to a disappointing season came in Jerez with a twelfth place.

Several rumours reported that Salo was linked with Ferrari as a possible replacement for Eddie Irvine, but they never bore fruition and the Finn opted for a drive with Tom Walkinshaw's Arrows team in the seat vacated by Damon Hill.

**Born:** 30/11/66, Helsinki, Finland. Single.

## Grand Prix 1997 Record

| Grand Prix | Grid | Qual Time | Fin | Laps | Race Time | Reason |
|---|---|---|---|---|---|---|
| Australian | 18 | 1:34.229 | – | 42 | | electric's |
| Brazilian | 22 | 1:19.274 | 13 | 71 | 1:37:20.538 | |
| Argentinian | 19 | 1:28.224 | 8 | 71 | 1:52:58.521 | |
| San Marino | 19 | 1:26.852 | 9 | 60 | 1:31:05.134 | |
| Monaco | 14 | 1:19.694 | 5 | 61 | 2:00:18.245 | |
| Spanish | 14 | 1:20.079 | – | 35 | | puncture |
| Canadian | 17 | 1:20.336 | – | 46 | | engine |
| French | 19 | 1:17.256 | – | 61 | | electrics |
| British | 17 | 1:24.478 | – | 44 | | engine |
| German | 19 | 1:45.372 | – | 33 | | clutch |
| Hungarian | 21 | 1:17.482 | 13 | 75 | 1:46:20.754 | |
| Belgian | 19 | 1:52.897 | 11 | 43 | 1:33:47.540 | |
| Italian | 19 | 1:25.693 | – | 33 | | engine |
| Austrian | 21 | 1:14.246 | – | 48 | | gearbox |
| Luxembourg | 20 | 1:19.526 | 10 | 66 | 1:32:18.927 | |
| Japanese | 22 | 1:40.529 | – | 46 | | engine |
| European | 21 | 1:24.222 | 12 | 68 | 1:39:15.015 | |

## 1997 Position Summary

| | | | |
|---|---|---|---|
| Contested: | 17 | Finished: | 8 |
| Pole Positions: | 0 | Fastest Laps: | 0 |
| Points: | 2 | | |
| 1st: | 0 | 2nd: | 0 |
| 3rd: | 0 | 4th: | 0 |
| 5th: | 1 | 6th: | 0 |

## Grand Prix Career Record

| | | |
|---|---|---|
| Contested: | 52 | (1994-1997) |
| Pole Positions: | 0 | |
| Fastest Laps: | 0 | |
| Points: | 12 | 1995 (5), 1996 (5), 1997 (2) |
| 1st: | 0 | |

| | | | |
|---|---|---|---|
| 2nd: | 0 | | |
| 3rd: | 0 | | |
| 4th: | 0 | | |
| 5th: | 5 | 1995 (Ita, Por), 1996 (Bra, Mon), 1997 (Mon) | |
| 6th: | 2 | 1995 (Jap), 1996 (Aus) | |

| Year | Team | No. | Grand Prix |
|------|------|-----|------------|
| 1994 | Lotus Mugen Honda | 2 | Jap, Aus |
| 1995 | Tyrrell Yamaha | 17 | Bra, Arg, San, Esp, Mon, Can, Fra, GB, Ger, Hun, Bel, Ita (2), Por, Eur, Pac, Jap (1), Aus (2) |
| 1996 | Tyrrell Yamaha | 16 | Aus (1), Bra (2), Arg, Eur, San, Mon (2), Esp, Can, Fra, GB, Ger, Hun, Bel, Ita, Por, Jap |
| 1997 | Tyrrell Ford | 17 | Aus, Bra, Arg, San, Mon (2), Esp, Can, Fra, GB, Ger, Hun, Bel, Ita, Aut, Lux, Jap, Eur |

# SCHUMACHER, Michael                    Germany

*1997: Ferrari*                                              *1998: Ferrari*

The *Sun* newspaper has hardly been at the centre of the literary establishment in recent years, but its comment the day after the final race of the 1997 season said it all: "Michael Schumacher ended the race with his car in the gravel and his reputation in the gutter." The prancing-horse pilot had seemingly ruined another outstanding year in which he used all his undoubted talents to bring his Ferrari to the brink of the world championship and the team in sight of the Constructors' Cup they last secured in 1983. Both were close-run things.

While his F310B car was a distinct improvement on his 1996 machine, Schumacher's ability to drag every last ounce of performance from it was exceptional. This was no better demonstrated than at Monaco and Spa where, in wet conditions, the German drove two magnificent races.

The former two-time world champion finished thirteen of his seventeen races and every single one of those finished scored points. No mean achievement. Qualifying was equally impressive and only three times did the German start away from the front two rows.

But for a bad start, Schumacher may well have won the season's opener at Melbourne. But he found himself behind Coulthard and then he wasn't helped by fuel-rig problems, so he was probably happy to settle for the fifteenth second place of his career. Despite being on the front row at the start of the Brazilian Grand Prix, Schumacher's Ferrari could not match the performance it had shown in Victoria. A lack of grip compounded matters and the reward for the weekend's efforts was just two points. Then, two weeks later an accident at the first corner with Rubens Barrichello brought the Argentine race to an end before the first lap had been completed.

The start of the European circuit saw a distinct improvement in form as Schumacher managed five successive finishes and three first places. Imola started the sequence with a second place in a race where he and the car looked in almost perfect harmony. The season's first win came also from the season's first pole position when he dominated in the wet conditions after having opened up a near 30-second lead inside just six laps.

Blistering tyres were one of the reasons that the domination couldn't be continued in Spain. A lack of grip affected qualifying but fourth place was won, and with it vital points in the quest for the championship.

Was it the French influence that then came in to play? Who knows, but the French speaking cities of Montreal and Magny-Cours proved to the distinct liking of Michael and resulted in him securing poles and victories at each. The latter venue proved to be the most dominant win with the new 046/2 engine working well with its additional 25 bhp. More importantly, the twenty points won in the two races gave the German a fourteen point lead over Villeneuve.

Having looked competitive in qualifying, the failure of his car's wheel bearings at Silverstone provided his first retirement of the season due to mechanical problems. The next race on the home 'turf' of Hockenheim provided an identical qualifying performance and he will have been more than satisfied with his second place, not withstanding tyre problems resurfacing and the loss of fifth gear.

Having qualified in pole position at the Hungaroring, blistering tyres once again took their toll to limit Schumacher's race competitiveness and he did well to come home fourth. At Spa, the rain once again intervened and, as at Monaco, Schumacher performed superbly to win in what was his drive of the season. Sixth positions at Monza and the A1-Ring were both achieved from a lowly ninth position on the starting grid. The race in Austria would have been more productive but for a Stop-Go penalty incurred by the German for not paying due attention to waved yellow flags.

The Luxembourg Grand Prix at the Nurburgring marked the start of Schumacher's 100th Grand Prix, but it ended without celebration after just two laps when he was shunted out of the race by no less a person than his younger brother Ralf.

With arch rival Villeneuve now back into a nine-point lead, Schumacher had to secure a win at Suzuka and hope for the best to take his title challenge down to the final race. He did so with another fine drive, and a magnificent contribution from his teammate Eddie Irvine who held Villeneuve back from scoring vital points. The perfect penultimate race was then soured by events in the final race at Jerez. Having secured a front-row position, he beat Villeneuve to the lead from the off. Villeneuve then attacked him late in the race in a move that ultimately lead to Schumacher touring the gravel and retiring from the race.

Subsequently, Schumacher had his second place in the final world championship table stripped from him in light of his 'instinctive' and 'intentional' actions on that fateful lap at Jerez. Deep down, the German must feel that he got off lightly and will be thankful that he will have started the 1998 season on level terms.

The 1998 season is the third in the Schumacher-Ferrari plan, the aim of which the aim was to win championships. With two years of improvisation and improving design, and having come so close in 1997, it is unlikely that Ferrari will stand a better chance of achieving that dream than now. For both though, it is more important that any win is achieved in a fair and sportsmanlike manner. Nothing else is likely to appease a disappointed tifosi and the symbol of the prancing horse.

**Born:** 3/1/69, Kerpen, Germany. Married with one child.

# Grand Prix 1997 Record

| Grand Prix | Grid | Qual Time | Fin | Laps | Race Time | Reason |
|---|---|---|---|---|---|---|
| Australian | 3 | 1:31.472 | 2 | 58 | 1:30:48.764 | |
| Brazilian | 2 | 1:16.594 | 5 | 72 | 1:36:40.721 | |
| Argentinian | 4 | 1:25.773 | – | 0 | | accident |
| San Marino | 3 | 1:23.955 | 2 | 62 | 1:31:01:910 | |
| Monaco | 2 | 1:18.943 | 1 | 62 | 2:00:05.654 | |
| Spanish | 7 | 1:18.313 | 4 | 64 | 1:30:53.975 | |
| Canadian | 1 | 1:18.095 | 1 | 54 | 1:17:40.646 | |
| French | 1 | 1:14.548 | 1 | 72 | 1:38:50.492 | |
| British | 4 | 1:21.977 | – | 38 | | wheel bearings |
| German | 4 | 1:42.181 | 2 | 45 | 1:21:16.573 | |
| Hungarian | 1 | 1:14.672 | 4 | 77 | 1:46:17.650 | |
| Belgian | 3 | 1:50.293 | 1 | 44 | 1:33:46.717 | |
| Italian | 9 | 1:23.624 | 6 | 53 | 1:17:16.090 | |
| Austrian | 9 | 1:11.056 | 6 | 71 | 1:28:09.409 | |
| Luxembourg | 5 | 1:17.385 | – | 2 | | suspension |
| Japanese | 2 | 1:36.133 | 1 | 53 | 1:29:48.446 | |
| European | 2 | 1:21.072 | – | 47 | | accident |

## 1997 Position Summary

| | | | |
|---|---|---|---|
| Contested: | 17 | Finished: | 13 |
| Pole Positions: | 3 | Fastest Laps: | 3 |
| Points: | 78 | | |
| 1st: | 5 | 2nd: | 3 |
| 3rd: | 0 | 4th: | 2 |
| 5th: | 1 | 6th: | 2 |

# Grand Prix Career Record

| | | |
|---|---|---|
| Contested: | 102 | |
| Pole Positions: | 17 | 1994 (Mon, Esp, Can, Hun, Eur, Jap), 1995 (San, Esp, Can, Jap), 1996 (San, Mon, Fra, Hun), 1997 (Can, Fra, Hun) |
| Fastest Laps: | 29 | 1992 (Bel, Aus), 1993 (Bra, Esp, Can, Fra, Ger), 1994 (Bra, Pac, Mon, Esp, Can, Hun, Eur, Aus), 1995 (Bra, Arg, Mon, Fra, Ger, Bel, Eur, Pac, Jap) 1996 (Esp, Ita), 1997 (Mon, Fra, GB) |
| Points: | 440 | 1991 (4), 1992 (53), 1993 (52), 1994 (92), 1995 (102), 1996 (59), 1997 (78) |
| 1st: | 27 | 1992 (Bel), 1993 (Por), 1994 (Bra, Pac, San, Can, Mon, Ger, Hun, Eur), 1995 (Bra, Esp, Mon, Fra, Ger, Bel, Eur, Pac, Jap), 1996 (Esp, Bel, Ita), 1997 (Mon, Can, Fra, Bel, Jap) |
| 2nd: | 17 | 1992 (Esp, Can, Aus), 1993 (San, Can, GB, Ger, Bel), 1994 (Esp, Jap), 1995 (Por), 1996 (Eur, San, Jap), 1997 (Aus, San, Ger) |
| 3rd: | 10 | 1992 (Mex, Bra, Ger, Ita), 1993 (Bra, Esp, Fra), 1995 (Arg), 1996 (Bra, Por) |
| 4th: | 6 | 1992 (SA, Mon, GB), 1996 (Ger), 1997 (Esp, Hun) |
| 5th: | 3 | 1991 (Ita), 1995 (Can), 1997 (Bra) |
| 6th: | 4 | 1991 (Por, Esp), 1997 (Ita, Aut) |

| Year | Team | No. | Grand Prix |
|---|---|---|---|
| 1991 | Jordan Ford | 1 | Bel |
| | Benetton Ford | 5 | Ita (2), Por (1), Esp (1), Jap, Aus |
| 1992 | Benetton Ford | 16 | SA (3), Mex (4), Bra (4), Esp (6), San, Mon (3), Can (6), Fra, GB (3), Ger (4), Hun, Bel (10), Ita (4), Por, Jap, Aus (6) |
| 1993 | Benetton Ford | 16 | SA, Bra (4), Eur, San (6), Esp (4), Mon, Can (6), Fra (4), GB (6), Ger (6), Hun, Bel (6), Ita, Por (10), Jap, Aus |
| 1994 | Benetton Ford | 14 | Bra (10), Pac (10), San (10), Mon (10), Esp (6), Can (10), Fra (10), GB, Ger, Hun (10), Bel, Eur (10), Jap (6), Aus |
| 1995 | Benetton Renault | 17 | Bra (10), Arg (4), San, Esp (10), Mon (10), Can (2), Fra (10), GB, Ger (10), Hun, Bel (10), Ita, Por (6), Eur (10), Pac (10), Jap (10), Aus |
| 1996 | Ferrari | 16 | Aus, Bra (4), Arg, Eur (6), San (6), |

| 1997 | Ferrari | 17 | Mon, Esp (10), Can, Fra, GB, Ger (3), Hun, Bel (10), Ita (10), Por (4), Jap (6) |
| | | | Aus (6), Bra (2), Arg, San (6), Mon (10), Esp (4), Can (10), Fra (10), GB, Ger (6), Hun (4), Bel (10), Ita (1), Aut (1), Lux, Jap (10), Eur |

# SCHUMACHER, Ralf                                                    Germany

*1997: Jordan Peugeot*                          *1998: Jordan Mugen-Honda*

Seven finishes from seventeen starts are hardly the sort of statistics that would endear a driver to an ambitious team. But, given that this was Schumacher Junior's first season in the top flight and the fact that six of those seven were points winners, the German won himself some breathing space.

The 1997 season was always going to be a learning process for Ralf Schumacher and the first two races indicated that to be true. Disappointing grid positions and mechanical failures on laps 2 and 53 respectively were frustrating to say the least. The Argentina Grand Prix – Jordan's 100th – provided him with not just his first points but also a first podium finish when he sailed home third, having also held second position at one point in the race.

Schumacher's qualifying performance set into a steady vein and, although he was never off the first five rows of the grid, during the next four races he failed to finish. He could point to two engine failures for two of those retirements but two avoidable accidents at Monaco and Canada added to the pressure he was coming under. One finish from seven races was less than had been expected from a driver who was always in the shadow of his older brother.

The French Grand Prix marked a distinct change in fortunes though. Having qualified an excellent third, he fell back in the race and had his leading brother to thank for being able to unlap himself, which ultimately led to a clash with Coulthard in which the McLaren was taken out, allowing Ralf to come home for a point. Two-point finishes came in each of the next three races even though his qualifying performance was increasingly erratic. He might have done better at Silverstone had he not been held up by cars on one-stop runs, and then slightly overshooting his pit position on one of his two stops.

After two non-finishes, the Austrian Grand Prix again provided a fifth-place finish, which was a distinct improvement on his eleventh place starting position and might have been even better notwithstanding several errors which cost him time. The Luxembourg race was best forgotten when he collided with his team-mate on the first corner. Following this he finished ninth in Japan, which was his worst placing of the year. A sixteenth place on the grid marked a disappointing end to the season that got worse when a water leak killed his car on lap 45.

Looking at the finishes in isolation make for impressive reading and, given that Schumacher can cut out some of the mistakes that cost him so dear during 1997, Ralf could well find himself as part of a top-running team. His partnership with Damon Hill, and how that develops in 1998, will be one of the interesting stories of the year.

**Born:** 30/6/75, Huerth, Germany. Single.

## Grand Prix 1997 Record

| Grand Prix | Grid | Qual Time | Fin | Laps | Race Time | Reason |
|---|---|---|---|---|---|---|
| Australian | 12 | 1:33.130 | – | 1 | | drive shaft |
| Brazilian | 10 | 1:17.175 | – | 52 | | electronics |
| Argentinian | 6 | 1:26.218 | 3 | 72 | 1:52:13.804 | |
| San Marino | 5 | 1:24.081 | – | 17 | | drive shaft |
| Monaco | 6 | 1:18.943 | – | 10 | | accident |
| Spanish | 9 | 1:18.423 | – | 50 | | engine |
| Canadian | 7 | 1:18.869 | – | 14 | | accident |
| French | 3 | 1:14.755 | 6 | 72 | 1:40:20.363 | |
| British | 5 | 1:22.277 | 5 | 59 | 1:28:33.545 | |
| German | 7 | 1:42.498 | 5 | 45 | 1:21:29.041 | |
| Hungarian | 14 | 1:16.686 | 5 | 77 | 1:46:17.864 | |
| Belgian | 6 | 1:50.520 | – | 21 | | spin |
| Italian | 8 | 1:23.603 | – | 39 | | damage |
| Austrian | 11 | 1:11.186 | 5 | 71 | 1:28:07.858 | |
| Luxembourg | 8 | 1:17.595 | – | 0 | | accident |
| Japanese | 13 | 1:37.443 | 9 | 53 | 1:31:10.482 | |
| European | 16 | 1:22.740 | – | 44 | | water leak |

## 1997 Position Summary

| | | | |
|---|---|---|---|
| Contested: | 17 | Finished: | 7 |
| Pole Positions: | 0 | Fastest Laps: | 0 |
| Points: | 13 | | |
| 1st: | 0 | 2nd: | 0 |
| 3rd: | 1 | 4th: | 0 |
| 5th: | 4 | 6th: | 1 |

## Grand Prix Career Record

| | | |
|---|---|---|
| Contested: | 17 | (1997) |
| Pole Positions: | 0 | |
| Fastest Laps: | 0 | |
| Points: | 13 | 1997 (13) |
| 1st: | 0 | |
| 2nd: | 0 | |
| 3rd: | 1 | 1997 (Arg) |
| 4th: | 0 | |
| 5th: | 4 | 1997 (GB, Ger, Hun, Aut) |
| 6th: | 1 | 1997 (Fra) |

| Year | Team | | No. | Grand Prix |
|------|------|---|-----|-----------|
| 1997 | Jordan Peugeot | | No | Aus, Bra, Arg (4), San, Mon, Esp, Can, Fra (1), GB (2), Ger (2), Hun (2), Bel, Ita, Aut (2), Lux, Jap, Eur |

# SOSPIRI, Vincenzo                                       Italy

*1997: Lola Ford*                                        *1998: –*

Sospiri deservedly received his call into the Formula One frame at the start of the 1997 season. A driver who had impressed in the lower ranks, his dream was provided and then dashed by the one-race wonder that was Lola F1. Qualifying in Melbourne was as far as it went, but some eleven seconds off the pace in an inadequate car proved too much and he was excluded from the start by the 107% qualification rule. There proved to be no further opportunities on the big circuit as his employers went into liquidation.

Sospiri got his 'chance' at Lola after a period as a successful test driver with Benetton in 1996. He started in karting and was four-times Italian Champion, twice European Champion and, in 1987, his final year, World Champion. He moved up through F3 and F3000 to become the International F3000 Champion in 1995.

After Lola, he raced in Indycar for the Dallara-Surora team before making his debut in Formula Nippon towards the end of the season – however, he spun off in his first race in the penultimate round at Fuji.

**Born:** 7/10/66, Forli, Italy. Single.

## Grand Prix 1997 Record

| Grand Prix | Grid | Qual Time | Fin | Laps | Race Time | Reason |
|-----------|------|-----------|-----|------|-----------|--------|
| Australian | 23 | 1:40.972 | | | 107% – did not qualify | |

### 1997 Position Summary

| | | | | |
|--|--|--|--|--|
| Contested: | 0 | | Finished: | 0 |
| Pole Positions: | 0 | | Fastest Laps: | 0 |
| Points: | 0 | | | |
| 1st–6th: | 0 | | | |

## Grand Prix Career Record

| | |
|--|--|
| Contested: | 0 |
| Pole Positions: | 0 |
| Fastest Laps: | 0 |
| 1st–6th: | 0 |

| Year | Team | No. | Grand Prix |
|------|------|-----|-----------|
| 1997 | Lola Ford | – | *Failed to qualify for Australian GP* |

# TAKAGI, Toranosuke                                    Japan

*1997: (Test Driver: Tyrrell Ford)*               *1998: Tyrrell Ford*

According to Tyrrell's commercial director Bob Tyrrell, Toranosuke Takagi
has the ability to become the best F1 driver Japan has produced. The 1998
season sees him make his debut in Formula One with Tyrrell for whom he
was test driver in 1997. During the year's testing, he completed over 1200
miles (2000 km) of circuit work and also competed in the 1997 Japanese
Formula Nippon competition.

Having gained his chance in the test driver role, he was to become the first
driver confirmed for the 1998 Tyrrell team as part of the Nakajima Planning
team – a sponsor of Tyrrell.

**Born:** 12/2/74, Shizuoka, Japan. Single.

## Grand Prix Career Record

Contested:          0
Pole Positions:     0
Fastest Laps:       0
1st–6th:            0

# TRULLI, Jarno                                         Italy

*1997: Minardi Hart / Prost Mugen Honda*          *1998: Prost Peugeot*

Fortunes can change quickly in Formula One racing, and Jarno Trulli
experienced the up-track in this respect. Having started the season in the
back-running Minardi-Hart car, he completed it impressing everyone in the
competitive Prost as a replacement for the injured Olivier Panis – and did
well enough to secure a full-time drive with the French team in 1998.

Trulli arrived in Melbourne for his F1 debut with a simple stated aim – to
gain experience in the race and get miles on the clock. He pretty much had his
wish granted. Having lined up seventeenth on the grid, he came home a
comfortable ninth, made all the more impressive by his successful handling of
nagging engine problems. The Brazilian Grand Prix told a very similar story
although this time Trulli was ahead of teammate Katayama on the grid.
Having made a good start, he eventually managed twelfth place. Consistency
from Trulli was clearly a factor in his early-season form and, despite starting
a place worse in 18th, he came home ninth having avoided accidents at the
start of the race.

The move into Europe proved difficult as the Italian failed to record a
finish at San Marino or Monaco. Both qualifying performances were below
par and at Imola a gearbox failure caused an early retirement, while in
Monaco, after several near misses, his car slid into a barrier at Mirabeau on
lap 7.

Having qualified eighteenth, Trulli was fighting the Spanish Grand Prix
from the back for much of the race, especially after a collision with Mika
Salo's Tyrrell that called for a pit stop to have a new nose cone fitted. Canada

proved to be Trulli's last drive in the Minardi and, having started a lowly twentieth on the grid, an engine failure on lap 33 put paid to a good drive that might have earned him his first points of the season.

With Olivier Panis suffering two broken legs in Montreal, the Prost team invited Trulli to test with them alongside their regular test driver, Frenchman Emmanuel Collard. It was the Italian who shone through though, and it was he who took the wheel of the number fourteen car for Prost's home race at Magny-Cours. Trulli went on to produce his best qualifying performance to date with a place on the third row of the grid. His start however, was less than perfect and he lost places. A gamble to go on to intermediate tyres late on, with rain threatening, didn't pay off – the rain stayed away – and he eventually finished tenth.

Thirteenth position on the grid was largely a result of brake problems hampering qualifying and eventually making Trulli opt for the T-car at the British Grand Prix, where he came home in eighth place after suffering a lack of grip with his first two sets of tyres. Things improved drastically in Germany when the Italian secured the first championship points of his career. Having lined up eleventh on the grid, Trulli drove aggressively and won though a great battle with Jacques Villeneuve, finishing less than half a minute behind the eventual race winner, Gerhard Berger.

Another top-ten finish in Hungary was again hampered by lack of grid but, after four good performances, fifteenth and tenth places at Spa and Monza respectively were a disappointment. At Spa though, an electrical problem left him standing at the start and a lap down by the time he had switched to the spare car.

With Olivier Panis due to return for the Luxembourg Grand Prix, Trulli clearly pulled out all the stops in his final race of the season at the Nurburgring in an effort to make a lasting impression. And so he did. In a fantastic qualifying run he secured a best-ever third place on the grid and, after a good start, he raced away in the lead after Hakkinen's McLaren expired. He held the lead from Villeneuve before eventually conceding to the Canadian at the pit stops but looked all set for second position until his Mugen Honda engine blew its top after 58 laps.

Jarno Trulli looks likely to revel in his Prost drive for 1998 and should make an ideal foil for Olivier Panis. If he can maintain the sort of qualifying performances he generally produced in his seven races for the team in 1997, a first podium finish, and a regular say in the points, is almost certain.

**Born:** 13/7/74, Pescara, Italy. Single.

# Grand Prix 1997 Record

| Grand Prix | Grid | Qual Time | Fin | Laps | Race Time | Reason |
|---|---|---|---|---|---|---|
| Australian | 17 | 1:34.120 | 9 | 55 | | |
| Brazilian | 17 | 1:18.335 | 12 | 71 | 1:36:54.101 | |
| Argentinian | 18 | 1:28.160 | 9 | 71 | 1:53:28.445 | |
| San Marino | 20 | 1:26.960 | – | 0 | | hydraulics |

| | | | | | | |
|---|---|---|---|---|---|---|
| Monaco | 18 | 1:20.349 | – | 7 | | accident |
| Spanish | 18 | 1:20.452 | 15 | 62 | 1:30:59.358 | |
| Canadian | 20 | 1:20.370 | – | 32 | | engine |
| French | 6 | 1:14.957 | 10 | 70 | 1:39:26.483 | |
| British | 13 | 1:23.366 | 8 | 58 | 1:28:14.818 | |
| German | 11 | 1:43.226 | 4 | 45 | 1:21:26.211 | |
| Hungarian | 12 | 1:16.297 | 7 | 77 | 1:47:02.701 | |
| Belgian | 14 | 1:52.274 | 15 | 42 | 1:35:02.667 | |
| Italian | 16 | 1:24.567 | 10 | 53 | 1:18:07.315 | |
| Austrian | 3 | 1:10.511 | – | 58 | | engine |

*Trulli drove for Minardi up to and including the Canadian Grand Prix and then for Prost from the French Grand Prix.*

## 1997 Position Summary

| | | | |
|---|---|---|---|
| Contested: | 14 | Finished: | 10 |
| Pole Positions: | 0 | Fastest Laps: | 0 |
| Points: | 3 | | |
| 1st: | 0 | 2nd: | 0 |
| 3rd: | 0 | 4th: | 1 |
| 5th: | 0 | 6th: | 0 |

## Grand Prix Career Record

| | | |
|---|---|---|
| Contested: | 14 | |
| Pole Positions: | 0 | |
| Fastest Laps: | 0 | |
| Points | 3 | 1997 (3) |
| 1st: | 0 | |
| 2nd: | 0 | |
| 3rd: | 0 | |
| 4th: | 1 | 1997 (Ger) |
| 5th: | 0 | |
| 6th: | 0 | |

| Year | Team | No. | Grand Prix |
|---|---|---|---|
| 1997 | Minardi Hart | 7 | Aus, Bra, Arg, San, Mon, Esp, Can |
| 1997 | Prost Mugen Honda | 7 | Fra, GB, Ger (3), Hun, Bel, Ita, Aut |

## TUERO, Esterban                                    Argentina

*1997: –*                                              *1998: Minardi*

At 19, Esteban Tuero will be the youngest regular driver in the FIA championship during 1998. He has tested for Minardi on several occasions since he first arrived in Europe in 1995. Tuero raced in Formula Nippon in Japan last year and is rumoured to be bringing £3.75 million to the Minardi team in sponsorship monies.

*1997: Tyrrell Ford*                                    *1998: –*

After four years and 48 Grands Prix, Jos Verstappen had seemingly decided to call it a day at the end of the 1997 season with a view to concentrating on his travel agency business. However during pre-season he was being re-linked with another drive for Tyrrell in 1998. Although never fulfilling the potential he showed in his debut year with Benetton, he remained one of the quickest drivers on the circuit but was never rewarded with the type of drive that might have suited his talents.

Last season, he failed to add to his total of eleven world championship points, never reaching higher than eighth place in an under-powered Tyrrell that was invariably towards the back end of the starting grid.

After an accident had curtailed his participation in Melbourne after just two laps, a finish in Brazil was followed by engine problems and retirement in Argentina. The move to Europe saw the most consistent run of the season for the Dutchman who came home tenth in San Marino and then a season's best eighth in Monaco despite walking the edge with a couple of spins. After an eleventh place in Spain, mechanical problems blighted the next three races, although in the first, in Montreal, Verstappen recorded what was to be his best grid position of the year – fourteenth.

Mechanical problems continued to hamper racing and under-steer also proved problematic in the later stages of the season but, even so, his car was marginally more reliable with five of the last eight races being completed.

**Born:** 4/3/72, Montford, Holland. Married with one son.

# Grand Prix 1997 Record

| Grand Prix | Grid | Qual Time | Fin | Laps | Race Time | Reason |
|------------|------|-----------|-----|------|-----------|--------|
| Australian | 21 | 1:34.943 | – | 2 | | accident |
| Brazilian | 21 | 1:18.885 | 15 | 70 | 1:36:15.893 | |
| Argentinian | 16 | 1:28.094 | – | 43 | | engine |
| San Marino | 21 | 1:27.428 | 10 | 60 | 1:31:11.741 | |
| Monaco | 22 | 1:21.290 | 8 | 60 | 2:00:20.197 | |
| Spanish | 19 | 1:20.502 | 11 | 63 | 1:31:03.478 | |
| Canadian | 14 | 1:20.102 | – | 42 | | gearbox |
| French | 18 | 1:16.941 | – | 15 | | stuck throttle |
| British | 19 | 1:25.010 | – | 45 | | engine |
| German | 20 | 1:45.811 | 10 | 44 | 1:22:05.839 | |
| Hungarian | 18 | 1:17.095 | – | 61 | | gearbox |
| Belgian | 21 | 1:53.725 | 16 | 25 | | spin |
| Italian | 20 | 1:25.845 | – | 12 | | hydraulics |
| Austrian | 20 | 1:12.230 | 12 | 69 | 1:28:19.144 | |
| Luxembourg | 21 | 1:19.531 | – | 50 | | engine |
| Japanese | 21 | 1:40.259 | 13 | 52 | 1:31:13.951 | |
| European | 22 | 1:24.301 | 16 | 68 | 1:40:06.201 | |

## 1997 Position Summary

| | | | |
|---|---|---|---|
| Contested: | 17 | Finished: | 9 |
| Pole Positions: | 0 | Fastest Laps: | 0 |
| Points: | 0 | | |
| 1st-6th: | 0 | | |
| Best Position: | 8th – Mon | | |

## Grand Prix Career Record

| | | |
|---|---|---|
| Contested: | 48 | (1994-1997) |
| Pole Positions: | 0 | |
| Fastest Laps: | 0 | |
| Points: | 11 | 1994 (10), 1996 (1) |
| 1st: | 0 | |
| 2nd: | 0 | |
| 3rd: | 2 | 1994 (Hun, Bel) |
| 4th: | 0 | |
| 5th: | 1 | 1994 (Por) |
| 6th: | 1 | 1996 (Arg) |

| Year | Team | No. | Grand Prix |
|---|---|---|---|
| 1994 | Benetton Ford | 10 | Bra, Pac, Fra, GB, Ger, Hun (4), Bel (4), Ita, Por (2), Eur |
| 1995 | Simtek Ford | 5 | Bra, Arg, San, Esp, Mon |
| 1996 | Arrows Hart | 16 | Aus, Bra, Arg (1), Eur, San, Mon, Esp, Can, Fra, GB, Ger, Hun, Bel, Ita, Por, Jap |
| 1997 | Tyrrell Ford | 17 | Aus, Bra, Arg, San, Mon, Esp, Can, Fra, GB, Ger, Hun, Bel, Ita, Aut, Lux, Jap, Eur |

## VILLENEUVE, Jacques                                          Canada

*1997: Williams Renault*                  *1998: Williams Mecachrome*

Taking and digesting Jacques Villeneuve's record across the two seasons he has competed in Formula One leads you to the assertion that he is the most successful driver over the past couple of years. Thirty-three starts, eleven victories, thirteen pole positions and 159 world championship points is a record nothing short of spectacular. Scoring on average one victory in every three races, the Canadian has also finished in the points in twenty-two of those thirty-three races.

However, Villeneuve has sometimes been painted as the bad boy of F1; certainly his outspoken views on a variety of subjects have courted the headlines and put him at odds with the governing bodies. But there seemed to be a distinct shift in feelings after those outrageous events in Jerez. Suddenly, even those who had wanted Michael Schumacher to take his third world title were championing Villeneuve's cause, not least because the world had at last woken up to the honesty and integrity of the son of one of the all-time greats of motor racing. A title that will ultimately be vested upon the son Jacques when current history has completed its course.

Out of these twelve finishes, his worst performance was fifth in a season that brought seven wins, ten poles and three fastest laps. Villeneuve started the season in sensational form by qualifying 1.7 seconds faster than new team-mate Heinz-Harald Frentzen in Melbourne. A clash with Eddie Irvine and Johnny Herbert at the first bend ended the race prematurely, but this perhaps inspired successive wins in South America. Then, a rear gearbox failure ended his attempts to record a first-ever points finish at Imola.

Points continued to evade him in Monaco, in a race where he qualified a 'lowly' third – the first time that Villeneuve had not secured pole for the season – and where retirement was enforced after sustaining damage in a collision with a guardrail at Ste Devote after sixteen laps. Another pole and another win came in Spain at Catalunya (which was also the 350th victory recorded on Goodyear tyres), but the desire to win his native Canadian meeting came apart after one lap – he later admitted to making 'a beginner's mistake' at the last corner.

Fourth on grid, and in race, at Magny Cours was followed up with number one figures at Silverstone. The victory at the British Grand Prix was also notable because it was the 100th achieved by the Williams team was also a close-run thing with a loose wheel nut slowing the number three car in the early stages.

The German Grand Prix was probably the worst meeting of the year for Villeneuve who suffered in qualifying and then spun out in the second half of the race. From that point though, the qualifying and race performances steadily improved with four poles and three wins on the final stretch.

Well on course for the Drivers' Championship, the Japanese Grand Prix gave another turn to the season's events and made sure the crowning of a new champion went right to the wire. Various transgressions throughout the season, which had lead to various warnings and suspended bans for ignoring waved yellow flags, ultimately resulted in Villeneuve racing in Suzuka under appeal. Villeneuve finished fifth and, on advice, dropped his appeal and so lost two vital points. The net effect was that the champion elect went into the final race of the season needing to score at least one point more than arch-rival Michael Schumacher to take his first championship in only his second attempt.

It got tighter all the way. Villeneuve, Schumacher and Frentzen all recorded identical qualifying times, but the Canadian took the final pole of the season by virtue of the fact that he did it first! Villeneuve started badly and found himself behind his previous equals, but pit-stop strategy worked in the Williams car's favour and, after Schumacher had 'instinctively' tried to ram the Canadian off the circuit, the former Indy Car Champion fairly coasted home to secure a final third placing, and a well-deserved Drivers' World Championship.

Villeneuve will race in 1998 as a hot favourite to retain his title, but it could also be his last year with Williams. Rumours continue to circulate that the Canadian may be employed in 1999 to drive for the Reynard/BAT-backed British-American Racing team that bought the Tyrrell team at the end of 1997. That may happen, but it is equally likely that Frank Williams will shuffle his drivers' pot, as is his wont.

**Born:** 9/4/71, St Jean-sur-Richelieu, Quebec, Canada. Single.

## Grand Prix 1997 Record

| Grand Prix | Grid | Qual Time | Fin | Laps | Race Time | Reason |
|---|---|---|---|---|---|---|
| Australian | 1 | 1:29.369 | – | 0 | | accident |
| Brazilian | 1 | 1:16.004 | 1 | 72 | 1:36:06.990 | |
| Argentinian | 1 | 1:24.473 | 1 | 72 | 1:52:01.715 | |
| San Marino | 1 | 1:23.303 | – | 40 | | gearbox |
| Monaco | 3 | 1:18.583 | – | 16 | | accident damage |
| Spanish | 1 | 1:16.525 | 1 | 64 | 1:30:35.896 | |
| Canadian | 2 | 1:18.108 | – | 1 | | accident |
| French | 4 | 1:14.800 | 4 | 72 | 1:40:12.276 | |
| British | 1 | 1:21.598 | 1 | 59 | 1.28:01.665 | |
| German | 9 | 1:42.967 | – | 33 | | spin |
| Hungarian | 2 | 1:14.859 | 1 | 77 | 1:45:47.149 | |
| Belgian | 1 | 1:49.450 | 5 | 44 | 1:34:28.820 | |
| Italian | 4 | 1:23.231 | 5 | 53 | 1:17:11.025 | |
| Austrian | 1 | 1:10.304 | 1 | 71 | 1:27:35.999 | |
| Luxembourg | 2 | 1:16.691 | 1 | 67 | 1:31:27.843 | |
| Japanese | 1 | 1:36.071 | dq (5th) | 53 | 1:30:28.222 | |
| European | 1 | 1:21.072 | 3 | 69 | 1:38:59.574 | |

## 1997 Position Summary

| | | | |
|---|---|---|---|
| Contested: | 17 | Finished: | 12 |
| Pole Positions: | 10 | Fastest Laps: | 3 |
| Points: | 81 | | |
| 1st: | 7 | 2nd: | 0 |
| 3rd: | 1 | 4th: | 1 |
| 5th: | 2 | 6th: | 0 |

## Grand Prix Career Record

| | | |
|---|---|---|
| Contested: | 33 | (1996-1997) |
| Pole Positions: | 13 | 1996 (Aus, Bel, Jap), 1997 (Aus, Bra, Arg, San, Esp, GB, Bel, Aut, Jap, Eur) |
| Fastest Laps: | 9 | 1996 (Aus, Can, Fra, GB, Por, Jap), 1997 (Bra, Bel, Aut) |
| Points: | 159 | 1996 (78), 1997 (81) |

| 1st: | 11 | 1996 (Eur, GB, Hun, Por), 1997 (Bra, Arg, Esp, GB, Hun, Aut, Lux) |
|------|-----|------|
| 2nd: | 5 | 1996 (Aus, Arg, Can, Fra, Bel) |
| 3rd: | 3 | 1996 (Esp, Ger), 1997 (Eur) |
| 4th: | 1 | 1997 (Fra) |
| 5th: | 2 | 1997 (Bel, Ita) |
| 6th: | 0 | |

| Year | Team | No. | Grand Prix |
|------|------|-----|-----------|
| 1996 | Williams Renault | 16 | Aus (6), Bra, Arg (6), Eur (10), San, Mon, Esp (4), Can (6), Fra (6), GB (10), Ger (4), Hun (10), Bel (6), Ita, Por (10), Jap |
| 1997 | Williams Renault | 17 | Aus, Bra (10), Arg (10), San, Mon, Esp (10), Can, Fra (3), GB (10), Ger, Hun (10), Bel (2), Ita (2), Aut (10), Lux (10), Jap, Eur (3) |

# WURZ, Alexander                                    Austria

*1997: (Test Driver: Benetton Renault)*          *1998: Benetton Mecachrome*

The 1997 season started off with Alexander Wurz holding the position of test driver for the Benetton team. By the end of the season, he had secured his first driving job in a new-look racing line-up for the 1998 season, partnering Italian Giancarlo Fisichella.

Wurz got his chance to prove his worth as a prospective driver when his fellow Austrian, Gerhard Berger, had to miss three races due to a sinus problem. Despite only finishing one of the trio – when he came home a superb third – Wurz did enough in qualifying to impress those in charge of his salary.

In the first Grand Prix of his career, he qualified just behind teammate Jean Alesi in Montreal and achieved third position for one lap before taking a kerb a little too high, which allowed Frentzen to pass him. Shortly afterwards transmission problems started to manifest, which ultimately ended his debut after 35 laps.

Qualifying at Magny-Cours for his second race went even better when his seventh grid place was one better than teammate Jean Alesi who was 0.2 seconds behind. In the race, Wurz led until the rain came, and a mistake on lap 60 saw him spin out.

With two starts and no finishes, it was a case of third time lucky for the precocious Austrian who enjoyed a magnificent weekend at Silverstone. He once again out-qualified his teammate Jean Alesi to take a place on the fourth row of the grid and, on a one-stop strategy, he moved up the field and looked likely to finish fourth until David Coulthard retired and allowed what should be the first of many podium finishes for Wurz.

Like many drivers before him, Wurz came through the normal karting ranks as a youngster before progressing to Formula Ford 1600 (1991-92) and Formula 3 (1993-95). In June 1996, he became the youngest driver ever to win at Le Mans and thus put himself in the world spotlight. In autumn 1996 he was given the chance to test for Benetton, and the team was so impressed with his technical feedback and lap times that he was subsequently asked to join as official test driver for the 1997 season.

**Born:** 15/2/74, Waithofen, Austria. Engaged.

## Grand Prix 1997 Record

| Grand Prix | Grid | Qual Time | Fin | Laps | Race Time | Reason |
|------------|------|-----------|-----|------|-----------|--------|
| Canadian | 11 | 1:19.268 | – | 35 | | transmission |
| French | 7 | 1:14.986 | – | 60 | | spin |
| British | 8 | 1:22.344 | 3 | 59 | 1:28:12.961 | |

## 1997 Position Summary

| | | | |
|---|---|---|---|
| Contested: | 3 | Finished: | 1 |
| Pole Positions: | 0 | Fastest Laps: | 0 |
| Points: | 4 | | |
| 1st: | 0 | 2nd: | 0 |
| 3rd: | 1 | 4th: | 0 |
| 5th: | 0 | 6th: | 0 |

## Grand Prix Career Record

| | | |
|---|---|---|
| Contested: | 3 | |
| Pole Positions: | 0 | |
| Fastest Laps: | 0 | |
| Points: | 4 | |
| 1st: | 0 | |
| 2nd: | 0 | |
| 3rd: | 1 | 1997 (GB) |
| 4th: | 0 | |
| 5th: | 0 | |
| 6th: | 0 | |

| Year | Team | No. | Grand Prix |
|------|------|-----|------------|
| 1997 | Benetton Renault | 3 | Can, Fra, GB (4) |

# Team Directory

# Arrows

## Danka Arrows
### Arrows Grand Prix International

TWR Group Ltd, Leafield Technical Centre, Leafield, Witney,
Oxon, OX8 5PF
Tel: +44 (0)1993 871000          Fax : +44 (0)1993 871100
Chairman/CEO:    Tom Walkinshaw
Designer:        Frank Dernie
Team Manager:    John Walton
Chief Mechanic:  Les Jones
Drivers/Engineers:Pedro Diniz (16)  /  Steve Clarke
                 Mika Salo (17)   /  Vincent Gaillardot
Test Driver:     –
Sponsors:        Danka, Zepter International, Parmalat, Power House,
                 Yamaha Motor Co., Bridgestone Corporation, Brastemp,
                 Remus, Quest International, Cadcentre, Kibon, Arisco,
                 Reporter Parfum, Amik, Packplast.

## Brief History

1977: Arrows Grand Prix founded. 1978: Riccardo Patrese scores Arrows'
first point with sixth at Long Beach; Patrese takes second in Sweden – the
team's best finish to date; Patrese banned for involvement in the accident that
killed Ronnie Peterson. 1981: Patrese takes only pole position to date at Long
Beach. 1984: Arrows switch to BMW Turbo engines. 1987: Megatron supply
engines to Arrows after BMW pulls out. 1989: Arrows open new $10 million
technical centre in Milton Keynes. 1989: Arrows are bought by Wataru
Ohashi's Footwork Corporation. 1995: Jackie Oliver takes control after
Footwork pull out. 1996: Tom Walkinshaw buys controlling interest in team
and relocates works; Reigning World Champion Damon Hill signs for team.
1997: Damon Hill equals team's best ever finish – 2nd after leading
Hungarian Grand Prix.

## Grand Prix Record

| | | |
|---|---|---|
| Contested: | 305 | |
| Victories: | 0 | (Best Finish: 2nd – 5 times) |
| Pole Positions: | 1 | |
| Fastest Laps: | 0 | |
| Constructors' World Titles: | 0 | (Best: 4th 1988) |

| Drivers' World Championships: | 0 | (Best: =7th 1988) |
|---|---|---|
| Most Points in a Season: | 23 | (1988) |
| Total World Championship Points: | 150 | |
| Average Points/Grand Prix: | 2.15 | |

## Review

The 1997 season got off to just about the worst possible start for the Arrows team. With all eyes on the then new world champion, Damon Hill only just qualified and then had to suffer the indignity of failure on the warm up lap when a throttle sensor failed at the very first corner. Diniz finished in tenth place but was only in the race after team boss Tom Walkinshaw appealed on the grounds of *force majeure* after gearbox problems had prevented the Brazilian getting a time inside the 107% rule.

Reliability was a major concern for both drivers throughout the season with less than half the races being completed and only at five of the 17 Grands Prix did both Hill and Diniz get past the chequered flag together. Qualifying also proved problematic and on only six occasions was there an Arrows car on one of the first five rows.

Having had just four finishes in total from the first eight Grands Prix, things improved on this significantly as the season progressed into its final stages. That in no small part was due to the arrival of John Barnard as technical director and his influence should have an impact during the 1998 season. The arrival of the British Grand Prix saw team boss Tom Walkinshaw being highly critical of his number one driver. Warranted or not, it had the desired result as Hill scooted home to record the team's first point of the season. The relief was there for all to see and you might have been forgiven for thinking that Hill had actually won the race given the post-race reaction from all sides.

The failures were often spectacular, but they were also often frustratingly trivial – none more so than at the Hungarian Grand Prix when, with a first-ever Arrows victory just two laps away thanks to a sensational driving performance by Damon Hill, a washer valued at just 50p failed. A runner seal inside the washer caused a tiny leak which eventually lead to a drop in hydraulic pressure. Despite being passed on the line by Villeneuve the second place was still a fine achievement and was only the fifth ever achieved by an Arrows car.

After the euphoria of the Hungaroring, Spa marked the start of four double finishes for the team from the final six races. Luxembourg also provided Pedro Diniz with his first and only two points of the season and followed on from respectable qualifying positions at both the Austrian and Luxembourg meetings.

By the time of the Austrian race, Hill had announced his departure to Jordan. That also seemed to have a soothing effect on his performances and in his final race he found himself just 0.054 seconds off what would have been a remarkable pole position. Hill's popularity might be better recognised by Arrows in 1998. It is doubtful they would be capable of drawing 18,000 for their open day in 1998 as they did last season.

Replacing Hill and joining Diniz will be Mika Salo, an under-rated and composed driver who might have hoped for a bigger team to whisk him away from Tyrrell. Nevertheless, the combination with John Bernard should prove effective and Salo will no doubt continue to score championship points with the reliable unit that Bernard should produce.

## Drivers and Results 1997

| Driver | Races | Com | Ret | Dnq | HP | Pts | Psn | Comp% |
|--------|-------|-----|-----|-----|-----|-----|-----|-------|
| Damon Hill | 17 | 10 | 7 | 0 | 2nd | 7 | 13/21 | 58.82% |
| Pedro Diniz | 17 | 6 | 11 | 0 | 5th | 2 | 17/21 | 35.29% |
| Aggregate | 34 | 16 | 18 | 0 | – | 9 | 8/10 | 47.06% |

| | Grand Prix | Damon Hill | Pedro Diniz |
|----|------------|------------|-------------|
| 1 | Australian | dns | 10th |
| 2 | Brazilian | 17th | Retired |
| 3 | Argentinian | Retired | Retired |
| 4 | San Marino | Retired | Retired |
| 5 | Monaco | Retired | Retired |
| 6 | Spanish | Retired | Retired |
| 7 | Canadian | 9th | 8th |
| 8 | French | 12th | Retired |
| 9 | British | 6th | Retired |
| 10 | German | 8th | Retired |
| 11 | Hungarian | 2nd | Retired |
| 12 | Belgian | 13th | 7th |
| 13 | Italian | Retired | Retired |
| 14 | Austrian | 7th | 13th |
| 15 | Luxembourg | 8th | 5th |
| 16 | Japanese | 11th | 12th |
| 17 | European | Retired | Retired |

## Arrows A19 Specifications

**Engine**
| | |
|---|---|
| Type: | V10 (72 degree) |
| Capacity: | 2996 cc |
| Valve mechanism: | DOHC, direct lifter type, cam gear drive |
| Fuel injection: | Zytek |
| Ignition: | Magneti Marelli |

**Car**

| | |
|---|---|
| Chassis: | Arrows manufactured Carbon Monocoque |
| Suspension: | Pushrod operated six damper system with dynamic dampers |
| Steering: | Arrows |
| Cooling system: | Secan oil and water radiators |
| Transmission: | Arrows 6-speed semi-automatic, in-line configuration |
| Clutch: | AP Racing (Carbon) |
| Brakes: | Brembo Al-Be composite callipers, Carbone Industrie discs and pads |
| Wheels: | BBS one piece 13" x12" front, 13" x13.7" rear |
| Tyres: | Bridgestone |
| Instruments: | Arrow data display |
| Seat belts: | Sabelt |
| Steering wheel: | Personal |
| Extinguisher: | SPA extinguishant/Arrows integral shaped container |

## Engines 1978-98

1978-83: Ford. 1984-86: BMW Turbo. 1987-88: Megatron Turbo. 1989-90: Ford Turbo. 1991: Porsche. 1992-94: Mugen-Honda. 1995-96: Hart. 1997-98: Yamaha.

## Drivers 1978-98

1978: R.Patrese. 1979: R.Patrese & J.Mass. 1980: R.Patrese & J.Mass. 1981: R.Patrese, S.Stohr & G.Villeneuve. 1982: M.Surer, M.Baldi & B.Henton. 1983: M.Surer, C.Serra, T.Boutsen. 1984: T.Boutsen, M.Surer. 1985: T.Boutsen & G.Berger. 1986: T.Boutsen, M.Sure & C.Danner. 1987: D.Warwick & E.Cheever. 1988: D.Warwick & E.Cheever. 1989: D.Warwick, E.Cheever & M.Donnelly. 1990: M.Alboreto & I.Capelli. 1991: M.Alboreto, A.Caffi & S.Johansson. 1992: M.Alboreto & A.Suzuki. 1993: D.Warwick & A.Suzuki. 1994: C.Fittipaldi & G.Morbidelli 1995: G.Morbidelli, T.Inoue & M.Papis. 1996: J.Verstappen & R.Rosset. 1997: D.Hill & P.Diniz. 1998: P.Diniz & M.Salo.

## Grand Prix Best Performance

2nd position five times: 1978 Sweden (Patrese), 1980 USA (Patrese), 1981 San Marino (Patrese), 1985 San Marino (Boutsen), 1997 Hungary (Damon Hill).

# Benetton

## Mild Seven Benetton
**Benetton Formula Ltd**
Whiteways Technical Centre, Enstone, Chipping Norton, Oxon, OX7 4EE
Tel: +44 (0)1608 678000    Fax: +44 (0)1608 678800

| | |
|---|---|
| Chairman: | Luciano Benetton |
| CEO: | David Richards |
| Tech. Director: | Pat Symonds |
| Team Manager: | Joan Villadelprat |
| Chief Mechanic: | Mick Ainsley-Cowlishaw |
| Chief Designer: | Nick Wirth |
| Drivers: | Giancarlo Fisichella (5) |
| | Alexander Wurz (6) |
| Test Driver: | – |
| Sponsors: | Mild Seven, Benetton Sportsystem, FedEx, Agip, Akai, Korean Air, Bridgestone, Hewlett Packard, A1, Minichamps. |

## Brief History

1986: Benetton Formula One established after taking over the old Toleman team. 1987: Gerhard Berger wins in Mexico to give Benetton their first victory. 1990: Nelson Piquet leads home fellow Brazilian Roberto Moreno for first one-two. 1992: Michael Schumacher wins his first Grand Prix in Belgium. 1994: Michael Schumacher wins the Drivers' World Championship. 1995: Michael Schumacher wins second Drivers' World Championship and Benetton win first Constructors' World Championship. 1997: Flavio Briatore resigns as CEO, David Richards appointed. 1998: Team switch to Bridgestone tyres.

## Grand Prix Record

| | | |
|---|---|---|
| Contested: | 251 | (178 excluding Toleman) |
| Victories: | 27 | |
| Pole Positions: | 15 | |
| Fastest Laps: | 35 | |
| Constructors' World Titles: | 1 | (1995) |
| Drivers' World Championships: | 2 | (1994, 1995) |
| Most Points in a Season: | 137 | (1995) |
| Total World Championship Points: | 772.5 | |
| Average Points/Grand Prix: | 2.88 | |

For the second year in succession, the Benetton team finished in third place in the Constructors' Cup although their tally of 67 points was one less than their 1996 total, but still some way off of the second-placed Ferrari team.

The main problem for the 1997 season seemed to lay in the inability to generate heat, and therefore grip, in their tyres when running on light fuel loads. This meant that, in qualifying, their main drivers, Jean Alesi and Gerhard Berger, experienced terrible problems in getting in the top half of the field. However, in races where heavy fuel loads and one-stop strategies were employed, they often did well. Despite these problems, a Benetton never failed to finish a race and there were eighteen points finishes from the thirty-four race starts.

Throughout the season, it was Jean Alesi who often looked more capable of scoring points, and so he did, contributing thirty-six of them. However, it was Gerhard Berger who was the most consistent finisher and he out-finished Alesi by a score of 8-6.

If the rumours are to be believed, the team suffered with behind-the-scenes disagreements which ultimately led to the departure of team boss Flavio Briatore on the weekend of the Luxembourg Grand Prix, and the departure of Alesi and Berger.

Both Alesi and Berger managed to capture a pole position apiece, which rather makes a mockery of the fact that qualifying overall was so poor. Alesi achieved his second career pole in Italy while Berger's twelfth came in Germany – also the scene of the team's only victory of the season. Berger's victory at Hockenheim was one of the most dominating of his career, and it came after his three-race sick leave, the death of his father and having been told the news that his services would not be required for the 1998 season.

While the start of the season in Melbourne was generally regarded as a disappointment, both drivers scored points, albeit just four between them. Berger secured the first of the team's five second places (Alesi secured the others). The best team performances came at Silverstone and the Nurburgring. At the British Grand Prix, Alesi came home second and Wurz, in his first-ever Grand Prix finish, an excellent third. In Luxembourg, Alesi again repeated his second place, with Berger coming home fourth.

The penultimate race of the season, at Suzuka, saw Benetton (including their Toleman record) make their 250th Grand Prix start.

For 1998, the Benetton team, along with rivals Williams, will make use of the Renault-sourced Mecachrome engines and the jury will remain out for some time until their performance and reliability can be gauged. Under new boss David Richards, founder of the engineering specialist Prodrive, the team have two of the most exciting drivers to emerge in F1 in recent years. After a prolonged court battle they were able to take up an option on Italian Giancarlo Fisichella, much to the disgust of Eddie Jordan who had given the driver his chance to shine, and Alexander Wurz, who performed admirably during the three-race absence of Gerhard Berger, not least in securing his first podium finish in only his third race.

For 1998 Benetton were one of the first teams to test pre-season under the new regulations and have chnaged to Bridgestone tyres for the 1998 season.

## Drivers and Results 1997

| Driver | Races | Com | Ret | Dnq | HP | Pts | Psn | Comp% |
|---|---|---|---|---|---|---|---|---|
| Jean Alesi | 17 | 14 | 3 | 0 | 2nd | 36 | 4/21 | 82.35% |
| Gerhard Berger | 14 | 13 | 1 | 0 | 1st | 27 | 6/21 | 92.86% |
| Alexander Wurz | 3 | 1 | 2 | 0 | 3rd | 4 | 15/21 | 33.33% |
| Aggregate | 34 | 28 | 6 | 0 | | 67 | 3/10 | 82.35% |

| Grand Prix | | Jean Alesi | Gerhard Berger | Alexander Wurz |
|---|---|---|---|---|
| 1 | Australian | Retired | 4th | – |
| 2 | Brazilian | 6th | 2nd | – |
| 3 | Argentinian | 7th | 6th | – |
| 4 | San Marino | 5th | Retired | – |
| 5 | Monaco | Retired | 9th | – |
| 6 | Spanish | 3rd | 10th | – |
| 7 | Canadian | 2nd | – | Retired |
| 8 | French | 5th | – | Retired |
| 9 | British | 2nd | – | 3rd |
| 10 | German | 6th | 1st | – |
| 11 | Hungarian | 11th | 8th | – |
| 12 | Belgian | 8th | 6th | – |
| 13 | Italian | 2nd | 7th | – |
| 14 | Austrian | Retired | 10th | – |
| 15 | Luxembourg | 2nd | 4th | – |
| 16 | Japanese | 5th | 8th | – |
| 17 | European | 13th | 4th | – |

## Benetton B198 Specifications

**Engine:** **Based on Renault RS9**

Cylinders: 10 cylinders (71 degree angle)

Valves: 40

Dimensions: 623 mm (length), 542 mm (width), 395 mm (height)

Management: Magneti Marelli electronic engine management and static ignition.

**Car**

Chassis: Carbon fibre composite monocoque manufactured by Benetton Formula

Suspension: Carbon fibre top and bottom wishbones operating a titanium rocker via a push rod system. Coil spring and

144

|                  |                                                                                      |
|------------------|--------------------------------------------------------------------------------------|
|                  | damper units mounted in recesses on top of monocoque. Titanium uprights and Benetton-designed axles. |
| Transmission:    | Benetton semi-automatic six-speed gearbox. Triple-plate clutch |
| Fuel system:     | ATL rubber fuel cell mounted within monocoque structure behind cockpit |
| Oil system:      | Oil tank within bell-housing providing two gallon/nine litres capacity |
| Cooling system:  | Separate water and oil cooling; water radiators in each sidepod |
| Electrical:      | Hardware and software developed jointly by Benetton and Magneti Marelli |
| Braking systems: | Carbon fibre discs and pads |
| Tyres:           | Bridgestone |

## Engines 1981-98

(1981-85: Toleman.) 1981-85: Hart Turbo. 1986: BMW Turbo. 1987: Ford Turbo. 1988-94: Ford. 1995-97: Renault. 1998: Mecachrome (Renault).

## Drivers 1981-98

1981: B.Henton & D.Warwick. 1982: D.Warwick & T.Fabi. 1983: D.Warwick & B.Giacomelli. 1984: A.Senna, J.Cecotto, S.Johansson & P.Martini. 1985: T.Fabi & P.Ghinzani. 1986: T.Fabi & G.Berger. 1987: T.Boutsen & T.Fabi. 1988: A.Nannini & T.Boutsen. 1989: A.Nannini, J.Herbert & E.Pirro. 1990: A.Nannini, N.Piquet & R.Moreno. 1991: N.Piquet, R.Moreno & M.Schumacher. 1992: M.Schumacher & M.Brundle. 1993: M.Schumacher & R.Patrese. 1994: M.Schumacher, J.Verstappen, J.J. Lehto & J.Herbert. 1995: M.Schumacher & J.Herbert. 1996-97: J.Alesi & G.Berger. 1998: G.Fisichella & A.Wurz. *NB: Team name Toleman 81-85.*

## Grand Prix Wins

1986 Mexico (Berger); 1989 Japan (Nannini); 1990 Japan (Piquet), Australia (Piquet); 1991 Canada (Piquet); 1992 Belgium (M.Schumacher); 1993 Portugal (M.Schumacher); 1994 Brazil (M.Schumacher), Pacific (M.Schumacher), San Marino (M.Schumacher), Monaco (M.Schumacher), Canada (M.Schumacher), France (M.Schumacher), Hungary (M.Schumacher), Europe (M.Schumacher); 1995 Brazil (M.Schumacher), Spain (M.Schumacher), Monaco (M.Schumacher), France (M.Schumacher), Britain (Herbert), Germany (M.Schumacher), Belgium (M.Schumacher), Italy (Herbert), Europe (M.Schumacher), Pacific (M.Schumacher), Japan (M.Schumacher); 1997 Germany (G.Berger).

# Ferrari

## Scuderia Ferrari Marlboro
**Ferrari SpR**
Via Ascari 55-57, 41053 Maranello, Modena, Italy
Tel: +39 536 949 111          Fax: +39 536 949 436

| | |
|---|---|
| Chairman: | Luca Di Montezemolo |
| Team Principle: | Jean Todt |
| Tech. Director: | Ross Brawn |
| Designers: | Rory Byrne, Paolo Martinelli (TD Engine Dept.) |
| Chief Mechanic: | Nigel Stepney |
| Drivers/Engineers: | Michael Schumacher (3)   /   G. Petterlini |
| | Eddie Irvine (4)   /   GL. Sociali |
| Test Driver: | Luca Badoer |
| Sponsors: | Marlboro, Fiat, Shell, Asprey, Magneti Marelli, Telecom Italia, Goodyear, Arexons, Brembo, SKF, TRW Sabelt, USAG, Veca. |

### *Brief History*

1898: Enzo Ferrari born in Modena, Italy. 1929: Enzo Ferrari forms his company. 1947: Franco Cortese wins the Grand Prix of Rome to record Ferrari's first race win. 1951: Jose Gonzalez records Ferrari's first Formula One victory. 1952: Alberto Ascari wins the Drivers' World Championship in a Ferrari. 1953: Ascari wins back-to-back titles driving for the Modena-based team. 1956: Juan-Manuel Fangio wins World Championship with Ferrari. 1958: Mike Hawthorn becomes the third Ferrari driver to win the title. 1961: Phil Hill leads Ferrari to the 'double' of both Drivers' and Constructors' titles. 1964: John Surtees takes the World Championship in a Ferrari. 1969: Lowest-ever Ferrari score of seven points achieved in Constructors' World Championship. 1975: Niki Lauda takes title in a Ferrari ahead of Emerson Fittipaldi. 1977: Lauda repeats his success of two years earlier. 1979: Jody Scheckter wins his only World Championship driving a Ferrari. 1983: Ferrari win the last of their eight World Constructors' Championships. 1996: Ferrari give double World Champion Michael Schumacher a record $25 million two-year contract.

## Grand Prix Record

| | |
|---|---|
| Contested: | 587 |
| Victories: | 113 |
| Pole Positions: | 121 |
| Fastest Laps: | 127 |
| Constructors' World Titles: | 8 (61, 64, 75, 76, 77, 79, 82, 83) |
| Drivers' World Championships: | 9 (52, 53, 56, 58, 61, 64, 75, 77, 79) |
| Most Points in a Season: | 113 (1979) |
| Total World Championship Points: | 2093.5 |
| Average Points/Grand Prix: | 3.47 |

## Review

After two years running with the Schumacher-Irvine combination, Ferrari came close to both championship titles. Although they were out of the running for the Constructors' Cup by the end of the penultimate race, the chance of a prancing horse-driver taking the Drivers' World Championship was very much a possibility when their cars took to the tarmac of Jerez. The dream fell short of realisation, and many Ferrari tifosi were less than happy about the conduct of Schumacher in that race. He remains, however, the team's best chance of achieving the dream of a Drivers' Championship in 1998.

The form of Eddie Irvine was perhaps even more encouraging. Schumacher, after all, is and was expected to make regular points contributions. But Irvine often excelled and it was surely only team orders that surely prevented his first race victory in a marvellous performance at Suzuka where he conceded the lead to his German teammate after having blasted the rest of the field out of sight early on.

Both drivers were helped by a much more reliable engine than in previous years. The F310B – designer John Barnard's last contribution as chief designer before moving to Arrows – proved to be a major step forward for the Ferrari, team as was the 046 engine. In fact, only Irvine's retirement from the Luxembourg Grand Prix could be directly attributed to a failure in the engine during the course of the season. The more powerful unit showed its potential early on in Melbourne with Schumacher qualifying third and Irvine fifth.

By the Imola meeting in San Marino, Ferrari started to make use of a new generation 046/2 engine in qualifying. With greater power and acceleration it helped Schumacher to third on the grid, but with reliability still questionable the 046/1 remained the choice for race use, although the 046/2 did come into race play for the first time at Magny-Cours.

With both drivers largely off the pace in Brazil, Argentina saw Irvine make his first contribution to the Scuderia cause with an excellent second, having led at one stage. Drivers and team pulled in the right direction for the races in San Marino and Monaco, taking 24 of the 30 points available. Schumacher's drive through the wet streets of Monte Carlo was to be one of the high points of the team's season.

Although Schumacher took fourth in Spain, Irvine struggled badly and came home in twelfth position. Both drivers had suffered with the effects of blistering tyres – something that was a cause for concern at points throughout the season.

The Canadian and French races provided two more wins with Schumacher in fine form. Irvine hadn't completed a single lap in the former before he tangled with the Stewart Ford of Jan Magnussen, but he came good back in Europe with an excellent third place, aided in no small part by a great start from his fifth position on the starting grid.

After both cars retired at Silverstone, Schumacher secured second place in his home Grand Prix and a second fourth position of the year at the Hungaroring. As the wet weather descended at Spa, the German once again showed, as he had done in Monaco, his racing prowess with a drive worthy of his first place.

Although Irvine finished out of the points in each of these races, Schumacher secured single points at Monza and the A1-Ring and, having failed to finish at the Nurburgring, arrived in Suzuka knowing that nothing short of victory would maintain his challenge for the championship. Under team orders, the race was certainly the most compelling as far as Ferrari were concerned. Irvine raced like a man possessed and flew past both Villeneuve and Schumacher early on. Then, he allowed his lead to be whittled away, and for his German teammate to take the lead to record the win needed to take the championship to the final race at Jerez.

With Schumacher needing to finish ahead of Villeneuve to ensure the title, the pressure was on and, despite a fine start from the grid which put him into the lead, the pressure finally took its toll. Having clashed with his challenger's car, he found himself sliding into the gravel and away from the title.

Schumacher later admitted to his 'mistake' and was stripped of his second place in the world championship, although his race positions and points accumulated along the way were allowed to stand.

Schumacher's actions in the European Grand Prix may have ultimately dug deep into the wounds that many already feel the Ferrari team have suffered with such a long barren spell without a title. Unless Schumacher can repair the damage with at least one title – with the help of the ever-improving Irvine – 1998 may mark the last season the two-times world champion has at Maranello.

## Drivers and Results 1997

| Driver | Races | Com | Ret | Dnq | HP | Pts | Psn | Comp% |
|--------|-------|-----|-----|-----|-----|-----|-----|-------|
| M. Schumacher | 17 | 13 | 4 | 0 | 1st | 78 | 2/21 | 76.47% |
| Eddie Irvine | 17 | 11 | 6 | 0 | 2nd | 24 | 8/21 | 64.71% |
| Aggregate | 34 | 24 | 10 | 0 | – | 102 | 2/10 | 70.59% |

| | Grand Prix | Michael Schumacher | Eddie Irvine |
|----|------------|--------------------|--------------| 
| 1 | Australian | 2nd | Retired |
| 2 | Brazilian | 5th | 16th |
| 3 | Argentinian | Retired | 2nd |
| 4 | San Marino | 2nd | 3rd |
| 5 | Monaco | 1st | 3rd |
| 6 | Spanish | 4th | 12th |
| 7 | Canadian | 1st | Retired |
| 8 | French | 1st | 3rd |
| 9 | British | Retired | Retired |
| 10 | German | 2nd | Retired |
| 11 | Hungarian | 4th | 9th |
| 12 | Belgian | 1st | 10th |
| 13 | Italian | 6th | 8th |
| 14 | Austrian | 6th | Retired |
| 15 | Luxembourg | Retired | Retired |
| 16 | Japanese | 1th | 3rd |
| 17 | European | Retired | 5th |

## Ferrari F300 Specifications

**Engine:** **Ferrari 047**

| | |
|---|---|
| Cylinders: | V10 (80 degrees) – 40 valves |
| Capacity: | 2997 cc |
| Power Output: | 700hp |
| Injection: | Magneti Marelli |
| Electronics: | Magneti Marelli |
| Dimensions: | Length: 620 cm, Width: –, Height: 380 cm. |

**Car**

| | |
|---|---|
| Gearbox: | Ferrari longitudinal gearbox – 7 gears plus reverse |
| Clutch: | Manual command on steering wheel |
| Front Suspension: | Push-Rod | Rear Suspension: | Push-Rod |
| Dampers: | Ferrari | Tyres: | Goodyear |
| Brakes: | Brembo | Instruments: | Magneti Marelli |

Wheel Diameter (Front/Rear): 13" & 13"

Dimensions: Length: 4340 mm   Width: 1795 mm   Wheelbase: 961 mm
Front/Rear Track: 1490 mm/1405 mm

## Engines 1950-98

1950-80: Ferrari. 1981-88: Ferrari Turbo. 1989-98: Ferrari.

## Drivers 1950-98

1950: A.Ascari, L.Villoresi, R.Sommer, D.Serafini, P.Whitehead. 1951: A.Ascari, L.Villoresi, J.Gonzalez, P.Taruffi. 1952: A.Ascari, G.Farina, L.Villoresi, P.Taruffi, P.Whitehead. 1953: A.Ascari, G.Farina, L.Villoresi, M.Hawthorn. 1954: G.Farina, J.Gonzalez, M.Hawthorn, U.Maglioli, M.Trintignant, R.Manzon. 1955: M.Hawthorn, M.Trintignant, G.Farina, U.Maglioli & J.Gonzalez. 1956: J.Fangio, P.Collins, E.Castellotti, L.Musso, O.Gendibien, A.de Portigo & M.Trintignant. 1957: P.Collins, M.Hawthorn, L.Musso, M.Trintignant, C.Perdisa, E.Castellotti, A.de Portigo & W.Von Trips. 1958: M.Hawthorn, P.Collins, L.Musso, W.Von Trips, P.Hill & O.Gendibien. 1959: T.Brooks, P.Hill, J.Behra, D.Gurney, C.Allison & O.Gendibien. 1960: P.Hill, W.Von Trips, R.Ginther, C.Allison & W.Mairesse. 1961: P.Hill, W.Von Trips, R.Ginther, G.Baghetti & W.Mairesse. 1962: P.Hill, W.Mairesse, G.Baghetti, L.Bandini & R.Rodriguez. 1963: W.Mairesse, J.Surtees, L.Bandini & L.Scarfiotti. 1964: J.Surtees & L.Bandini. 1965: J.Surtees & L.Bandini. 1966: J.Surtees, L.Bandini, M.Parkes & L.Scarfiotti. 1967: L.Bandini, C.Amon, M.Parkes & L.Scarfiotti. 1968: J.Ickx, C.Amon & A.de Adamich. 1969: C.Amon & P.Rodriguez. 1970: J.Ickx, I.Giunti & C.Regazzoni. 1971: J.Ickx, C.Regazzoni & M.Andretti. 1972: J.Ickx, C.Regazzoni & M.Andretti. 1973: J.Ickx & A. Merzario. 1974: C.Regazzoni & N.Lauda. 1975: C.Regazzoni & N.Lauda. 1976: N.Lauda, C.Regazzoni & C.Reutemann. 1977: N.Lauda, C.Reutemann & G.Villeneuve. 1978: C.Reutemann & G.Villeneuve. 1979: J.Scheckter & G.Villeneuve. 1980: J.Scheckter & G.Villeneuve. 1981: G.Villeneuve & D.Pironi. 1982: G.Villeneuve, D.Pironi, P.Tambay & M.Andretti. 1983: P.Tambay & R.Arnoux. 1984: M.Alboreto & R.Arnoux. 1985: M.Alboreto, R.Arnoux & S.Johansson. 1986: M.Alboreto & S.Johansson. 1987: M. Alboreto & G.Berger. 1988: M.Alboreto & G.Berger. 1989: N.Mansell & G.Berger. 1990: A.Prost & N.Mansell. 1991: A.Prost, J.Alesi & G.Morbidelli. 1992: J.Alesi, I.Capelli & N.Larini. 1993: J.Alesi & G.Berger. 1994: J.Alesi, G.Berger & N.Larini. 1995: J.Alesi & G.Berger. 1996-98: M.Schumacher & E.Irvine.

## Grand Prix Wins

1951 Britain (Gonzalez), Germany (Ascari), Italy (Ascari); 1952 Switzerland (Taruffi), Belgium (Ascari), Britain (Ascari), Germany (Ascari), Netherlands (Ascari), Italy (Ascari); 1953 Argentina (Ascari), Netherlands (Ascari), Belgium (Ascari), France (Hawthorn), Britain (Ascari), Germany (Farina), Switzerland (Ascari); 1954 Britain (Gonzalez), Spain (Hawthorn); 1955

Monaco (Trintignant); 1956 Argentina (Musso/Fangio), Belgium (Collins), France (Collins), Britain (Fangio), Germany (Fangio); 1958 France (Hawthorn), Britain (Collins); 1959 France (Brooks), Germany (Brooks); 1960 Italy (Hill); 1961 Netherlands (von Trips), Belgium (Hill), France (Baghetti), Britain (von Trips), Italy (Hill); 1963 Germany (Surtees); 1964 Germany (Surtees), Austria (Bandini), Italy (Surtees); 1966 Belgium (Surtees), Italy (Scarfiotti); 1968 France (Ickx); 1970 Austria (Ickx), Italy (Regazzoni), Canada (Ickx), Mexico (Ickx); 1971 South Africa (Andretti), Netherlands (Ickx); 1972 Germany (Ickx); 1974 Spain (Lauda), Netherlands (Lauda), Germany (Regazzoni); 1975 Monaco (Lauda), Belgium (Lauda), Sweden (Lauda), France (Lauda), Italy (Regazzoni), United States (Lauda); 1976 Brazil (Lauda), South Africa (Lauda), Long Beach (Regazzoni), Belgium (Lauda), Monaco (Lauda), Britain (Lauda); 1977 Brazil (Reutemann), South Africa (Lauda), Germany (Lauda), Netherlands (Lauda); 1978 Brazil (Reutemann), Long Beach (Reutemann), Britain TP (Reutemann), United States (Reutemann), Canada (G.Villeneuve); 1979 South Africa (G.Villeneuve), Long Beach (G.Villeneuve), Belgium (Scheckter), Monaco (Scheckter), Italy (Scheckter), United States (G.Villeneuve); 1981 Monaco (Villeneuve), Spain (G.Villeneuve); 1982 San Marino (Pironi), Netherlands (Pironi), Germany (Tambay); 1983 San Marino (Tambay), Canada (Arnoux), Germany (Arnoux); 1984 Belgium (Alboreto); 1985 Canada (Alboreto), Germany (Alboreto); 1987 Japan (Berger), Australia (Berger); 1988 Italy (Berger); 1989 Brazil (Mansell), Hungary (Mansell), Portugal (Berger); 1990 Brazil (Prost), France (Prost), Britain (Prost), Portugal (Mansell), Spain (Prost); 1994 Germany (Berger); 1995 Canada (Alesi); 1996 Spain, Belgium, Italy (M.Schumacher); 1997 Monaco, Canada, France, Belgium, Japan (M.Schumacher).

**Michael and Eddie share the podium with Heinz-Harald at Imola.**

# Jordan

## Benson & Hedges Jordan Mugen Honda

**Jordan Grand Prix Ltd**
Buckingham Road, Silverstone, Towcester, Northants, NN12 8JT
Tel: +44 (0)1327 857153          Fax: +44 (0)1327 858120

| | |
|---|---|
| Chairman: | Eddie Jordan |
| Race Team Dir: | Trevor Foster |
| Team Manager: | Jim Vale |
| Designer: | Gary Anderson |
| Chief Mechanic: | Tim Edwards |
| Drivers/Engineers: | Damon Hill (9)          /   Nick Burrows & Dino Toso |
| | Ralf Schumacher (10)   /   Andrew Stevenson & Sam Michael |
| Test Driver: | – |
| Sponsors: | Benson & Hedges, Mastercard, S.Oliver, Pearl Assurance, Diavia, Hewlett-Packard, GdeZ, Scania, ARmor All, Beta, Cadtek, Cargo Express, Esat Digifone, Goodyear, HDC, Keihin, Laidlaw Colourgraphics, NGK Spark Plug, OS Integration, RST, Rockport, Serengeti, Showa, Tie. |

## Brief History

1980: Eddie Jordan forms Jordan Motor Racing Team. 1987: Johnny Herbert wins British Formula 3 Championship driving a Jordan. 1988: Jean Alesi takes the International F3000 title for Jordan. 1990: Jordan F1 formed. 1991: Jordan score their first F1 points with Andrea de Cesaris fourth in Canada. 1993: Jordan signs a deal to use Hart engines until the end of the 1994 season. 1995: Exclusive deal with Peugeot engines. 1998: Switch to Mugen-Honda engines.

## Grand Prix Record

| | | |
|---|---|---|
| Contested: | 114 | |
| Victories: | 0 | (Best Finish: 2nd – twice) |
| Pole Positions: | 1 | |
| Fastest Laps: | 1 | |
| Constructors' World Titles: | 0 | (Best: 5th 1994 & 1997) |
| Drivers' World Championships: | 0 | (Best: 6th 1994) |
| Most Points in a Season: | 33 | (1997) |
| Total World Championship Points: | 121 | |
| Average Points/Grand Prix: | 1.06 | |

The Jordan team celebrated its 100th Grand Prix in Argentina but ended the 1997 season still looking for that elusive first Grand Prix victory. Since the team's first race at Phoenix in 1991 it has secured just one pole and one fastest lap. There were distinct points in the season though when the team looked set to gain that first-ever win thanks to the burgeoning form of Italian Giancarlo Fisichella.

There was little doubt last year that the 197 was the best car ever produced by the Jordan factory, and with distinct aerodynamic improvements it was often one of the most competitive on the circuit. There were problems though and straight-line speed and tyre wear were often cause for concern.

Then there was the problem of having two young and inexperienced drivers in their starting line-up. Ralf Schumacher failed to complete a number of races simply by trying too hard too soon and the pit lane air will have been red with rage when the two conspired to take each other out, especially at the Argentine Grand Prix at a time when both were challenging for the lead.

While Giancarlo Fisichella scored close on twice as many points as Ralf Schumacher, and finished more than twice as many races, it was the German who proved that, when he could finish races, he was the more consistent points scorer. Even so he finished just one of his first seven races and despite scoring a remarkable third in the team's 100th race he found himself under pressure as the season moved into its second half. He responded well though and managed top six finishes in all but one of those completed races, despite not always having the best qualifying position. Fisichella, on the other hand, finished all but four races and managed two podium places. He almost secured a first-ever win at Hockenheim, where he led before the pressure from the pursuing, and eventual race winner, Gerhard Berger seemed to finally take its toll.

Performance wasn't always assured though, and the races at the Hungaroring and Jerez were particularly disappointing, especially as they both came at times when there had been a marked improvement in performance.

As the season came to a close the Benetton team won the battle for the signature of Giancarlo Fisichella, which lead the way to the £5 million per year signing of Damon Hill. Hill signed for one year with the option of a second. It wasn't the only change at Jordan; with Peugeot opting to supply the French-based Prost team, Jordan signed a two-year deal to use the Japanese Mugen Honda V10 engine.

The design evolution by Gary Anderson will have continued through the close season and the arrival of the aforementioned Hill, and his often under-rated talents, could well ensure that first Grand Prix win – don't be surprised if it happens in Hungary. And if Ralf Schumacher can add a cool patient head to his driving, Jordan could also improve on their record 33 secured last season.

## Drivers and Results 1997

| Driver | Races | Com | Ret | Dnq | HP | Pts | Psn | Comp% |
|--------|-------|-----|-----|-----|-----|-----|------|-------|
| G'carlo Fisichella | 17 | 13 | 4 | 0 | 2nd | 20 | 9/21 | 76.47% |
| Ralf Schumacher | 17 | 7 | 10 | 0 | 3rd | 13 | 12/21 | 41.12% |
| Aggregate | 34 | 20 | 14 | 0 | – | 33 | 5/10 | 58.82% |

| | Grand Prix | Giancarlo Fisichella | Ralf Schumacher |
|---|---|---|---|
| 1 | Australian | Retired | Retired |
| 2 | Brazilian | 8th | Retired |
| 3 | Argentinian | Retired | 3rd |
| 4 | San Marino | 4th | Retired |
| 5 | Monaco | 6th | Retired |
| 6 | Spanish | 9th | Retired |
| 7 | Canadian | 3rd | Retired |
| 8 | French | 9th | 6th |
| 9 | British | 7th | 5th |
| 10 | German | 11th | 5th |
| 11 | Hungarian | Retired | 5th |
| 12 | Belgian | 2nd | Retired |
| 13 | Italian | 4th | Retired |
| 14 | Austrian | 4th | 5th |
| 15 | Luxembourg | Retired | Retired |
| 16 | Japanese | 7th | 9th |
| 17 | European | 11th | Retired |

## Jordan Mugen-Honda 198 Specifications

**Engine:** **Mugen-Honda MF301HC**

| | |
|---|---|
| Cylinders: | V10 (72 degrees) |
| Valves: | 40 – 4 per cylinder, with pneumatic return |
| Injection: | Honda PGM-F1 |
| Ignition System: | Honda PGM-IG |
| Capacity: | 3000 cc |
| Dimensions: | 625 mm (length), 525 mm (width), 470 mm (height) |

**Car**

| | |
|---|---|
| Chassis: | Full carbon fibre composite monocoque |
| Suspension: | Showa dampers |
| Transmission: | In-house Jordan GP design. Six-speed and reverse longitudinal gearbox with electro-hydraulic sequential gear change |
| Clutch: | Triple plate Jordan/AP racing clutch |
| Brakes: | Brembo braking systems. SEP carbon discs and pads. |
| Wheel rims: | OZ Racing forged according to Jordan's specifications. |

| | | | |
|---|---|---|---|
| Tyres: | Goodyear | | |
| Fuel tank: | ATL | | |
| Oil System: | In-house Jordan design, tank integral with gearbox | | |
| Cooling System: | Secan Radiator | | |
| Electrical: | TAG | | |

**Dimensions**

| | | | |
|---|---|---|---|
| Overall Length: | 4400mm | Wheelbase: | 2900mm |
| Front Track: | 1500mm | Rear Track: | 1418mm |
| Height: | 950mm | | |

## Engines 1991-98

1991: Ford. 1992: Yamaha. 1993-94: Hart. 1995-97: Peugeot. 1998: Mugen-Honda.

## Drivers 1991-97

1991: A.de Cesaris, B.Gachot, R.Moreno, M.Schumacher & A.Zanardi. 1992: S.Modena & M.Gugelmin. 1993: R.Barrichello, I.Capelli, T.Boutsen, M.Apicella, E.Nespatti & E.Irvine. 1994: R.Barrichello, E.Irvine, A.Suzuki & A.de Cesaris. 1995: R.Barrichello & E.Irvine. 1996: R.Barrichello & M. Brundle. 1997: R.Schumacher & G.Fisichella. 1998: D.Hill & R.Schumacher.

## Grand Prix Best Performance

2nd Position twice: 1995 Canada (Barrichello), 1997 Belgium (Fisichella).

*Eddie Jordan (centre) with his 1998 drivers – Ralf and Damon.*

# McLaren

## West McLaren Mercedes

**McLaren International Ltd**
Unit 22, Woking Business Park, Albert Drive, Woking, Surrey, GU21 5JY
Tel: +44 (0)1483 728211          Fax: +44 (0)1483 720157

| | |
|---|---|
| Chairman: | Ron Dennis |
| MD: | Martin Whitmarsh |
| Chief Designers: | Neil Oatley |
| | Mario Illien (engine) |
| | Henri Durand (aerodynamics), Dieter Gundel (systems), Patric Lowe (R&D), Steve Nichols (vehicle engineering), Jim Coates (electronic systems) |
| Drivers/Engineers: | Mika Hakkinen (7)    /    Roger Higgins |
| | David Coulthard (8)    /    Tim White |
| Test Driver: | Ricardo Zonta |
| Sponsors: | West, Mercedes-Benz, Mobil, Tag Heuer, Loctite, Boss, Camozzi, Goodyear, British Aerospace, SAP, Sun Microsystems, Cadence, Targetti, Kenwood, Eibach Springs, Enkei, Computervision. |

## Brief History

1959: Bruce McLaren makes his F1 debut driving for the Cooper works team. 1963: Bruce McLaren Motor Racing Ltd founded. 1966: McLaren make their Grand Prix debut at Monaco. 1968: Bruce McLaren wins in Belgium for his own team's first F1 victory. McLaren finish second behind Lotus in Constructors' World Championship. 1970: Bruce McLaren killed at Goodwood whilst testing a CanAm sportscar. 1973: Emerson Fittipaldi leads McLaren to the Drivers' & Constructors' Championship double. 1976: James Hunt takes the Drivers' World Championship by a point from Niki Lauda. 1984: Niki Lauda beats teammate Alain Prost by just half a point to take the Drivers' title. 1985: Alain Prost takes the title ahead of Michele Alboreto. 1986: Prost retains his title after Nigel Mansell goes out in the final race at Adelaide. 1988: Senna takes the title by three points from Prost. McLaren post a record Constructors' Championship score of 199 points. 1989: Prost takes the title from Senna by sixteen points for another McLaren double. 1990: Senna regains the title from Prost by seven points. 1991: Senna wins his third World Drivers' Championship. 1997: McLaren win first and last Grands Prix of the season.

## Grand Prix Record

| | |
|---|---|
| Contested: | 460 |
| Victories: | 107 |
| Pole Positions: | 80 |
| Fastest Laps: | 71 |
| Constructors' World Titles: | 7 (74, 84, 85, 88, 89, 90, 91) |
| Drivers' World Championships: | 9 (74, 76, 84, 85, 86, 88, 89, 90, 91) |
| Most Points in a Season: | 199 (1988) |
| Total World Championship Points: | 2047.5 |
| Average Points/Grand Prix: | 4.29 |

## Review

The McLaren team may have had to wait 50 Grands Prix between victories until their opening season win in the streets of Melbourne, but by the end of the season they had added another two wins. They were also only one of two teams who could boast the fact that both their drivers had taken that number one spot during the season – the other being Williams of course.

The Woking-based team ended the season as they had started it – with a win – but also in the knowledge that they had made significant progress with the development of car and drivers. There was an increasingly better performance in qualifying and they were never that far off the pace in the final calendar of races. The team's upturn in performance in those final stages of the season could be put down in no small part to the aerodynamic changes introduced since the mid-season arrival of Adrian Newey from Williams as technical director, and this will ultimately pay the sort of dividends that were apparent when Newey was chief designer at Williams.

Strategically, McLaren were often helped by their cars' larger than average fuel tank capacity that allowed both Coulthard and Hakkinen to run for longer without having to pit – something that was especially helpful in single-stop races. It will be interesting to see if other teams sacrifice weight for larger capacity in 1998.

Right from the start of the season the portents looked promising. Coulthard's unexpected but richly deserved victory in the Australian Grand Prix was enhanced by Mika Hakkinen's third place and ensured both McLaren's drivers were on the podium – a rare sight in recent years. After a further two finishes in Brazil, the team only managed to get both drivers across the finish line once in the next ten races and, although that bare statistic sounds bad, there was still significant progress being made despite problems with blistering tyres and oil. Mika Hakkinen for example had looked set to win at Silverstone, such was his command of the race, but engine problems took their toll seven laps from the finish line.

Hakkinen matched his third placing of Melbourne at Spa, but it was achieved under the threat of a ban that was subsequently upheld after he had been found guilty of using a fuel mix in qualifying that did not match the sample the team had supplied. McLaren were also fined £30,000 for the discrepancy.

The final five races of the season saw a distinct improvement in fortunes, with five points finishes recorded by the team. Coulthard was victorious at Monza and this was then matched by Hakkinen in Jerez for that first-ever race win.

Off the track, Ron Dennis took on the role of Chairman of McLaren and Martin Whitmarsh was appointed as MD. Then, in the middle of November, the team were cleared by the World Motor Sport Council of any sort of collusion with the Williams team to arrange the result of the final race of the season – a race in which Williams driver Jacques Villeneuve secured the Drivers' World Championship title.

With two in-form drivers and the not inconsiderable experience of aerodynamicist Adrian Newey on board, McLaren look set to be an even more formidable unit in 1998 and may not be that far off challenging on a regular basis for top billing in both qualifying and racing.

## Drivers and Results 1997

| Driver | Races | Com | Ret | Dnq | HP | Pts | Psn | Comp% |
|---|---|---|---|---|---|---|---|---|
| David Coulthard | 17 | 10 | 7 | 0 | 1st | 36 | 4/21 | 58.82% |
| Mika Hakkinen | 17 | 10 | 7 | 0 | 1st | 27 | 6/21 | 58.82% |
| Aggregate | 34 | 20 | 14 | 0 | – | 63 | 4/10 | 58.82% |

| Grand Prix | | David Coulthard | Mika Hakkinen |
|---|---|---|---|
| 1 | Australian | 1st | 3rd |
| 2 | Brazilian | 10th | 4th |
| 3 | Argentinian | Retired | 5th |
| 4 | San Marino | Retired | 6th |
| 5 | Monaco | Retired | Retired |
| 6 | Spanish | 6th | 7th |
| 7 | Canadian | 7th | Retired |
| 8 | French | 7th | Retired |
| 9 | British | 4th | Retired |
| 10 | German | Retired | 3rd |
| 11 | Hungarian | Retired | Retired |
| 12 | Belgian | Retired | dq (3rd) |
| 13 | Italian | 1st | 9th |
| 14 | Austrian | 2nd | Retired |
| 15 | Luxembourg | Retired | Retired |
| 16 | Japanese | 10th | 4th |
| 17 | European | 2nd | 1st |

## McLaren MP4-13 Specifications

**Engine:**       **Mercedes-Benz**
Type:       V10 (75 degree)
Cylinders:       10 – 4 valves per cylinder
Injection:       TAG 2000 electronic system

**Car**
Chassis:       McLaren moulded carbon fibre/honeycombed composite
Transmission:       McLaren longitudinal six speed semi-automatic. Control by TAG electronic system. McLaren drive shafts and CV assemblies
Suspension:       Inboard spring/damper operated by pushrod and bellcrank with a double wishbone system
Springs:       Eibach
Dampers:       Penske
Brakes:       AP Racing callipers and master cylinders
Tyres:       Bridgestone
Race wheels:       Enkei
Water Radiators:       McLaren/Calsonic
Oil Radiators:       McLaren/Calsonic

## Engines 1966-98

1966-82: Ford. 1983-87: TAG-Porsche Turbo. 1988: Honda Turbo. 1989-92: Honda. 1993: Ford. 1994: Peugeot. 1995-98: Mercedes.

## Drivers 1966-98

1966: B.McLaren. 1967: B.McLaren. 1968: D.Hulme & D.Gurney. 1969: B.McLaren, D.Hulme & V.Elford. 1970: B.McLaren, D.Hulme, D.Gurney & J.Surtees. 1971: D.Hulme, P.Gethin & J.Oliver. 1972: D.Hulme & P.Revson. 1973: D.Hulme, P.Revson, J.Scheckter. 1974: E.Fittipaldi & D.Hulme. 1975: E.Fittipaldi & E.Mass. 1976: J.Hunt & E.Mass. 1977: J.Hunt & E.Mass. 1978: J.Hunt & P.Tambay. 1979: J.Watson & P.Tambay. 1980: J.Watson & A.Prost. 1981: J.Watson & A.de Cesaris. 1982: N.Lauda & J.Watson. 1983: N.Lauda & J.Watson. 1984: N.Lauda & A.Prost. 1985: N.Lauda, A.Prost & J.Watson. 1986: A.Prost & K.Rosberg. 1987: A.Prost & S.Johansson. 1988: A.Prost & A.Senna. 1989: A.Prost & A.Senna. 1990: A.Senna & G.Berger. 1991: A.Senna & G.Berger. 1992: A.Senna & G.Berger. 1993: A.Senna, M.Andretti & M.Hakkinen. 1994: M.Hakkinen, M.Brundle & P.Alliot. 1995: M.Hakkinen, N.Mansell, M.Blundell & J.Magnussen. 1996-98: M. Hakkinen & D. Coulthard.

## Grand Prix Wins

1968 Belgium (McLaren), Italy (Hulme), Canada (Hulme); 1969 Mexico (Hulme); 1972 South Africa (Hulme); 1973 Sweden (Hulme), Britain (Revson), Canada (Revson); 1974 Argentina (Hulme), Brazil (Fittipaldi), Belgium (Fittipaldi), Canada (Fittipaldi); 1975 Argentina (Fittipaldi), Spain (Mass), Britain (Fittipaldi); 1976 Spain (Hunt), France (Hunt), Germany (Hunt), Canada (Hunt), United States (Hunt); 1977 Britain (Hunt), United States (Hunt), Japan (Hunt); 1981 Britain (Watson); 1982 Long Beach (Lauda), Belgium (Watson), Detroit (Watson), Britain (Lauda); 1983 Long Beach (Watson); 1984 Brazil (Prost), South Africa (Lauda), San Marino (Prost), France (Lauda), Monaco (Prost), Britain (Lauda), Germany (Prost), Austria (Lauda), Netherlands (Prost), Italy (Lauda), Europe (Prost), Portugal (Prost); 1985 Brazil (Prost), Monaco (Prost), Britain (Prost), Austria (Prost), Netherlands (Lauda), Italy (Prost); 1986 San Marino (Prost), Monaco (Prost), Austria (Prost), Australia (Prost); 1987 Brazil (Prost), Belgium (Prost), Portugal (Prost); 1988 Brazil (Prost), San Marino (Senna), Monaco (Prost), Mexico (Prost), Canada (Senna), Detroit (Senna), France (Prost), Britain (Senna), Germany (Senna), Hungary (Senna), Belgium (Senna), Portugal (Prost), Spain (Prost), Japan (Senna), Australia (Prost); 1989 San Marino (Senna), Monaco (Senna), Mexico (Senna), United States (Prost), France (Prost), Britain (Prost), Germany (Senna), Belgium (Senna), Italy (Prost), Spain (Senna); 1990 United States (Senna), Monaco (Senna), Canada (Senna), Germany (Senna), Belgium (Senna), Italy (Senna); 1991 United States (Senna), Brazil (Senna), San Marino (Senna), Monaco (Senna), Hungary (Senna), Belgium (Senna), Japan (Berger), Australia (Senna); 1992 Monaco (Senna), Canada (Berger), Hungary (Senna), Italy (Senna), Australia (Berger); 1993 Brazil (Senna), Europe (Senna), Monaco (Senna), Japan (Senna), Australia (Senna); 1997 Australia (Coulthard), Italy (Coulthard), Europe (Hakkinen).

# Minardi

## Minardi Team

**Minardi Scuderia Italia**
Minardi Team SpA, Via Spalenzani 21, 48018 Faunze, Ravenna, Italy
Tel: +39 546 620480          Fax: +39 546 620998

| | |
|---|---|
| President: | Gian Carlo Minardi |
| Vice President: | Gabriele Rumi |
| Team Manager: | Frederic Dhainaut |
| Chief Designer: | Mauro Gennari |
| Tech. Coord: | Gabbriele Tredozi |
| Electronics: | Alessandro Iacoponi |
| Drivers: | Esterban Tuero |
| | tbc |
| Test Driver: | – |
| Sponsors: | Bossini, Brembo, Bridgestone, Carbone Industrie, Cimatron, Diemme, Doimo, Donatl, Fiamm, Fondmetal, Hartpower, Hewlett Packard, Ircis, Magneti Marelli, Microsystem, Mild Seven, Milpass, RBM, Setrans, Sparco, TRW Sabelt, Valleverde. |

## Brief History

**1979:** Minardi formed by Giancarlo Minardi. **1985:** Minardi make their Formula One debut in Brazil. **1988:** Pierluigi Martini picks up Minardi's first points with sixth in Canada. **1990:** Minardi record their only front row start with Martini behind Gerhard Berger in America. **1993:** Christian Fittipaldi takes Minardi's highest placing of fourth in South Africa. Minardi's best finish of eighth with seven points in the Constructors' World Championship.

## Grand Prix Results

| | | |
|---|---|---|
| Contested: | 205 | |
| Victories: | 0 | (Best Finish: 4th – three times) |
| Pole Positions: | 0 | |
| Fastest Laps: | 0 | |
| Constructors' World Titles: | 0 | (Best: 7th 1991) |
| Drivers' World Championships: | 0 | (Best: 10th 1994) |
| Most Points in a Season: | 7 | (1993) |
| Total World Championship Points: | 27 | |
| Average Points/Grand Prix: | 0.13 | |

## Review

The Minardi-Hart team finished the season as the only finishing team not to record a championship point during the course of the year. Indeed, it was the second successive year without a point scored for the Italian team whose best result was posted by Jarno Trulli when he came home in ninth place at both the Australian and Argentinian Grands Prix

For the majority of the season the Minardi M197 was way off the pace and, more often than not, the drivers found themselves on the last two rows of the grid. Only half of the races were completed and only on four occasions throughout the season did both Minardis finish the race together.

In Austria, the car of Tarso Marques was disqualified after qualifying when it was found to be 3 kg under weight.

The season had offered reasonable encouragement, especially early on when Trulli looked capable of getting the most from the car. When he left for Prost in mid-season, as cover for the injured Olivier Panis, the best chance of championship points seemed to go with him. Ukyo Katayama, in his final year as a Formula One driver, could only manage tenth position twice and was often well outside this in his 47% of race completions. At Spa, the team had their 200th Grand Prix race and they will be hoping for a big improvement in 1998, no doubt looking to a first-ever podium finish as their next milestone.

## Drivers and Results 1997

| Driver | Races | Com | Ret | Dnq | HP | Pts | Psn | Comp% |
|--------|-------|-----|-----|-----|-----|-----|-----|-------|
| Ukyo Katayama | 17 | 8 | 9 | 0 | 10th | 0 | – | 47.06% |
| Jarno Trulli | 8 | 5 | 3 | 0 | 9th | 0 | – | 62.50% |
| Tarso Marques | 9 | 4 | 5 | 0 | 10th | 0 | – | 44.44% |
| Aggregate | 34 | 17 | 17 | 0 | – | 0 | – | 50.00% |

| | Grand Prix | U.Katayama | J.Trulli | T.Marques |
|----|------------|------------|----------|-----------|
| 1 | Australian | Retired | 9th | – |
| 2 | Brazilian | 18th | 12th | – |
| 3 | Argentinian | Retired | 9th | – |
| 4 | San Marino | 11th | Retired | – |
| 5 | Monaco | 10th | Retired | – |
| 6 | Spanish | Retired | 15th | – |
| 7 | Canadian | Retired | Retired | – |
| 8 | French | 11th | 10th | – |
| 9 | British | Retired | – | 10th |
| 10 | German | Retired | – | Retired |
| 11 | Hungarian | 10th | – | 12th |
| 12 | Belgian | 14th | – | Retired |
| 13 | Italian | Retired | – | 14th |

| 14 | Austrian | 11th | – | dns |
| 15 | Luxembourg | Retired | – | Retired |
| 16 | Japanese | Retired | – | Retired |
| 17 | European | 17th | – | 15th |

## Minardi M198 Specifications

**Engine:**

| | |
|---|---|
| Injection: | Magneti Marelli electronic |
| Electronics: | Magneti Marelli |
| Fuel tank: | ALT |
| Fuel: | Minardi |

**Car**

| | |
|---|---|
| Chassis: | Carbon fibre monocoque |
| Suspension: | Inboard spring via rocker and pushrod to wishbone |
| Brake Pads: | Carbon Industrie |
| Brake Discs: | Brembo |
| Cooling system: | Water radiators (x2), oil radiator (x1) |
| Gearbox: | 6 speed plus reverse. Longitudinal Minardi Xrtac gearbox with Minardi electrohydraulic system |
| Wheels: | Fondmetal: 11"x13" (front), 13.7"x13" (rear) |
| Tyres: | Bridgestone |
| Seatbelts: | TRW Sabelt |

## Engines 1985-97

1985-87: Motori Moderni Turbo. 1988-90: Ford Cosworth. 1991: Ferrari. 1992: Lamborghini. 1993-96: Ford Cosworth. 1997: Hart.

## Drivers 1985-97

1985: P.Martini. 1986: A.de Cesaris & A.Nannini. 1987: A.Nannini & A.Campos. 1988: L.Perez Sala, A.Campos & P.Martini. 1989: P.Martini, L.Perez Sala & P.Barilla. 1990: P.Martini, P.Barilla & G.Morbidelli. 1991: P.Martini, G.Morbidelli & R.Moreno. 1992: G.Morbidelli, C.Fittipaldi & A.Zanardi. 1993: C.Fittipaldi, F.Barbazza, P.Martini & J-M.Gounon. 1994: P.Martini & M.Alboreto. 1995: P.Lamy, L.Badoer & P.Martini. 1996: P. Lamy & T.Inoue. 1997: U.Katayama & J.Trulli.

## Grand Prix Best Performance

4th position three times: 1991 San Marino (Martini), Portugal (Martini); 1993 South Africa (Martini).

# Prost

## Equipe Prost Peugeot

Technopole de la Nievre, 58470 Magny-Cours, France
Tel: +33 3 86 60 62 00        Fax: +33 3 86 21 22 96

| | |
|---|---|
| Owner: | Alain Prost |
| MD: | Bruno Michel |
| Sporting Manager: | Cesare Fiorio |
| Chief Mechanic: | Robert Dassaud |
| Chief Designer: | Loic Bigois |
| Drivers/Engineers: | Olivier Panis (11)  /  Renato Muscati |
| | Jarno Trulli (12)  /  Humphrey Corbett |
| Test Driver: | – |

### Brief History

1976: Ligier enter F1 at the end of the 1976 season. Jacques Laffite takes pole and sets the fastest lap in Italy. 1979: Laffite wins the opening two Grands Prix in Argentina and Brazil. 1980: Ligier finish second in the Constructors' World Championship behind Williams. 1983: Ligier fail to score a point in the season for the first time in their history. 1996: Tom Walkinshaw leaves for Arrows. 1997: Alain Prost takes control of Ligier and renames team to Prost Grand Prix. 1998: Secure Peugeot engine for cars.

### Grand Prix Record

| | | |
|---|---|---|
| Contested: | 343 | |
| Victories: | 9 | |
| Pole Positions: | 9 | |
| Fastest Laps: | 11 | |
| Constructors' World Titles: | 0 | (Best: 2nd 1980) |
| Drivers' World Championships: | 0 | (Best: 4th 1979, 1980, 1981) |
| Most Points in a Season: | 66 | (1980) |
| Total World Championship Points: | 410 | |
| Average Points/Grand Prix | 1.14 | |

### Review

The high hopes that the Prost team had for the 1997 season were tempered by the awful accident that left them without their number one driver, Olivier Panis, for much of it. Up until the accident in Canada, which left the

Frenchman with both legs broken, the Alain Prost lead team had looked competitive and were showing that they could live in the top drawer. Indeed, at the time of Panis' accident, the driver himself was running third in the Drivers' Championship with the team a close fifth in the Constructors' Cup. This latter position was achieved despite some indifferent performances from Shinji Nakano who had a completion rate of less than 50% and included five retirements in the first seven races.

Nakano's position in the team had been part of the deal that secured the Mugen Honda engine for Prost for the 1997 season. A rookie in his first year, his two points were clearly less than had been anticipated in what was a competitive car and the rumours were rife well before the end of the 1997 season that a replacement was being sort.

Ironically, it was the accident to Panis that brought the French outfit's new driver to the fore. Having out-performed the regular Prost test driver Emmanuel Collard in trials, Italian Jarno Trulli was offered what amounted to seven drives in the absence of Panis. Trulli, who had started the season at Minardi in good form, produced some consistent qualifying performances and managed a points finish in only his third race for the team. The icing might well have come in his final race of the year, prior to the pending return of Panis, when he qualified third in Austria and had been leading the race only to give way to engine problems before its conclusion.

It was Panis though who produced the bulk of the Prost points, completing 80% of his races and retiring just twice. Five points finishes included a second in Spain and a third in Brazil.

The introduction of Peugeot engines for the 1998 season should provide greater straight-line speed and a more reliable performance. Both factors should help both team and drivers and allow Olivier Panis a bigger say in the Drivers' Championship. If Jarno Trulli can build on the form shown in his brief spell in 1997, the team could be challenging for a top-five place in the Constructors' Championship.

Development off the track was also continuing apace and the team were hoping to move from their Magny-Cours base to a new state-of-the-art facility on the Satory industrial estate near Versailles prior to the start of the 1998 season.

## Drivers and Results 1997

| Driver | Races | Com | Ret | Dnq | HP | Pts | Psn | Comp% |
|--------|-------|-----|-----|-----|-----|-----|------|-------|
| Olivier Panis | 10 | 8 | 2 | 0 | 2nd | 16 | 10/21 | 80.00% |
| Shinji Nakano | 17 | 8 | 9 | 0 | 6th | 2 | 17/21 | 47.06% |
| Jarno Trulli | 7 | 5 | 2 | 0 | 4th | 3 | 16/21 | 71.43% |
| Aggregate | 34 | 21 | 13 | 0 | – | 21 | 6/10 | 67.74% |

| Grand Prix | | Olivier Panis | Shinji Nakano | Jarno Trulli |
|---|---|---|---|---|
| 1 | Australian | 5th | 7th | – |
| 2 | Brazilian | 3rd | 14th | – |
| 3 | Argentinian | Retired | Retired | – |
| 4 | San Marino | 8th | Retired | – |
| 5 | Monaco | 4th | Retired | – |
| 6 | Spanish | 2nd | Retired | – |
| 7 | Canadian | 11th | 6th | – |
| 8 | French | – | Retired | Retired |
| 9 | British | – | 11th | 8th |
| 10 | German | – | 7th | 4th |
| 11 | Hungarian | – | 6th | 7th |
| 12 | Belgian | – | Retired | 15th |
| 13 | Italian | – | 11th | 10th |
| 14 | Austrian | – | Retired | Retired |
| 15 | Luxembourg | 6th | Retired | – |
| 16 | Japanese | Retired | Retired | – |
| 17 | European | 7th | 10th | – |

## Prost AP01 Specifications

**Car**

| | |
|---|---|
| Chassis: | Carbon fibre composite monocoque manufactured by Prost Grand Prix |
| Suspension: | Double wishbone and push-rod (rear) with suspension units located on top of monocoque (front) |
| Brakes: | Brembo and/or AP one-piece callipers and master cylinders with Carbone Industries carbon fibre discs |
| Transmission: | Transverse semi-automatic six-speed gearbox. Multi-plate clutch |
| Fuel system: | ATL rubber fuel cell mounted within the monocoque structure behind the cockpit |
| Oil system: | Eight litre capacity oil tank |
| Cooling system: | Separate water radiators in each side pod plus oil radiator on right-hand side of engine |
| Tyres: | Bridgestone |

## Engines 1976-98

1978-78: Matra. 1979-80: Ford. 1981-84: Matra. 1984-86: Renault Turbo. 1987: Megatron Turbo. 1988: Judd. 1989-90: Ford. 1991: Lamborghini. 1992-94: Renault. 1995-97: Mugen-Honda. 1998: Peugeot.

## Drivers 1976–98

1976: J.Laffite. 1977: J.Laffite. 1978: J.Laffite. 1979: J.Laffite, P.Depailler & J.Ickx. 1980: J.Laffite & D.Pironi. 1981: J.Laffite, J-P Jarier, J-P Jabouille & P.Tambay. 1982: J.Laffite & E.Cheever. 1983: J-P Jarier & R.Boesel. 1984: A.de Cesaris & F.Hesnault. 1985: J.Laffite, A.de Cesaris & P.Streiff. 1986: R.Arnoux, J.Laffite & P.Alliot. 1987: R.Arnoux & P.Ghinzani. 1988: R.Arnoux & S.Johansson. 1989: R.Arnoux & O.Grouillard. 1990: P.Alliot & N.Larini. 1991: T.Boutsen & E.Comas. 1992: T.Boutsen & E.Comas. 1993: M.Brundle & M.Blundell. 1994: E.Bernard, O.Panis, J.Herbert & F.Lagorce. 1995: M.Brundle, A.Suzuki & O.Panis. 1996: P.Diniz & O.Panis. 1997: O.Panis & S.Nakano. 1998: O.Panis & J.Trulli.

## Grand Prix Wins

1977 Sweden (Laffite); 1979 Argentina (Laffite), Brazil (Laffite), Spain (Depailler); 1980 Belgium (Pironi), Germany (Laffite); 1981 Austria (Laffite), Canada (Laffite); 1996 Monaco (Panis).

# Sauber

## Red Bull Sauber Petronas

**Team Sauber Formel 1**
Wildbachstrasse 9, 8340 Hinwil, Switzerland
Tel: +41 1 938 1400                    Fax: +41 1 938 1670

| | |
|---|---|
| Team Principal: | Peter Sauber |
| Team Director: | Max Welti |
| Chief Designer: | Leo Ress |
| Team Manager: | Beat Zehnder |
| Chief Mechanic: | Ernst Keller |
| Drivers: | Jean Alesi (14) |
| | Johnny Herbert (15) |
| Test Driver: | Jorg Muller |
| Sponsors: | Red Bull, Baumier, Brembo, Emil Frey, Giroflex, Goodyear, Helbling Informatik, IBM, Lista, MacNeal-Schwendler, Magneti Marelli, Man Nutzfahrzeuge, Modellbau Bubeckk, OMP, Sachs, Silicon Graphics, Speedline. |

### Brief History

1993: Sauber record a scoring finish in their first Grand Prix with J.J. Lehto taking fifth in South Africa. The team end the season sixth in the Constructors' World Championship with twelve points. 1995: Achieve first podium finish when Frentzen finishes third at Monza. 1996: Herbert finishes third at Monaco. 1997: Herbert finishes third in Hungary.

### Grand Prix Record

| | | |
|---|---|---|
| Contested: | 82 | |
| Victories: | 0 | (Best Finish: 3rd – three times) |
| Pole Positions: | 0 | |
| Fastest Laps: | 0 | |
| Constructors' World Titles: | 0 | (Best: 6th 1993) |
| Drivers' World Championships: | 0 | (Best: 8th 1994) |
| Most Points in a Season: | 18 | (1995) |
| Total World Championship Points: | 69 | |
| Average Points/Grand Prix: | 0.70 | |

The competitive edge that the Sauber team exhibited in 1997 was nothing short of sensational. With just five years of Formula One history behind them, they could be on the verge of upstarting the more established 'new' teams who have yet to win their first Grand Prix race. The relative success of 1997 was down to three factors: the continuing development of the aerodynamic performance of the car, the reliability and additional power provided by the Ferrari-sourced Peteronas engines and Johnny Herbert.

Herbert was the veritable Mr Steady, never finishing outside a top-eight place and having his most successful points haul since 1994. The downside was the team's inability to find a suitable partner for the Englishman. Having started the season with the Italian Nicola Larini – who in truth had done pretty well in his rookie season – there was a parting of the ways after one of several outbursts by the Italian to his native press about team affairs. His replacement, Gianni Morbidelli, never made up the ground and often found himself at the centre of a jinx that, in turn, forced him to miss five races and forced the team to use test driver Norberto Fontana as a second replacement.

Herbert's best performance came at the Hungaroring where he finished third. The lowest step on the podium proved to be Sauber's highest finish of the season, and the highest of their short history. The feat had only been achieved twice before in a Sauber car, and one of those was again down to Herbert.

Herbert secured fifteen of the team's points – the only other coming from Larini who finished sixth at Melbourne in his first Formula One. At that point Larini looked set for a promising career, but a seventh place was the best he recorded after than one, at Imola, in what proved to be his penultimate race. The best position that either of his replacements managed was ninth. Herbert though, continued to lead the way and fourth places in Argentina and at Spa were the other highlights.

Despite the track performance, qualifying was often erratic. The best Herbert himself managed was seventh and he even started as low as sixteenth. Clearly, an improvement in qualifying position could reap even bigger benefits than the ones already being achieved from rather average positions.

The 1998 season does look as though it can hold some promise, with Frenchman Jean Alesi joining Herbert at the Swiss team. If the former Ferrari and Benetton driver can bring his experience rather than impetuosity to bear, then Sauber could prove to be the real dark horses during 1998.

## Drivers and Results 1997

| Driver | Races | Com | Ret | Dnq | HP | Pts | Psn | Comp% |
|--------|-------|-----|-----|-----|-----|-----|-----|-------|
| Johnny Herbert | 17 | 11 | 6 | 0 | 3rd | 15 | 11/21 | 64.71% |
| Nicola Larini | 5 | 3 | 2 | 0 | 6th | 1 | 21/21 | 60.00% |
| Gianni Morbidelli | 8 | 6 | 2 | 0 | 9th | 0 | – | 75.00% |
| Norberto Fontana | 4 | 3 | 1 | 0 | 9th | 0 | – | 75.00% |
| Aggregate | 34 | 23 | 11 | 0 | – | 16 | 7/10 | 67.65% |

| | Grand Prix | J.Herbert | N.Larini | G.Morbidelli | N.Fontana |
|---|-----------|-----------|----------|--------------|-----------|
| 1 | Australian | Retired | 6th | – | – |
| 2 | Brazilian | 7th | 11th | – | |
| 3 | Argentinian | 4th | Retired | – | |
| 4 | San Marino | Retired | 7th | – | |
| 5 | Monaco | Retired | Retired | – | |
| 6 | Spanish | 5th | – | 14th | |
| 7 | Canadian | 5th | – | 10th | |
| 8 | French | 8th | – | – | Retired |
| 9 | British | Retired | – | – | 9th |
| 10 | German | Retired | – | – | 9th |
| 11 | Hungarian | 3rd | – | Retired | – |
| 12 | Belgian | 4th | – | 9th | – |
| 13 | Italian | Retired | – | 12th | – |
| 14 | Austrian | 8th | – | 9th | – |
| 15 | Luxembourg | 7th | – | 9th | – |
| 16 | Japanese | 6th | – | dns | – |
| 17 | European | 8th | – | – | 14th |

## Sauber Petronas C16 Specifications

**Engine:** **Sauber-Petronas**
Type: V10 (75 degrees)
Valves: 40
Valve Mechanism: Pneumatic
Management: Magneti Marelli
Ignition System: Magneti Marelli, static

**Car**
Chassis: Carbon fibre monocoque
Suspension: Upper and lower wishbones, combined spring/damper units (Sachs), mounted inboard with pushrod actuation
Brakes: Eight-piston callipers (Brembo) front and six-piston callipers rear; carbon pads and discs (Carbone Industrie)
Transmission: Semi-automatic, longitudinally mounted, six-speed transmission (Sauber), carbon clutch (Sachs)
Tyres: Goodyear

## Engines 1993-98

1993: Sauber. 1994: Mercedes. 1995-96: Ford. 1997-98: Sauber-Petronas.

## Drivers 1993-97

1993: K. Wendlinger & J. J.Lehto. 1994: K.Wendlinger, H-H.Frentzen, J.J.Lehto & A.de Cesaris. 1995: H-H.Frentzen, J-C.Boullion & K.Wendlinger. 1996: J. Herbert & H-H.Frentzen. 1997: J.Herbert & N.Larini. 1998: J.Herbert & Jean Alesi

## Grand Prix Best Performance

3rd position twice: 1995 Italy (Frentzen), 1996 Monaco (Herbert), 1997 Hungary (Herbert).

# Stewart

## Stewart Ford
**Stewart Grand Prix Ltd**
16 Tanners Drive, Blakelands, Milton Keynes, Bucks, MK14 5BW
Tel: +44 (0)1908 216122          Fax: +44 (0)1908 216892
Chairman:           Jackie Stewart OBE
Managing Director: Paul Stewart
Team Managers:   David Stubbs
Designer:            Alan Jenkins
Drivers/Engineers: Rubens Barrichello (18)  / Christophe Bouqueniaux
                    Jan Magnussen (19)      / Darren Nicolls
Test Driver:         –
Sponsors:           Ford Motor Company, HSBC Holdings Ltd, MCI, Texaco,
                    Lear Coporation, Bridgestone, Hewlett-Packard, EDS
                    Unigaphics.

## Brief History

1996: Stewart Grand Prix formed. 1997: First season F1 racing. Finished 2nd
in Monaco Grand Prix.

## Grand Prix Record

| | | |
|---|---|---|
| Contested: | 17 | |
| Victories: | 0 | (Best Finish: 2nd) |
| Pole Positions: | 0 | |
| Fastest Laps: | 0 | |
| Constructors' World Titles: | 0 | (Best: 9th 1997) |
| Drivers' World Championships: | 0 | (Best: 14th 1997 |
| Most Points in a Season: | 6 | 1997 |
| Total World Championship Points: | 6 | |
| Average Points/Grand Prix | 0.18 | |

## Review

The Stewart team's generally impressive debut on the F1 scene owed a lot to
the workaholic nature of the Stewart family and their willingness to tread the
boards to ensure the healthy stream of funds they required to get the Stewart
Formula 1 show on the road. Team Stewart also brought a freshness to the
circuit, which in many ways revitalised many aspects of the competition.

More importantly, they re-established the fact that new teams can succeed and be taken seriously, and this was especially important to the sport given the several notable failures in recent years.

With the backing of Ford engines, but without any testing history, the Stewart team found themselves in the unenviable position of having to do their engine and car development on the fly, and most fully in the public eye, and by the end of the season the power pack had already progressed through many phases of development. This invariably led to some spectacular failures. An example of this came at the British Grand Prix where the team had a disastrous qualifying session, which saw three engine problems including one failure. Both engines then blew up in the race – Barrichello's Phase Six engine after 37 laps and Magnussen's Phase Seven engine on lap 51.

Not all problems were engine related and some were simply associated with teething problems one would expect with any applied new technology. In the Brazilian Grand Prix for example, Barrichello was left on the starting grid after his engine suddenly powered up to 16,000 rpm and was then automatically shut down by safety systems – the fault was eventually traced to the governing software.

But, amongst all this, there was some outstanding success. The second place at Monaco will probably remain the highlight for many seasons to come, even if it is matched or surpassed in the foreseeable future. Monaco was also the only meeting where both cars managed to finish the course, although this is not really surprising given that this circuit is one of the least testing for engines.

Nevertheless, despite the failures, the engine and its performances looked to improve as the season drew to a close and it is generally regarded as being ahead of the more established Yamaha and closing in on Mugen Honda. Stewart supporters will be looking for an increase in power performance from the SF-2 and the means to improve on a generally poor qualifying performance that persisted through much of the 1997 season. But, beyond that, reliability will remain the main concern for the 1998 season (as a team, Stewart finished less than 25% of their 1997 races) and, while grid and finishing position will be targets, a consistent finish must be the first priority for the 1998 season. Furthermore a driver of the calibre of Rubens Barrichello will always be there or thereabouts when the points are handed out.

## Drivers and Results 1997

| Driver | Races | Com | Ret | Dnq | HP | Pts | Psn | Comp% |
|---|---|---|---|---|---|---|---|---|
| Rubens Barrichello | 17 | 3 | 14 | 0 | 2nd | 6 | 14/21 | 17.65% |
| Jan Magnussen | 17 | 5 | 12 | 0 | 7th | 0 | – | 29.41% |
| Aggregate | 34 | 8 | 26 | 0 | – | 6 | 9/10 | 23.53% |

| Grand Prix | | Rubens Barrichello | Jan Magnussen |
|---|---|---|---|
| 1 | Australian | Retired | Retired |
| 2 | Brazilian | Retired | dns |
| 3 | Argentinian | Retired | 10th |
| 4 | San Marino | Retired | Retired |
| 5 | Monaco | 2nd | 7th |
| 6 | Spanish | Retired | 13th |
| 7 | Canadian | Retired | Retired |
| 8 | French | Retired | Retired |
| 9 | British | Retired | Retired |
| 10 | German | Retired | Retired |
| 11 | Hungarian | Retired | Retired |
| 12 | Belgian | Retired | 12th |
| 13 | Italian | 13th | Retired |
| 14 | Austrian | 14th | Retired |
| 15 | Luxembourg | Retired | Retired |
| 16 | Japanese | Retired | Retired |
| 17 | European | Retired | 9th |

## Stewart Ford SF2 Specifications

**Engine:**   **Ford Zetec-R V10**
Cylinders: 10 (72 degree) – 40 valves
Capacity: 2998 cc
Management: Ford electronics
Ignition: Cosworth
Fuel Injection: Visteon
Valve Mechanism: Pneumatic
Dimensions: 605 mm (length), 520 mm (width), 460 mm (height)

**Car**
Chassis: Carbon fibre monocoque designed and built in-house
Transmission: Stewart Carbon-caped six-speed gearbox
Clutch: High-pressure hydraulic system, AP Racing triple-plate clutch
Suspension: Upper and lower wishbones, combined spring/damper units mounted with pushrod actuation. Choice of twin or triple Stewart/Penske damper layout
Brakes: Twin AP Racing four-piston callipers (front). Twin AP Racing six-piston callipers (rear)
Brake pads: Carbone Industrie carbon fibre discs and pads
Tyres: Bridgestone

## Engines 1997-98

1997-98: Ford.

## Drivers 1997-98

1997-98: R.Barrichello & J.Magnussen.

## Grand Prix Best Performance

2nd position once: 1997 Monaco (Barrichello).

*In the rain at Monaco and on the way to second place – Rubens Barrichello.*

# Tyrrell

## Tyrrell Ford

**Tyrrell Racing Organisation Ltd**
Long Reach, Ockham, Woking, Surrey, GU23 6PE
Tel: +44 (0)1483 284955      Fax: +44 (0)1483 284892

| | |
|---|---|
| Chairman: | Ken Tyrrell |
| MD Commercial: | Bob Tyrrell |
| MD Engineering: | Dr Harvey Postlethwaite |
| Sporting Director: | Satoru Nakajima |
| Dep.Tech.Dir: | Mike Gascoyne |
| Team Manager: | Steve Nielsen |
| Chief Mechanic: | Nigel Steer |
| Drivers: | Toranosuke Takagi |
| | tbc |
| Test Driver: | – |
| Sponsors: | PIAA Corporation, Ford, Goodyear, Koni, Parametric Technology, Motion Systems, Mitech, Morse, Tamiya. |

## Brief History

1970: Jackie Stewart takes pole position for Tyrrell in Montreal in their first race in Formula One. 1971: Stewart wins the second race of the season in Spain to record Tyrrell's first win in only their fifth race; they go on to win the Constructors' World Championship with more than double the points of second-placed BRM. 1972: Tyrrell win four races but finish second to Lotus in the Championship. 1973: Five races won but runners-up to Lotus for the second year running. 1978: Patrick Depailler wins in Monaco for his only Grand Prix win for Tyrrell. 1982: Michele Alboreto wins in Las Vegas for Tyrrell's first win for four years. 1983: Alboreto wins in Detroit for Tyrrell's last victory to date. 1984: Tyrrell fail to score a point in the Constructors' Championship for the first time. 1989: After six years without success, Jonathan Palmer records the fastest lap in the Canadian Grand Prix.

## Grand Prix Record

| | | |
|---|---|---|
| Contested: | 402 | |
| Victories: | 23 | |
| Pole Positions: | 14 | |
| Fastest Laps: | 20 | |
| Constructors' World Titles: | 1 | (1971) |

| | | |
|---|---|---|
| Drivers' World Championships: | 2 | (1971, 1973) |
| Most Points in a Season: | 82 | (1973) |
| Total World Championship Points: | 617 | |
| Average Points/Grand Prix: | 1.47 | |

## Review

The 1997 season proved to be another disappointing one for the Tyrrell team and this was one of the main points of reflection that came to the fore and was instrumental in prompting Ken Tyrrell to sell his team to British American Racing (BAR) in early December last year. The Reynard/British American Tobacco offer of some £22 million proved too much to pass over for one of the stalwarts of the F1 racing scene.

On the track in 1997, the Ford Cosworth ED V8 engine lacked the power that had been hoped for and, for much of the season, it was a battle between the two Tyrrells and Minardis for the final grid positions.

Grip, or rather lack of it, provided the early problems, however much the driver duo of Salo and Verstappen struggled to generate heat in their tyres. After both cars had failed to complete the Melbourne race, Brazil brought the first finish for both. The driving of Mika Salo improved and he took fifth place in Monaco, where he drove the whole race without a stop. A brave decision that worked. With Verstappen coming home in eighth place, things were looking distinctly better for Tyrrell at that point.

It proved a false dawn though, and the team had only two finishes from its next ten starts. The final phase of the season saw both drivers struggling at the back end of the grid and passing the chequered flag in the tail end of the field of finishers. The only landmark came in Luxembourg when the team competed in its 400th Grand Prix race.

With Salo moving to Arrows and Verstappen retiring, Tyrrell will have a new driver line-up for 1998. They will also have a new Ford V10 engine which should bridge the power gap that hindered performance in 1997.

Prior to the BAR buy-out, the team have also invested heavily by purchasing their own wind tunnel. The 50% tunnel is based at Bournemouth International Airport where it will be shared with team sponsor European Aviation.

For 1998, Tyrrell will continue to compete as such, with the BAR management coming into play for the 1999 season. At the time of writing, it is unclear how much of a role the current Tyrrell management will have to play in its future. One thing is for certain though – the Tyrrell name will continue to be used for the forseeable future to allow the new team to continue to make use of FIA and Concorde signatory funds.

## Drivers and Results 1997

| Driver | Races | Com | Ret | Dnq | HP | Pts | Psn | Comp% |
|--------|-------|-----|-----|-----|-----|-----|------|-------|
| Mika Salo | 17 | 8 | 9 | 0 | 5th | 2 | 17/21 | 47.06% |
| Jos Verstappen | 17 | 9 | 8 | 0 | 8th | 0 | – | 52.94% |
| Aggregate | 34 | 17 | 17 | 0 | – | 2 | 10/10 | 50.00% |

| Grand Prix | | Mika Salo | Jos Verstappen |
|------------|--|-----------|----------------|
| 1 | Australian | Retired | Retired |
| 2 | Brazilian | 13th | 15th |
| 3 | Argentinian | 8th | Retired |
| 4 | San Marino | 9th | 10th |
| 5 | Monaco | 5th | 8th |
| 6 | Spanish | Retired | 11th |
| 7 | Canadian | Retired | Retired |
| 8 | French | Retired | Retired |
| 9 | British | Retired | Retired |
| 10 | German | Retired | 10th |
| 11 | Hungarian | 13th | Retired |
| 12 | Belgian | 11th | 16th |
| 13 | Italian | Retired | Retired |
| 14 | Austrian | Retired | 12th |
| 15 | Luxembourg | 10th | Retired |
| 16 | Japanese | Retired | 13th |
| 17 | European | 12th | 16th |

## Tyrrell 026 Specifications

**Engine:** **Ford ED3 V8**
Injection: Cosworth
Ignition: Cosworth
Spark Plugs: Champion

**Car**
Chassis: Moulded carbon fibre and honeycomb structure
Suspension: Combined spring and damper units operated by push rods and rockers
Brakes: AP Racing.
Instruments: Pi Research System, integrated digital display
Gearbox: Tyrrell longitudinal three-shaft 6-speed unit
Gear Selection: Pneumatic, sequential, semi-automatic
Drive Shafts: Tyrrell Trilobe
Clutch: AP Racing carbon plate
Differential: Tyrrell Viscous Coupling
Tyres: Goodyear

## Engines 1970-98

1970-85: Ford. 1985-86: Renault Turbo. 1987-90: Ford. 1991: Honda. 1992: Ilmor. 1993-96: Yamaha. 1997-98: Ford.

## Drivers 1970-98

1970: J.Stewart & F.Cevert. 1971: J.Stewart & F.Cevert. 1972: J.Stewart & F.Cevert. 1973: J.Stewart & F.Cevert. 1974: J.Scheckter & P.Depailler. 1975: J.Scheckter & P.Depailler. 1976: J.Scheckter & P.Depailler. 1977: R.Peterson & P.Depailler. 1978: P.Depailler & D.Pironi. 1979: J-P.Jarier & D.Pironi. 1980: J-P.Jarrier, D.Daly & M.Thackwell. 1981: E.Cheever, R.Zunino & M.Alboreto. 1982: M.Alboreto, B.Henton & S.Borgudd. 1983: M.Alboreto & D.Sullivan. 1984: S.Bellof, M.Brundle, S.Johansson & M.Thackwell. 1985: M.Brundle, S.Johansson, S.Bellof, I.Capelli & P.Streiff. 1986: M.Brundle & P.Streiff. 1987: J.Palmer & P.Streiff. 1988: J.Palmer & J.Bailey. 1989: J.Palmer, M.Alboreto, J.Alesi & J.Herbert. 1990: S.Nakajima & J.Alesi. 1991: S.Nakajima & S.Modena. 1992: A.de Cesaris & O.Grouillard. 1993: A.de Cesaris & U.Katayama. 1994: U.Katayama & M.Blundell. 1995: U.Katayama, M.Salo & G.Tarquini. 1996: U.Katayama & M.Salo. 1997: J.Verstappen & M.Salo.

## Grand Prix Wins

1971 Spain (Stewart), Monaco (Stewart), France (Stewart), Britain (Stewart), Canada (Stewart), United States (Cevert); 1972 Argentina (Stewart), France (Stewart), Canada (Stewart), United States (Stewart); 1973 South Africa (Stewart), Belgium (Stewart), Monaco (Stewart), Netherlands (Stewart), Germany (Stewart); 1974 Sweden (Scheckter), Britain (Scheckter); 1975 South Africa (Scheckter); 1976 Sweden (Scheckter); 1978 Monaco (Depailler); 1982 Las Vegas (Alboreto); 1983 Detroit (Alboreto).

# Williams

## Winfield Williams

**Williams Grand Prix Engineering Ltd**
Grove, Wantage, Oxfordshire, OX12 0QD
Tel: +44 (0)1235 777700          Fax: +44 (0)1235 764705

| | |
|---|---|
| MD: | Frank Williams |
| Tech. Director: | Patrick Head |
| Team Manager: | Dickie Stanford |
| Chief Designer: | Gavin Fisher |
| Aerodynamicist: | Geoff Willis |
| Senior Ops Eng: | James Robinson |
| Chief Mechanic: | Carl Gaden |
| Drivers/Engineers: | Jacques Villeneuve (1)    /    Jock Clear |
| | Heinz-Harald Frentzen (2)    /    tbc |
| Test Driver: | Juan Pablo Montoya |
| Sponsors: | Winfield, Castrol, Goodyear, Komatsu, Automotive Products, Magneti Marelli, Champion, Sparco, Petrobras, Andersen Consulting, Auto Motor und Sport, Falke, Sonox, Universal Studios, Sparco, Du Pont, OZ Racing, Renault VI, Digital, Telxon, Largotim, Burg-Wachter, Snap-on Tools |

## Brief History

1969: After building his business up, Frank Williams starts running cars. 1970: Piers Courage killed during the Dutch Grand Prix driving a private session. 1973: Entered Formula One under the name of ISO. 1976: Disappointing partnership with oil man Walter Wolf. 1978: Williams Grand Prix Engineering founded. Australian Alan Jones signed to drive. 1979: Clay Regazzoni wins in Britain for Williams' first Grand Prix victory. 1980: Alan Jones wins the Drivers' World Championship with Williams taking the Constructors' title for the first time. 1986: Frank Williams seriously injured in a car crash and confined to a wheelchair. 1992: Nigel Mansell becomes the first driver to win the opening five rounds of a season and achieves a record of nine victories in total as Williams take the Drivers' and Constructors' World Championships. 1993: Alain Prost wins his fourth world title and announces his retirement from the sport. 1994: Williams record their seventh Constructors' Championship victory to bring them level with Lotus in the all-time record. 1996: Williams win eighth Constructors' Championship, Damon Hill wins first Drivers' World Championship, Jacques Villeneuve runner-up in first season. 1997: Williams win ninth Constructors' Championship,

Jacques Villeneuve wins first Drivers' World Championship in only his second season.

## Grand Prix Record

| | | |
|---|---|---|
| Contested: | 316 | |
| Victories: | 103 | |
| Pole Positions: | 108 | |
| Fastest Laps: | 109 | |
| Constructors' World Titles: | 9 | (80, 81, 86, 87, 92, 93, 94, 96, 97) |
| Drivers' World Championships: | 7 | (80, 82, 87, 92, 93, 96, 97) |
| Most Points in a Season: | 175 | (1996) |
| Total World Championship Points: | 1910.5 | |
| Average Points/Grand Prix: | 5.74 | |

## Review

A record ninth Constructors' Cup victory, a second successive World Championship driver and the top two drivers in the World Championship. Yes, another typical year at Williams Grand Prix Engineering Limited. At the end it all came good, but it didn't always look that way during the course of the season.

New boy Heinz-Harald Frentzen took some considerable time to settle in to the team, and it was only in the second half, and in particular the final races of the season, that he looked the driver that had made team owner Frank Williams opt for his signature in place of the then newly crowned world champion Damon Hill. Even so, his lone victory at San Marino was less than what was expected of him, but it came at a time when he was under intense pressure for his lack of form in the opening stages of the season.

Jacques Villeneuve's performance was as expected and, although he failed to finish five races, he won seven victories and was never out of the points in the twelve races he did complete. The Williams tally of 123 points was some way off the 175 that won them the 1997 Constructors' Cup. That, however, was in no small way due to the improvement of Ferrari, who took points on a regular basis and look set to be one of the main rivals to Williams in 1998.

Williams dominated the qualifying in the first half of the season: of the eighteen front row grid positions up until the British Grand Prix, fourteen were occupied by Williams drivers and that included seven pole positions, with the meeting in Buenos Aires being the 100th pole secured by a Williams car. That was recorded by Villeneuve, who made the position his own for the first four races.

Despite some early season reliability problems, which saw five non-finishes up until and including Monaco, the wins, lead by Villeneuve, came quickly to help open up a lead in the championship.

The German Grand Prix at Hockenheim proved to be one of the worst of the season for Williams. It was the first race since Suzuka 1995 that a Williams car hadn't started from the front row of the grid and neither driver managed to finish the race.

Things got back on track at the Hungaroring when Villeneuve took another win. Following the race at Spa, both drivers finished in the points in the remaining races, even though Villeneuve ultimately found himself disqualified from his fifth place at Suzuka when a season of cautions and suspended bans for ignoring waved yellow flags finally caught up with him. By this time, Frentzen had found his form and secured the points in Japan that retained the Constructors' Cup for Williams.

Villeneuve came through his final hurdle in Jerez and deservedly won the Drivers' World Championship, having survived the attentions of the prancing horse, and thus completed the Williams' double-double.

The Jerez race saw the last use of the Renault engine, and their considerable expertise, for some years to come. The team, along with Benetton, will use the Renault-sourced Mecachrome engines for 1998, and this will be an unknown factor in their championship challenge. Villeneuve has proved himself to be an outstanding driver and his record in just two seasons of Formula One would match, if not surpass, that of any other driver of the same period. He knows, and is not afraid to speak, his own mind. Given that the new engine and car match up to the normal Williams specifications, he will undoubtedly be a front-runner during 1998.

Heinz-Harald took time to come to terms with moving from a small team such as Sauber to the pressure cooker world of the top team. Perhaps he was too over-awed about his new status, but given the confidence to impose his own needs and requirements on his team, and his ever-improving form in the final stages of the season, the basis for a more successful season is there. The pressure, though, is unlikely to abate and, in many respects, he will be driving for a 1999 contract.

## Drivers and Results 1997

| Driver | Races | Com | Ret | Dnq | HP | Pts | Psn | Comp% |
|---|---|---|---|---|---|---|---|---|
| Jacques Villeneuve | 17 | 12 | 5 | 0 | 1st | 81 | 1/21 | 70.59% |
| H-H. Frentzen | 17 | 12 | 5 | 0 | 1st | 42 | 3/21 | 70.59% |
| Aggregate | 34 | 24 | 10 | 0 | – | 123 | 1/10 | 70.59% |

| | Grand Prix | Jacques Villeneuve | Heinz-Harald Frentzen |
|---|---|---|---|
| 1 | Australian | Retired | 8th |
| 2 | Brazilian | 1st | 9th |
| 3 | Argentinian | 1st | Retired |
| 4 | San Marino | Retired | 1st |
| 5 | Monaco | Retired | Retired |
| 6 | Spanish | 1st | 8th |

| 7 | Canadian | Retired | 4th |
|---|---|---|---|
| 8 | French | 4th | 2nd |
| 9 | British | 1st | Retired |
| 10 | German | Retired | Retired |
| 11 | Hungarian | 1st | Retired |
| 12 | Belgian | 5th | 3rd |
| 13 | Italian | 5th | 3rd |
| 14 | Austrian | 1st | 3rd |
| 15 | Luxembourg | 1st | 3rd |
| 16 | Japanese | dq (5th) | 2nd |
| 17 | European | 3rd | 6th |

## Williams FW20 Specifications

**Engine:**

| | |
|---|---|
| Cylinders: | 10 in V configuration 67 degrees |
| Valves: | Pneumatically controlled |
| Electronics: | Magneti Marelli |

**Car**

| | |
|---|---|
| Chassis: | Carbon Aramid epoxy composite, manufactured by Williams using Fiberite products |
| Transmission: | Six-speed Williams transverse semi-automatic |
| Clutch: | AP Racing |
| Cooling system: | Two Secan water radiators either side of chassis; two IMI oil radiators |
| Brakes: | Carbone Industrie discs and pads operated by AP callipers |
| Lubricants: | Castrol |
| Tyres: | Goodyear |

## Engines 1973-98

1973-83: Ford. 1984-87: Honda Turbo. 1988: Judd. 1989-97: Renault. 1998: Mecachrome.

## Drivers 1973-97

1973: H.Ganley, H.Pescarolo & N.Galli. 1974: A.Merzario, J-P.Jabouille & T.Belso. 1975: A.Merzario, J.Laffite & J.Scheckter. 1976: J.Ickx, M.Leclerc & A.Merzario. 1977: P.Neve. 1978: A.Jones. 1979: A.Jones & C.Regazzoni. 1980: A.Jones & C.Reutemann. 1981: A.Jones & C.Reutemann. 1982: K.Rosberg, D.Daly, C.Reutemann & M.Andretti. 1983: K.Rosberg, J.Laffite & J.Palmer. 1984: K.Rosberg & J.Laffite. 1985: K.Rosberg & N.Mansell. 1986: N.Mansell & N.Piquet. 1987: N.Mansell, N.Piquet & R.Patrese. 1988: N.Mansell, R.Patrese, M.Brundle & J.Schlesser. 1989: T.Boutsen &

R.Patrese. 1990: T.Boutsen & R.Patrese. 1991: N.Mansell & R.Patrese. 1992: N.Mansell & R.Patrese. 1993: A.Prost & D.Hill. 1994: A.Senna, D.Hill, D.Coulthard & N.Mansell. 1995: D.Hill & D.Coulthard. 1996: D.Hill & J.Villeneuve. 1997-98: J.Villeneuve & H-H.Frentzen.

## Grand Prix Wins

1979 Britain (Regazzoni), Germany (Jones), Austria (Jones), Netherlands (Jones), Canada (Jones); 1980 Argentina (Jones), Monaco (Reutemann), France (Jones), Britain (Jones), Canada (Jones), United States (Jones); 1981 Long Beach (Jones), Brazil (Reutemann), Belgium (Reutemann), Las Vegas (Jones); 1982 Switzerland (Rosberg); 1983 Monaco (Rosberg), 1984 Dallas (Rosberg), 1985 Detroit (Rosberg), Europe (Mansell), South Africa (Mansell), Australia (Rosberg); 1986 Brazil (Piquet), Belgium (Mansell), Canada (Mansell), France (Mansell), Britain (Mansell), Germany (Piquet), Hungary (Piquet), Italy (Piquet), Portugal (Mansell); 1987 San Marino (Mansell), France (Mansell), Britain (Mansell), Germany (Piquet), Hungary (Piquet), Austria (Mansell), Italy (Piquet), Spain (Mansell), Mexico (Mansell); 1989 Canada (Boutsen), Australia (Boutsen); 1990 San Marino (Patrese), Hungary (Boutsen); 1991 Mexico (Patrese), France (Mansell), Britain (Mansell), Germany (Mansell), Italy (Mansell), Portugal (Patrese), Spain (Mansell); 1992 South Africa (Mansell), Mexico (Mansell), Brazil (Mansell), Spain (Mansell), San Marino (Mansell), France (Mansell), Britain (Mansell), Germany (Mansell), Portugal (Mansell), Japan (Riccardo Patrese); 1993 South Africa (Prost), San Marino (Prost), Spain (Prost), Canada (Prost), France (Prost), Britain (Prost), Germany (Prost), Hungary (Hill), Belgium (D.Hill), Italy (D.Hill); 1994 Spain (D.Hill), Britain (D.Hill), Belgium (D.Hill), Italy (D.Hill), Portugal (D.Hill), Japan (D.Hill), Australia (Mansell); 1995 Argentina (D.Hill), San Marino (D.Hill), Hungary (D.Hill), Portugal (Coulthard), Australia (D.Hill); 1996: Australia (D.Hill), Brazil (D.Hill), Argentina (D.Hill), Europe (J.Villeneuve), San Marino (D.Hill), Canada (D.Hill), France (D.Hill), Britain (J.Villeneuve), Germany (D.Hill), Hungary (J.Villeneuve), Portugal (J.Villeneuve), Japan (D.Hill). 1997: Brazil (J.Villeneuve), Argentina (J.Villeneuve), San Marino (Frentzen), Spain (J.Villeneuve), Britain (J.Villeneuve), Hungary (J.Villeneuve), Austria (J.Villeneuve), Luxembourg (J.Villeneuve).

# Retired Teams

# Lola

## Mastercard Lola Formula One Team

**Lola Cars**
Cleb Road, St Peters Hill, Huntingdon, Cambridgeshire, PE18 7DS
Tel: +44 (0)1480 451301          Fax: +44 (0)1480 456722

### Grand Prix Record

| | | |
|---|---|---|
| Contested: | 0 | (158) |
| Victories: | 0 | (0) |
| Pole Positions: | 0 | (1) |
| Fastest Laps: | 0 | (0) |
| Constructors' World Titles: | 0 | (Best: 4th 1962) |
| Drivers' World Championships: | 0 | |
| Most Points in a Season: | 0 | |
| Total World Championship Points: | 0 | (46) |

*(Figures in brackets are those achieved by teams using Lola chassis.)*

### Review

When the Huntingdon-based Lola team declared they were going to enter the 1997 Formula One championship, there was a good deal of mixed reaction. Here was one of the world's leading racing car manufacturers with over 40 years in the business, with great pedigree and no little success in areas such as IndyCar racing. Yet, the announcement to many came too close to the start of the season without any chance to run, plan and develop or to secure the sort of multi-million-pound deals required to run a mediocre team, let alone one looking to challenge in the tradition of Lola.

The key to it all was the announcement of a sponsorship coup by luring credit card giant Mastercard to become its main provider. Yet the deal, which seemed to have been based around selling new credit card subscriptions to F1 enthusiasts, ultimately proved problematic according to Lola Boss Eric Broadley, because funding was 'not forthcoming'.

The car, the T97/30, had little chance. Without any development or testing with the aid of a wind tunnel it was always going to be hopelessly off the pace. So it proved with drivers Sospiri and Rosset, finishing qualifying in Melbourne well outside the 107% qualifying cut-off. Handling and a problem in the software controlling the semi-automatic gearbox were reported as being the primary problems that caused qualifying failure, but the team had completed just a handful of laps with the Ford-powered engine and was generally regarded as too new by one and all. Sospiri and Rosset had tried their best, but they were an amazing eleven seconds off the qualifying pace.

Following Australia, the team pulled out of the two South American Grands Prix with an aim to re-launch their challenge on the European circuit. But, by the time the Brazilian meeting dawned, the team was almost no more, owing some £6 million and with less than £500,000 in assets. Half of the debt was owed to the parent company, Lola Cars, which itself went into receivership with the F1 arm not long after. Lola Cars were, thankfully, eventually saved, but this will serve as a lesson for any prospective new teams looking to enter the fray too soon and too quickly in the future.

## Drivers and Results 1997

| Driver | Races | Com | Ret | Dnq | HP | Pts | Psn | Comp% |
|--------|-------|-----|-----|-----|-----|-----|-----|-------|
| Ricardo Rossett | 0 | – | – | – | – | – | – | 0.00 |
| Vincenzo Sospiri | 0 | – | – | – | – | – | – | 0.00 |
| Aggregate | 0 | – | – | – | – | – | – | 0.00 |

| Grand Prix | Ricardo Rossett | Vincenzo Sospiri |
|------------|-----------------|------------------|
| 1  Australian | dnq – 107% | dnq – 107% |

## Engines 1997

1997: Ford.

## Drivers 1997

1997: R.Rosset & V.Sospiri.

# Circuit Directory

# A1-Ring

**A1-Ring**
**Austrian Grand Prix – 26 July 1998**
**Lap Distance:**   2.684 miles/4.321 km – Clockwise
**Race Distance:**  190.564 miles/306.808 km – 71 laps

The A1-Ring is an updated and re-designed version of the famous old Österreichring. It lies in a green, hilly area of Austria known as Styria, roughly central in a triangle formed by the cities of Vienna, Salzburg and Graz.

Originally built in 1968, a total of eighteen Grands Prix were held there between 1970 and 1987, with the final event needing three starts to get it underway! It came back onto the calender last season after £17 million had been spent on it to turn the circuit into one of the most modern in the world. The circuit has a square feel to it and combines a number of long straights with tight and sweeping corners that will test drivers and keep teams on their toes when it comes to car set-ups.

## The Circuit

The starting line and grid are located in front of the medical centre and from here the cars power their way down past the garages in top gear at 180 mph. Changing down and braking hard, the **Castrol Kurve** is a sharp right-hand turn that is taken in 2nd gear at 70 mph. Once through the turn the cars come out on to the fastest part of the circuit and a near straight that is over half a mile in length. At a top speed of 180 mph, the stands of the Naturtribune West flash past on the left as the track curves slightly out to the left.

At the end of the straight the **Remus Kurve** looms – very tight, it takes the cars through 150 degrees. It is the hardest braking point in the circuit with drivers pulling -3.6 g as they decelerate hard to 40 mph at the apex of the corner. Out of here is another long straight, only slightly shorter than the one leading into the Remus Kurve and just as as fast as it passes in front of the Naturtribune Nord stands. The end of this straight marks the entry to the most curvaceous part of the circuit which swings inside and out.

The **Gosset Kurve** is a double right-hand turn, the 50 mph 2nd-gear entry being slower than the shallower exit which can be negotiated in 4th gear at 110 mph. The **Niki Lauda Kurve** is an open sweeping turn around to the left, taken at 90 mph in 3rd gear, and leading into another similar turn called the **Power Horse Kurve** which is marginally faster at 100 mph.

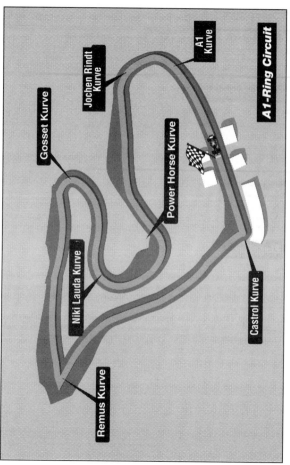

A1-Ring Circuit

A1 Kurve

Jochen Rindt Kurve

Gosset Kurve

Power Horse Kurve

Niki Lauda Kurve

Castrol Kurve

Remus Kurve

Out on to a shorter straight, the cars run parallel to the Start-Finish line at 175 mph as they approach the **Jochen Rindt Kurve**. This is an open right-hand turn that is taken in 4th gear at 105 mph and leads into a short straight from where cars can re-enter the pit lane. The **A1 Kurve** slows the cars down through 3rd gear at 85 mph as they turn right before accelerating out along the straight across the Start-Finish line.

## 5-Year Record

| Year | 1st | 2nd | 3rd | 4th | 5th | 6th |
|------|-----|-----|-----|-----|-----|-----|
| 1987 | Mansell | Piquet | Fabi | Boutsen | Senna | Prost |
| | (Williams) | (Williams) | (Benetton) | (Benetton) | (Lotus) | (McLaren) |

*1988-1996 no races held at circuit.*

| | | | | | | |
|------|-----|-----|-----|-----|-----|-----|
| 1997 | Villeneuve | Coulthard | Frentzen | Fisichella | R.Schumacher | M.Schumacher |
| | (Williams) | (McLaren) | (Williams) | (Jordan) | (Jordan) | (Ferrari) |

## Qualifying

*1997*
Villeneuve (Williams)
1:10.304

## Notebook

Jacques Villeneuve's win last season was his sixth of the season and pole position was eighth of the year. Gerhard Berger was the only driver on the grid who had previously competed in an Austrian Grand Prix. Heinz-Harald Frentzen's third place was the third successive finish in that position following races at Spa and Monza.

Brazilian Tarso Marques was not allowed to start last year's Austrian Grand Prix after his Minardi was found to be underweight when it was weighed after the qualifying session. He had qualified in 21st place.

# Buenos Aires

## Autodromo de la Ciudad de Buenos Aires
## Argentine Grand Prix – 12 April 1998
**Lap Distance:**  2.64 miles/4.259 km – Clockwise
**Race Distance:** 190.08 miles/306.654 km – 72 laps

The Autodromo is located in the park Almirante Brown on the southern outskirts of the city of Buenos Aires. The track was originally built with the support of President Peron, in the era of the legendary Juan Manuel Fangio. First used in 1952, the Grand Prix returned to Buenos Aires after an absence of fourteen years. It was the site of the first F1 race to incur fatalities when Farina's Ferrari killed nine spectators in the first race to be held there in 1953.

Grip, grip, grip! The overriding factor at the Autodromo in three words. It is one of the smallest circuits but is technically difficult because of its low speed corners, twisty nature and also the change in gradient – the track goes up and down and as such can be a little bumpy. Because of these factors, cars need to be set up for maximum grip so they tend to be set with a high degree of wing level to ensure maximum downforce. Passing is not impossible but very difficult and is often best attempted on the Start/Finish straight.

## The Circuit

Off the starting straight and up to top gear and 180 mph as drivers approach the **Curvón**. Braking hard and pulling -3.4g into this first corner, turning to the right at 60 mph in 2nd gear. Cars accelerate out into a shallow right-hand bend which is taken at 140 mph. After a short straight the **Curva de la Confiteria** is an inner left-hand loop that is entered at 155 mph in 5th gear, quickly changing down to 2nd gear and 60 mph at its apex. A change to 3rd gear and the loop is exited at about 110 mph.

The **No 8 Curvon** marks the end of the inner loop as the cars sweep tightly back round on themselves in 3rd gear at 80 mph. Coming out of the turn, the drivers find themselves on the second longest straight (0.25 miles) which is taken at 180 mph slowing to 165 mph as they enter the sweeping right-hander of the **Curva de Ascari**. As the curve straightens out the entry to the Esses approaches fast and cars are hard on the brakes (-3.1g).

The **Entrata a los mixtos** (Extrada a Esses) is a tight hairpin which is taken in 2nd gear at a sedate 55 mph before entering the Esses at **Viborita** which is a double sweep left and then right, both in 3rd gear, but slowing from 95 mph to about 75 mph as the Esses are completed.

**Curva del Ombú** is a bend taken in 2nd gear at about 75 mph. This used to signal the end of the lap before the circuit was re-designed. Now though , the drivers continue down a shortened version of the old pit lane to the left right wiggle that marks the **Senna S**. What used to be called Tobogan is approached in 5th gear at 150 mph, after which a rapid change down reduces speed to 55 mph through the S bend. Hard on the accelerator out of Senna, up to 155 mph in 5th gear, and then comes **Horquilla**, braking hard back down to 2nd gear and 55 mph. The final 90-degree bend brings the cars out onto **Tribunas** the longest straight (about 0.5 miles) and it's full speed ahead and across the finishing line in 6th gear at 180 mph.

## 3-Year Record

| Year | 1st | 2nd | 3rd | 4th | 5th | 6th |
|------|-----|-----|-----|-----|-----|-----|
| 1995 | Hill | Alesi | M.Schumacher | Herbert | Frentzen | Berger |
| | (Williams) | (Ferrari) | (Benetton) | (Benetton) | (Sauber) | (Ferrari) |
| 1996 | Hill | Villeneuve | Alesi | Barrichello | Irvine | Verstappen |
| | (Williams) | (Williams) | (Benetton) | (Jordan) | (Ferrari) | (Arrows) |
| 1997 | Villeneuve | Irvine | R.Schumacher | Herbert | Hakkinen | Berger |
| | (Williams) | (Ferrari) | (Jordan) | (Sauber) | (McLaren) | (Benetton) |

## Qualifying

| 1997 | 1996 | 1995 |
|------|------|------|
| Villeneuve (Williams) | Hill (Williams) | Coulthard (Williams) |
| 1:24.473 | 1:30.346 | 1:53.241 |

## Notebook

Jacques Villeneuve's pole position was the 100th won by a Williams driver – it was also the 125th pole position secured by a Renault engine. It was the Jordan team's 100th Grand Prix appearance and the 600th Grand Prix held. No less than nine drivers on the grid for the Argentine Grand Prix had previously driven for the Jordan team at some level. Jacques Villeneuve's win equalled that of his late father Gilles' record of six Grand Prix victories.

Damon Hill was the only previous winner of the Argentine Grand Prix on the grid in1997. Of the fourteen drivers who have won the Argentine Grand Prix, only three have failed to win a World Championship title. They are Stirling Moss, Bruce McLaren and Jacques Laffite.

The organisers of the Argentine Grand Prix were fined $10,000 after the red flag was shown instead of a yellow flag following a collision involving Michael Schumacher, Rubens Barrichello and David Coulthard at the first bend.

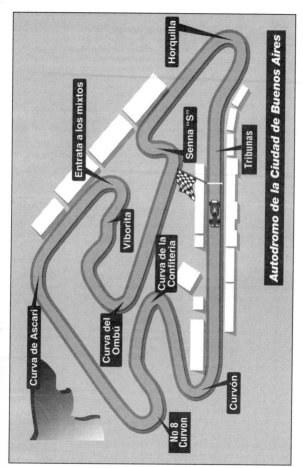

**Autodromo de la Ciudad de Buenos Aires**

Horquilla

Entrata a los mixtos

Senna "S"

Tribunas

Viborita

Curva de la Confitería

Curva de Ascari

Curva del Ombú

Curvón

No 8 Curvon

193

# Catalunya

**Circuit de Catalunya**
**Spanish Grand Prix, Barcelona – 5 May 1998**
**Lap Distance:**   2.937 miles/4.727 km – Clockwise
**Race Distance:** 191.69 miles/307.255 km – 65 laps

Located twelve miles north-east of Barcelona, Catalunya is one of five circuits to play host to the Spanish Grand Prix. Held here since 1991, the circuit continues to be improved and upgraded on an annual basis, making it one of the most advanced circuits in the world. Despite that, it remains bumpy and the track surface has ripples on it, complete with demanding fast corners and long high straights. In many respects the circuit is like Estoril, but it has many more run-off areas which make it popular with the drivers from a safety point of view.

Technically, the circuit is challenging with a good mixture of slow 2nd-gear and fast 4th-gear corners. Setup is of paramount importance as teams try to trade the downforce they require for corners with reduction in drag for the fast straights. Generally, a neutral chassis setting is opted for which helps with understeer in the long corners. Tyre wear is high due to the abrasive nature of the track surface.

## The Circuit

From the starting line cars accelerate downhill at 190 mph to **Elf**. The approach to Elf is downhill until almost the corner itself when it rises to the left. Braking hard at -3.8 g, this corner is taken in 3rd gear at 85 mph on the inside so that the car can drift out to the left for the next bend taken in 4th at around 100 mph. **Curvone Renault** is the first long, sweeping 180-degree right-hander, entered in 4th gear at 100 mph with 140 mph attained during its course.

Out of Renault and accelerating to about 180 mph before the circuit loops back on itself at **Revolt Repsol**. Entered in 2nd gear at 85 mph, cars catapult out up to 155 mph and in 5th gear along a short straight to **Revolt Seat**. Hard on the brakes, this tight left-hand hairpin drops the cars downhill at around 60 mph through a gentle left-handed sweep at 160 mph before braking again to enter **Revolt Würth**. Here, the track takes a sharp left-hand turn which is almost 90 degrees and is entered in 2nd gear at 85 mph. On exit, the circuit turns slightly right as 5th gear and 155 mph is reached.

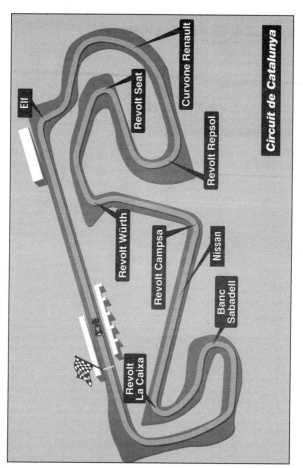

Circuit de Catalunya

Curvone Renault

Revolt Seat

Elf

Revolt Repsol

Revolt Würth

Revolt Campsa

Nissan

Banc Sabadell

Revolt La Caixa

**Revolt Campsa** is a blind right-hander but can be navigated safely in 5th at 135 mph. Then it's down the short straight called **Nissan** in top gear at 185 mph, on the run into 180 degree hairpin **Revolt La Caixa,** which is taken in 2nd gear at 65 mph as it climbs to the right into the two 100-degree bends at **Banc Sabadell**. Entered in 3rd at 80 mph, it is exited in 5th gear as the car accelerates towards the penultimate corner, another right-hander that turns into a short straight leading to the final bend which is taken in 5th gear at about 140 mph. On to the Start-Finish straight where cars reach a maximum of 190 mph on the kilometre-long straight.

## 3-Year Record

| Year | 1st | 2nd | 3rd | 4th | 5th | 6th |
|------|-----|-----|-----|-----|-----|-----|
| 1995 | M.Schumacher (Benetton) | Herbert (Benetton) | Berger (Ferrari) | Hill (Williams) | Irvine (Jordan) | Panis (Ligier) |
| 1996 | M.Schumacher (Ferrari) | Alesi (Benetton) | Villeneuve (Williams) | Frentzen (Sauber) | Hakkinen (Jordan) | Diniz (Ligier) |
| 1997 | Villeneuve (Williams) | Panis (Prost) | Alesi (Benetton) | M.Schumacher (Ferrari) | Herbert (Sauber) | Coulthard (McLaren) |

## Qualifying

| 1997 | 1996 | 1995 |
|------|------|------|
| Villeneuve (Williams) | Hill (Williams) | M.Schumacher (Benetton) |
| 1:16.525 | 1:20.650 | 1:21.452 |

## Notebook

Williams gained their tenth consecutive pole position in Barcelona at the 1997 race. Both front row positions were occupied by Williams drivers for the fourth time in the season. Jacques Villeneuve's win gave Goodyear their 350th Grand Prix victory.

The Spanish Grand Prix has produced both the largest and shortest winning margins in Grand Prix history. Jackie Stewart finished two laps in front of second-placed McLaren at Montjuic Park in 1968. Eighteen years later Ayrton Senna beat Nigel Mansell by just 0.014 of a second at Jerez.

# Hockenheim

**Hockenheimring**
**German Grand Prix – 2 August 1998**
**Lap Distance:**   4.239 miles/6.829 km – Clockwise
**Race Distance:** 190.755 miles/309.305 km – 45 laps

Located some fifty miles south of Frankfurt and fifteen miles west of Heidelberg, the circuit was originally built as a test circuit for Mercedes cars. The German Grand Prix has been staged here since 1986 and it is, for the majority, an open circuit that is very fast throughout. The exception to this is the stadium complex near the starting grid where the track twists back and forth through 360 degrees in front of the grandstands.

This makes it a very difficult circuit to set up for. Car settings are compromised for top speeds down the straights and downforce on the slow corners. At over four miles in length, it is one of the longest Grand Prix circuits, and it is often more infamously remembered as the circuit that took the life of Jim Clarke in April 1968. Weather is often very changeable as the circuit winds its way through dense pine forests which can create dangerous patches of fog and mist.

## The Circuit

From the Start-Finish line, cars approach **Nord Kurve**, a fast right-hander that is taken in 4th gear at 125 mph and exited in 5th ready to move up to top gear and accelerating to around 210 mph for the long run to the first chicane. The posthumously named **Jim Clark Kurve** slows cars to 2nd gear as they brake hard at -3.2g, decelerating to 60 mph before accelerating back up to 200 mph deep into the forest.

Before the **Ostkurve**, the drivers get busy. The previous straight turns into a sharp right-left turn taken in 2nd gear at 50 mph before it becomes a long right-hand bend about 350 metres before Ostkurve is entered – a chicane which is a right-left taken in 2nd gear leading into a long, fast right-hander and on to the next straight. The **Ayrton Senna Kurve**, which is also known as Bremskurve 3, is approached down the back straight at 205 mph. The left-right turn slows the cars drastically to 60 mph as it's taken in 2nd gear and then it's full-power as the cars accelerate back up to 195 mph before the stadium complex begins to come into view.

The Agip Kurve is a fast right-hander that is taken in 4th gear at 105 mph and leads quickly into the **Sachs Kurve** as drivers shift down to a 60 mph 2nd gear for the hairpin that has a well-earned reputation for being slippery. The final section in the stadium complex that leads back to the start line, the **Süd** or **Opel Kurve**, is a double-apex hairpin with both right-handers taken in 3rd gear at an average of 90 mph and leading into the finishing straight where cars can accelerate to 175 mph.

## 5-Year Record

| Year | 1st | 2nd | 3rd | 4th | 5th | 6th |
|------|-----|-----|-----|-----|-----|-----|
| 1993 | Prost (Williams) | M.Schumacher (Benetton) | Brundell (Ligier) | Senna (McLaren) | Patrese (Benetton) | Berger (Ferrari) |
| 1994 | Berger (Ferrari) | Panis (Ligier) | Bernard (Ligier) | Fittipaldi (Arrows) | Morbidelli (Arrows) | Comas (Larrousse) |
| 1995 | M.Schumacher (Benetton) | Coulthard (Williams) | Berger (Ferrari) | Herbert (Benetton) | Boullion (Sauber) | Suzuki (Ligier) |
| 1996 | Hill (Williams) | Alesi (Benetton) | Villeneuve (Williams) | M.Schumacher (Ferrari) | Coulthard (McLaren) | Barrichello (Jordan) |
| 1997 | Berger (Benetton) | M.Schumacher (Ferrari) | Hakkinen (Benetton) | Trulli (Mclaren) | R.Schumacher (Prost) | Alesi (Ligier) |

## Qualifying

| 1997 | 1996 | 1995 |
|------|------|------|
| Berger (Benetton) | Hill (Williams) | Hill (Williams) |
| 1:41.873 | 1:43.912 | 1:44.385 |

## Notebook

Having had a victory in 1996 taken from him when his car failed just two laps from victory, Gerhard Berger marked his return to F1 racing, after a three-race lay-off through illness and the loss of his father, with a win. His pole position was the twelfth of his career. The victory was his tenth and he also recorded the twenty-first fastest lap of his career.

Jarno Trulli, driving a Prost, scored his first championship points when he finished in fourth place. Michael Schumacher was fined $5,000 after last year's race for speeding in the pit lane on the Saturday.

Grand Prix racing was first staged in Hungary in 1986 with Nelson Piquet winning for Williams.

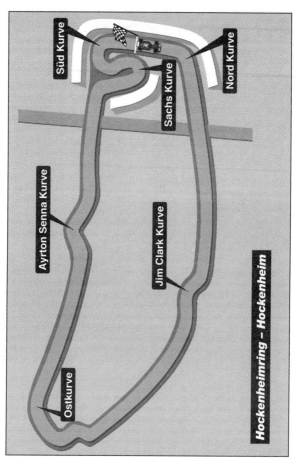

Süd Kurve

Nord Kurve

Sachs Kurve

Ayrton Senna Kurve

Jim Clark Kurve

Ostkurve

*Hockenheimring – Hockenheim*

199

# Hungaroring

**Hungaroring**
**Hungarian Grand Prix – 16 August 1998**
**Lap Distance**   2.465 miles/3.968 km – Clockwise
**Race Distance**   189.805 miles/305.586 km – 77 laps

Just twelve miles to the north-east of Budapest, Hungaroring is a modern Grand Prix complex that has been created with F1 in mind. It has hosted the Hungarian Grand Prix since 1986 but is not the best liked of tracks amongst the drivers. Bumpy and slippery, there is limited scope for overtaking with no fast corners, which can make the race rather processional in nature. Grid position is therefore all important, as is a high downforce and the circuit is second only to Monaco in this respect.

## The Circuit

From the Start-Finish line it's full power to **Turn 1** with speeds approaching 175 mph. Turn 1 is a long, right-hand downhill bend taking the drivers through 180 degrees, entered in 3rd gear at 75 mph, exited in 4th at 135 mph. The camber on this corner can also catch drivers out or, at the very least, see them slipping out of the drive line and into the dirty sections of the track, which does not benefit their tyres or subsequent grip. Entry and exit positions are also important as the corner is blind. A short straight brings the cars into **Turn 2** and then **Turn 3** and here there is a choice of two lines, but whether the car turns in early or late makes little difference to the amount of oversteer experienced as this long left-hander begins to sweep right. Turn 2 is entered at 135 mph, slowing to 70 mph before accelerating out of Turn 3 at 115 mph.

Cars approach **Turn 4** leaving the straight at around 170 mph, changing down from top to 4th gear while braking to 110 mph before climbing uphill on the approach to **Turn 5** – another long right-hander negotiated in 3rd gear at 80 mph and accelerated out of in 4th gear to 150 mph.

**Turn 6** leads to the highest part of the circuit and is a right-left chicane that is entered in 2nd gear at 55 mph and exited in 5th at 115 mph. **Turn 7** comes quickly and the approach to this left-hander is bumpy. Third gear maintained throughout, 75 mph being the slowest point at the apex of the curve. **Turn 8** is a right-hander and is taken in 3rd gear at 85 mph with the left-hander taken flat out. A curving straight forms **Turn 9** and leads into **Turn 10** which is not as fast as it looks as the corner suddenly tightens. It is taken in 4th at 110 mph.

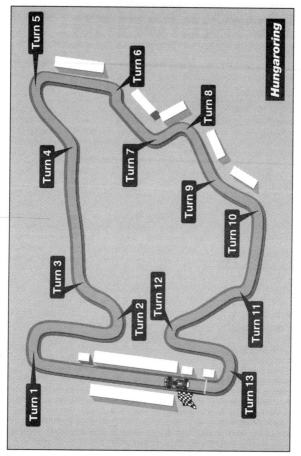

**Turn 11** is an off-camber and downhill right-left chicane which always seems to gather particles of grit, whilst a high kerb awaits the unsuspecting at the second apex. It is taken in 3rd gear at 90 mph. **Turn 12** is almost a hairpin-like corner directly behind the pits and it's taken in 2nd at 60 mph. A long right-hander marks **Turn 13**, which mirrors Turn 1. Through it, the cars first oversteer, turning to understeer by the time they exit on to the straight via the kerb. Around 80 mph sees the cars through the apex of the curve from which they power towards 175 mph as they flash across the Start-Finish line.

## 5-Year Record

| Year | 1st | 2nd | 3rd | 4th | 5th | 6th |
|------|-----|-----|-----|-----|-----|-----|
| 1993 | Hill (Williams) | Patrese (Benetton) | Berger (Ferrari) | Warwick (Footwork) | Brundle (Ligier) | Wendlinger (Sauber) |
| 1994 | M.Schumacher (Benetton) | Hill (Williams) | Verstappen (Benetton) | Brundle (McLaren) | Blundell (Tyrrell) | Panis (Ligier) |
| 1995 | Hill (Williams) | Coulthard (Williams) | Berger (Ferrari) | Herbert (Benetton) | Frentzen (Sauber) | Panis (Ligier) |
| 1996 | Villeneuve (Williams) | Hill (Williams) | Alesi (Benetton) | Hakkinen (McLaren) | Panis (Ligier) | Barrichello (Jordan) |
| 1997 | Villeneuve (Williams) | Hill (Arrows) | Herbert (Sauber) | M.Schumacher (Ferrari) | R.Schumacher (Jordan) | Nakano (Prost) |

## Qualifying

| 1997 | 1996 | 1995 |
|------|------|------|
| M.Schumacher (Ferrari) | M.Schumacher (Ferrari) | Hill (Williams) |
| 1:14.672 | 1:17.129s | 1:16.982 |

## Notebook

Jacques Villeneuve secured his second successive win at the Hungarian Grand Prix in 1997 and will be looking for his hat-trick in 1998. Last year's race though, will be remembered as the one where Damon Hill nearly pulled off what would have been arguably his greatest-ever victory. Leading the race with under two laps to go, a hydraulic problem slowed his car and allowed Villeneuve to overtake him almost on the line. Hill became only the fifth Arrows driver to secure a second-place finish. Hill has never finished outside of the top two positions in a Hungarian Grand Prix.

The Sauber team were fined $25,000 by FIA stewards after fuel samples taken from their cars after practice were not the same as the fuel that had been approved for them prior to the event. Jos Verstappen was fined $5,000 for speeding in the pit lane.

# Imola

## Autodromo Enzo and Dino Ferrari
## San Marino Grand Prix – 26 April 1998

**Lap Distance:**  3.063 miles/4.931 km – Anticlockwise
**Race Distance:** 189.906 miles/305.749 km – 62 laps

Located in north-central Italy in the principality of San Marino, Imola provides one of the most atmospheric race days anywhere in the World. Major modifications have been made to the very fast circuit in the wake of the 1994 event in which Ayrton Senna and Roland Ratzenberger lost their lives. This brought revision to Tamburello, Villeneuve and Variante Bassa which have now made the circuit a low-to-medium speed track which requires a lot of heavy braking. Medium downforce is required and teams usually have stiffer than normal settings for stability when braking; as such, this can hinder grip.

## The Circuit

**Tamburello** is the first corner from the start and cars brake heavily at its entrance. The corner is a left-handed S-bend which is entered in 3rd gear at 75 mph and exited in 4th gear at 125 mph as cars power up the straight to **Villeneuve**. This is a second S-bend that slows the approach to the forthcoming hairpin and slows cars down from 130 mph to 105 mph in 4th gear. Accelerating quickly up to 150 mph, cars almost immediately brake for **Tosa**, a tight hairpin from right to left taken in 2nd gear at around 55 mph. On exit, cars accelerate to 175 mph and climb towards **Piratella**. This is a somewhat blind left-hander that pulls -3.5g as drivers brake at its entrance, it is taken in 4th gear at 100 mph and accelerated away from at 160 mph. Despite its nature it is a corner well liked by most drivers.

The approach to **Acque Minerali** is downhill at 130 mph – a very bumpy and uncomfortable chicane that turns slowly right and finally sharply right with cars down to 70 mph and 3rd gear at its tightest point. Pulling away the track swings slightly left at 100 mph.

**Variante Alta** is next and, coming off a short straight, it is a fast chicane that can be tackled in 3rd gear – it certainly requires a 3rd-gear exit. It is entered in 6th gear at 170 mph and speeds of 75 mph are maintained through it. Drivers tend to take more chances at this chicane because it does have a safe run-off area.

Out of the chicane and the track plunges downhill through some stunning countryside, arriving at a sharpish double left-hander called **Rivazza** which swings the cars through 180 degrees. This requires very hard braking, down from 6th (180 mph) to 3rd gear (60 mph) at its entrance where a massive -3.8 g really tests the driver's strength. Shifting up briefly before changing down to tackle the final turn, which is taken at 80 mph, the cars arrive on a curving right-hand line and fly through the **Variante Bassa**, accelerating all the time up to 170 mph. The **Tragurdo** then looms up as a left-right chicane that feeds the pits and is taken in 2nd gear at around 55 mph. Cars then accelerate to 185 mph across the Start-Finish line.

## 3-Year Record

| Year | 1st | 2nd | 3rd | 4th | 5th | 6th |
|------|-----|-----|-----|-----|-----|-----|
| 1995 | Hill (Williams) | Alesi (Ferrari) | Berger (Ferrari) | Coulthard (Williams) | Hakkinen (McLaren) | Frentzen (Sauber) |
| 1996 | Hill (Williams) | M.Schumacher (Ferrari) | Berger (Benetton) | Irvine (Ferrari) | Barrichello (Jordan) | Alesi (Benetton) |
| 1997 | Frentzen (Williams) | M.Schumacher (Ferrari) | Irvine (Ferrari) | Fisichella (Jordan) | Alesi (Benetton) | Hakkinen (McLaren) |

## Qualifying

| 1997 | 1996 | 1995 |
|------|------|------|
| Villeneuve (Williams) | M.Schumacher (Ferrari) | M.Schumacher (Benetton) |
| 1:23.303 | 1:26.890 | 1:27.274 |

## Notebook

Jacques Villeneuve gained his fifth consecutive pole position at Imola in 1997 and Damon Hill and Michael Schumacher were the only two previous winners of the race on the grid at Imola. Heinz-Harald Frentzen's first Grand Prix victory came in his fourth Grand Prix for Williams – Jacques Villeneuve had also secured his first Williams win in his fourth race.

Johnny Herbert celebrated his 100th Grand Prix appearance at last year's race while Gerhard Berger made his 200th Grand Prix appearance.

Both Williams drivers (Frentzen and Villeneuve) received a one-race ban, suspended for two races, after the Imola stewards found them guilty of failing to observe a waved yellow flag. Italian Nicola Larini was fined $5,000 for speeding in the pit lane during qualifying.

Ralf Schumacher, Shinji Nakano, Jarno Trulli and Jan Magnussen all made their San Marino debuts.

Gilles Villeneuve completed his last Grand Prix at Imola in 1982.

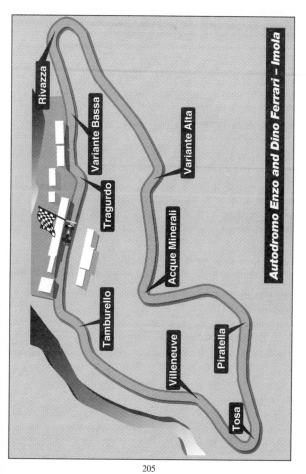

**Autodromo Enzo and Dino Ferrari – Imola**

Rivazza

Variante Bassa

Tragurdo

Variante Alta

Acque Minerali

Tamburello

Villeneuve

Piratella

Tosa

# Interlagos

**Autodromo Jose Carlos Pace**
**Brazilian Grand Prix – 29 March 1998**
**Lap Distance:**   2.684 miles/4.325 km – Anticlockwise
**Race Distance:** 190.77 miles/306.075 km – 71 laps

Located ten miles south of central Sao Paulo, the track is named after Carlos Pace who won here in 1975. It has staged the Brazilian GP since 1991. The track was resurfaced for the 1995 season and re-worked for the 1997 race, but the majority of drivers complain that it is still extremely bumpy. It remains one of the most tiring circuits that taxes even the fittest of drivers, not least because it undulates throughout its course. Cars will generally be set with a medium amount of wing, with downforce settings ranging from medium to high. The high humidity and track temperatures during March normally ensure that cars are set to maintain maximum grip on the track.

## The Circuit

At the start, the cars race down to the **Descida do Sol** which drops downhill to the left. It is approached in 6/7th gear at about 180 mph. Then braking very hard (-3.3g), the cars approach the **S do Senna** – a left-right-left section which begins with Curva 1, one of just two places were you might get to see overtaking manoeuvres as they try to out-brake one another. Cars take this corner in 2nd gear at 60 mph changing up to 3rd gear and accelerating through 100 mph towards the final turn in the sequence (Curva do Sol) and a 4th gear 140 mph. Hard on the throttle, cars accelerate to 180 mph along the **Reta Oposta** straight in top gear at 180 mph.

The **Descida do Lago** is a tight left-hand corner to which there is a bumpy entrance, which often throws rash drivers into a spin. Those who get through it take it in 3rd gear at 85 mph, having braked hard at its entrance. Drivers who get it right can often get past those who don't at this point. After a short straight, another left-hander (135 mph in 4th gear) swings the cars back on themselves as they accelerate to 170 mph before braking hard at the entrance to Ferradura.

The **Ferradura** is a sweeping, double apex right-hander with an extremely bumpy entrance. Probably the most difficult corner on the circuit as it is approached downhill and at speed – 5th gear at 165 mph. After going through the first apex in 3rd gear at around 100 mph, the car drifts out for the second apex and, on exiting at the top in 3rd, another right-hander is on top of you

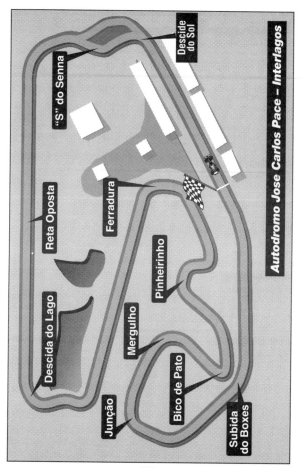

Autodromo Jose Carlos Pace – Interlagos

Descide do Sol

"S" do Senna

Reta Oposta

Ferradura

Descida do Lago

Pinheirinho

Mergulho

Junção

Bico de Pato

Subida do Boxes

almost immediately as Pinheirinho approaches which is taken in 2nd gear at about 55 mph.

The **Pinheirinho** is a very tight left-hander that is only taken in 2nd gear at 60 mph, exited in 3rd gear, and then it's up to 4th for the approach to another tight corner, this time with a right-hand turn. The **Bico de Pato** (also known as Cotovêlo) is taken in 2nd at just over 70 mph and exited in 3rd gear, climbing to 5th as the car makes for a left-hander prior to turning for **Mergulho**. This sweeping corner is taken in 4th gear at 145 mph before accelerating along to the 3rd-gear **Junção**.

**Subida do Boxes** marks the entrance to two left-handed curves, both banked and going up hill. The first is approached at 110 mph and is followed by **Arquebancada**, which is taken in 5th gear at 160 mph. Acceleration continues as the Start-Finish line straight comes into view and is crossed at about 185 mph.

## 3-Year Record

| Year | 1st | 2nd | 3rd | 4th | 5th | 6th |
|------|-----|-----|-----|-----|-----|-----|
| 1995 | M.Schumacher (Benetton) | Coulthard (Williams) | Berger (Ferrari) | Hakkinen (McLaren) | Alesi (Ferrari) | Blundell (McLaren) |
| 1996 | Hill (Williams) | Alesi (Benetton) | M.Schumacher (Ferrari) | Hakkinen (McLaren) | Salo (Tyrrell) | Panis (Ligier) |
| 1997 | Villeneuve (Williams) | Berger (Benetton) | Panis (Prost) | Hakkinen (McLaren) | M.Schumacher (Ferrari) | Alesi (Benetton) |

## Qualifying

| 1997 | 1996 | 1995 |
|------|------|------|
| Villeneuve (Williams) | Hill (Williams) | Hill (Williams) |
| 1:16.004 | 1:18.111 | 1:20.081 |

## Notebook

Last year's race had to be restarted – it was stopped on the first lap – so the stricken Stewart Ford of local hero Rubens Barrichello could be removed after it failed to leave the starting grid. Teammate Jan Magnussen was one of several drivers to spin out on the first lap, but Magnussen was unable to join the restart as Barrichello took the spare car. The driver to profit the most though was Jacques Villeneuve who went off at the first bend but made the re-start and went on to win the race! One team who weren't on the starting grid in 1997 were Lola who announced their withdrawal from F1 just two days before the start of practice. Jos Verstappen was officially awarded the title of the Heaviest F1 Driver for 1997. He tipped the scales at 79.5 kg.

# Kyalami

**Kyalami Race Track**
**South African Grand Prix – Reserve Grand Prix**
**Lap Distance:** 2.648 miles/4.263 km
**Race Distance:** tbc

Kyalami, which means 'my home' in Zulu, is located sixteen miles north of Johannesburg and eighteen miles south or Pretoria. The circuit was opened in 1961 and used to stage the South African Grand Prix from 1967 through to 1985. At that time, due to financial difficulties and the political problems in the country, the race was removed from the FIA calender. Williams started to test at the circuit in 1989 and the Grand Prix returned for 1992 and 1993 – the latter being won by Alain Prost in a Williams.

The circuit is located some 6,000 feet above sea level and nestles on the Highveld plain where temperatures at race time are often in the 90s and often lead to afternoon thunderstorms.

## The Circuit

The original circuit, before it fell into disrepair, was one of the most glamourous on the calender but has been completely rebuilt in recent years – in fact it has gone through two facelifts since it was originally discarded in 1984. The remodelling has made overtaking a near impossibility and grid position and race strategy are of prime consideration for teams.

The Start-Finish line is now located in the Gestetner Straight, from which the cars turn to the right and then turn through 180 degrees via two stepped turns. The cars turn on to the Old Pits Straight following a quick left-hander. Past the old pits comes the Goodyear Deep, a sweeping 90-degree right-hander which is followed by a similar, but tighter, left-hander – the Goodyear Corner.

This brings cars into the more complex part of the track, which sees them wiggle their way through a sequence of sharp left- and right-hand turns with the Westbank Corner turning the cars through 180 degrees back towards the Start-Finish line.

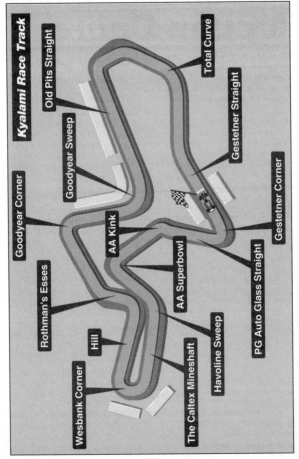

**Kyalami Race Track**

- Total Curve
- Gestetner Straight
- Old Pits Straight
- Goodyear Sweep
- Goodyear Corner
- Gestetner Corner
- AA Kink
- AA Superbowl
- PG Auto Glass Straight
- Rothman's Esses
- Hill
- Havoline Sweep
- Wesbank Corner
- The Caltex Mineshaft

# Magny-Cours

**Circuit de Nevers**
**French Grand Prix – 28 June 1998 (tbc)**
**Lap Distance**    2.64 miles/4.25 km – Clockwise
**Race Distance**   190.08 miles/306.029 km – 72 laps

Located about half way between Paris and Lyon, Circuit de Nevers was opened to Grand Prix racing in 1991 following a massive refurbishment. Its smooth surface makes it a favourite with the drivers but it is often difficult for teams to set the car up for, simply because there is no other circuit like it. Teams therefore normally opt for medium downforce with a lower than normal ride height, which helps to increase downforce whilst producing minimal drag. The circuit has a mix of high- and low-speed corners with relatively low grip.

## The Circuit

From the starting grid, cars accelerate up to 170 mph before entering **Grande Courbe**, a long, left-hand bend which is driven in 4th gear at 125 mph. Drivers take great care to get the right line out of the curve into **Estoril**, which is a sweeping right-hand turn that goes through 180 degrees. Here, 5th gear is maintained at a speed of 110 mph. Understeer can be a real problem for drivers and time can be lost if the entry into **Golf** is not right. Golf itself is very nearly a straight but has a gentle curve to the right throughout its length. As such, it is taken full-out in top gear with speeds around 180 mph.

   **Adelaide** is a 2nd-gear hairpin that brings the drivers back to earth. Braking hard at -3.2g, and at 40 mph, it turns through 180 degrees and takes the vehicle back in the direction from which it has just come with the track immediately to the right. This leads straight into a fast right-left that is cleared in 4th and which leads to **Nurburgring**, a chicane that wriggles the cars left and right – not as tight as Adelaide but, nevertheless, tricky because it closes up in the middle. Hard on the throttle, cars approach 150 mph and brake hard at the entrance to **180 Degrees.** This is another hairpin and again brings the cars through 180 degrees and back upon themselves – taken in 2nd gear at 50 mph.

   From the 180 it's up quickly through the gears to 6th and 170 mph before changing down to meet the challenge of **Imola** at 110 mph, a right-left that protects the **Chateau d'Eau**, a virtual 90-degree turn entered in 4th and exited in 2nd at 55 mph on to a straight that allows the car to accelerate to 155 mph towards the 2nd-gear **Chicane**. This is a very tight right-left turn where drivers have to be very careful to avoid the kerbs, especially on the second part of the corner. Immediately following the chicane is the sharp **Lycée** right-hander taken in 2nd gear as the cars slow to 40 mph. Positioning for exit out of Lycée is important as it affects the driver's ability to get on the throttle quickly to ensure maximum speed down the straight. The corner also provides the entry to the pit lane.

## 3-Year Record

| Year | 1st | 2nd | 3rd | 4th | 5th | 6th |
|------|-----|-----|-----|-----|-----|-----|
| 1995 | M.Schumacher (Benetton) | Hill (Williams) | Coulthard (Williams) | Brundle (Ligier) | Alesi (Ferrari) | Barrichello (Jordan) |
| 1996 | Hill (Williams) | Villeneuve (Williams) | Alesi (Benetton) | Berger (Benetton) | Hakkinen (McLaren) | Coulthard (McLaren) |
| 1997 | M.Schumacher (Ferrari) | Frentzen (Williams) | Irvine (Ferrari) | Villeneuve (Williams) | Alesi (Benetton) | R.Schumacher (Jordan) |

## Qualifying

| 1997 | 1996 | 1995 |
|------|------|------|
| M.Schumacher (Ferrari) | M.Schumacher (Ferrari) | Hill (Williams) |
| 1:14.548s | 1:15.989 | 1:17.225 |

## Notebook

Michael Schumacher will be looking for his third consecutive pole position in 1998, and also for his third win at the French Grand Prix and his 25th Grand Prix victory overall. At the 1997 event, the pole position was his 16th and Ferrari's 120th overall. The two Schumachers finished in the points together for the first time and also finished in the top three of qualifying – the first brothers ever to do so. Heinz-Harald Frentzen finished second in qualifying, giving Germany a 1,2,3 on the grid.

Jacques Villeneuve arrived at last year's event with his hair dyed blond and saying, "I don't want to look the same for the next 40 years!"

The 1926 French Grand Prix produced the smallest grid in Grand Prix history when just three Bugattis made it to the start. It also produced the biggest winning margin – an amazing 15 laps! The French Grand Prix also boasts an aviation record – in 1992, 48,880 helicopters either took off or landed in a ten-hour period, which is a world record.

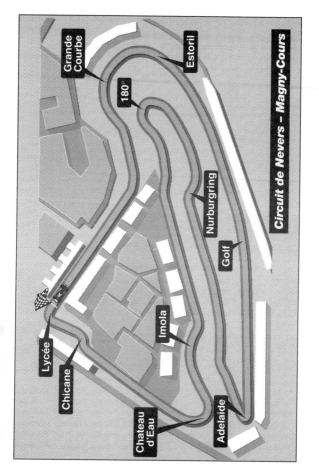

*Circuit de Nevers – Magny-Cours*

Grande Courbe

Estoril

180°

Nurburgring

Golf

Imola

Adelaide

Lycée

Chicane

Chateau d'Eau

213

# Melbourne

## Albert Park Grand Prix Circuit
## Australian Grand Prix – 8 March 1998
**Lap Distance:**   3.274 miles/5.269 km – Clockwise
**Race Distance:** 189.89 miles/305.6 km – 58 laps

Melbourne hosts its third Grand Prix in 1998. A street circuit situated in a park, the track is a combination of fast corners and tight hairpins along with sweeping curves. Not particularly challenging as a race circuit, but most drivers do consider it amongst their favourites. The approaches to some of the corners are a little bumpy and can create problems for the drivers. Expect to see cars with a high wing level to produce maximum downforce. The circuit can be heavy on tyres so teams often opt for soft set-ups that will prolong tyre life.

## *The Circuit*

From the start, cars accelerate to 185 mph as they reach the **Fangio Stand**. Flanked by the Fangio and Brabham Stands are two 45-degree right- and left-handers – Turns 1 and 2. Turn 1 is the hardest braking point in the circuit pulling -3.5 g. A change down to 2nd gear sees the first turn taken at 70 mph before a short acceleration into Turn 2, which is taken at 100 mph. Turn 2 and Turn 3 mark the bumpiest parts of the circuit. From here the cars accelerate to 180 mph before braking hard again (-3.4g) towards a sharp right-left S-bend, taking Turn 3 in 2nd gear at around 55 mph. Accelerating again the cars catapult out through Turn 4 at 80 mph, accelerating past the **Whitford Stand** in 5th gear at 170 mph.

A short, sharp right-hander marks Turn 6 with cars again braking hard (-3.0g) and slowing to 70 mph. The circuit then loops round to the right, negotiating Turn 8 at 155 mph, and then past the **Clark Stand** at 175 mph. The **Fittipaldi Stand** is at Turn 9 where cars brake hard again (-3.3g) before setting off to a long, inner-loop curve turning the cars left at a speed of 160 mph. They slow to 90 mph and swing right, past the **Waite Stand** and changing up to 5th and 140 mph before passing the **Hill Stand** at 160 mph. Braking hard again (-3.5g) the cars change down to 3rd gear and enter the right-hand Turn 13 at 80 mph. Accelerating to 100 mph in front of the **Stewart Stand**, Turn 14, another right-hander, is taken in 3rd gear at 100 mph.

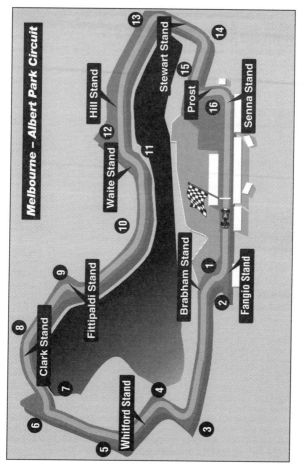

*Melbourne – Albert Park Circuit*

The **Prost Stand** marks the entrance to the most difficult section of the circuit with the cars turning through two sharp 90-degree turns, going first left (Turn 15) and then right (Turn 16). Cars approach Turn 15 at 130 mph, braking hard and changing down from 4th to 2nd to negotiate the near hair-pin turn at 50 mph. Turn 16 is less demanding but still requires 2nd gear with cars accelerating in front of the **Senna Stand** from 80 mph on to the finishing straight. The longest section of straight on the circuit, cars can go flat out in 6th gear at 180 mph as they flash across the Start-Finish line.

## 3-Year Record

| Year | 1st | 2nd | 3rd | 4th | 5th | 6th |
|------|-----|-----|-----|-----|-----|-----|
| 1995 | Hill (Williams) | Panis (Ligier) | Morbidelli (Arrows) | Blundell (McLaren) | Salo (Tyrrell) | Lamy (Minardi) |
| 1996 | Hill (Williams) | Villeneuve (Williams) | Irvine (Ferrari) | Berger (Benetton) | Hakkinen (McLaren) | Salo (Tyrrell) |
| 1997 | Coulthard (McLaren) | M.Schumacher (Ferrari) | Hakkinen (McLaren) | Berger (Benetton) | Panis (Prost) | Larini (Sauber) |

*1995 race held at Adelaide*

## Qualifying

| 1997 | 1996 | 1995 |
|------|------|------|
| Villeneuve (Williams) | Villeneuve (Williams) | – |
| 1:29.369s | 1:32.371 | |

## Notebook

Gerhard Berger and Mika Hakkinen were the only drivers to have scored points in both the 1996 and 1997 Melbourne Grands Prix. Damon Hill and Gerhard Berger were the only previous winners of the Australian GP on the grid in Melbourne. Hill, however, failed to complete even the warm-up lap in his Arrows debut. Jacques Villeneuve, having taken successive pole positions, failed to complete a single lap of the 1997 event when he tangled with Herbert and Irvine at the very first corner.

David Coulthard's win was the 105th for McLaren and the team's first since Ayrton Senna won the event in Adelaide in 1993. Sir Jack Brabham waved the chequered flag to announce Coulthard's victory.

Melbourne 1997 saw a new start procedure used for the first time with five red lights coming on and the race getting underway when they were extinguished. Between them, Bridgestone and Goodyear took 3,800 tyres to Albert Park. Olivier Panis scored the first points won with Bridgestone tyres.

# Monaco

**Circuit de Monaco**
**Monaco Grand Prix Monte Carlo – 24 May 1998**
**Lap Distance:** 2.082 miles/3.352 km – Clockwise
**Race Distance:** 162.24 miles/261.478 km – 78 laps

Probably the most famous Grand Prix circuit in the world, taking its macadam from the busy city streets and harbour-front of Monte Carlo in the south of France. A tight, demanding circuit, there is little room on the track with overtaking a near impossibility – as such, pole position can be decisive. The circuit is not hard on the engines as they are never operating at full power; it is demanding on the drivers however – a typical lap of the circuit requires 36 gear changes, and that's over 2800 per race! Teams look for maximum downforce as mechanical grip is vital because the roads that comprise the circuit have very low grip. When wet weather prevails, look out for cars sliding into the armco barriers that surround most of the circuit.

## The Circuit

The start of the Monaco Grand Prix is all about getting to, and through, the very first corner safely. Do that and you have a chance! The **Virage de Sainte Devote** is a near 90-degree right-hander that is approached from the Start-Finish line at 170 mph. Then, it's a hard brake at -3.6 g and down to a 2nd-gear 55 mph for cornering. The **Montée du Beau Rivage** is a short straight that takes the cars past the world famous Rosie's Bar in 6th gear at 165 mph and then it's over the crest of the hill and down to 4th gear as **Virage Massenet** beckons. A long left-hander, the car must be kept close to the inside kerb in 3rd gear at 80 mph. The cars then come to **Virage Casino** which is a quick right-hander that is taken in 2nd gear at 70 mph.

Coming out of Casino the cars get a chance to accelerate briefly along a short straight before they enter one of the most complex sections of the course. The **Virage Mirabeau** is approached downhill in 4th at 130 mph, requiring fast gear changes to get into 2nd gear for this bumpy right-hander, taken slowly at 30 mph. Out of this comes the short approach to the **Virage Loews**, a left-hand hairpin negotiated in 2nd gear at about 20 mph with the steering turned full lock, then right – this is one of the most famous TV and photographic views in F1. The turns are ended by the **Virage du Portier**, another sharp right-hander cleared in 2nd gear at 50 mph.

Coming out of the turns, the cars start on a long sweep through the **Tunnel**. Noise and sparks fly as the cars change up to 5th gear and 145 mph. Once out of the tunnel, left-right **Nouvelle Chicane** is approached at 175 mph before drivers change down to 2nd gear and a sedate 30 mph.

The most spectacular and glamourous part of the course is **Tabac**, lying, as it does, alongside the harbour, which is driven through at 95 mph in 4th gear. Piscine or the **Swimming Pool** complex provides a short kink in the circuit which pushes the drivers through a succession of gear changes and speeds ranging from 50 mph to 100 mph. This section of the circuit underwent major revision prior to the 1997 Grand Prix to make it safer.

**Virage de la Rascasse** is the slowest part of the circuit with a very tight hairpin that is taken in 1st gear at a crawling 20 mph. Along a very short straight and a faster right-hander, **Virage Anthony Noghes**, is taken in 2nd at 45 mph before accelerating and climbing upwards into the Start-Finish straight.

## 3-Year Record

| Year | 1st | 2nd | 3rd | 4th | 5th | 6th |
|------|-----|-----|-----|-----|-----|-----|
| 1995 | M.Schumacher (Benetton) | Hill (Williams) | Berger (Ferrari) | Herbert (Benetton) | Blundell (McLaren) | Frentzen (Sauber) |
| 1996 | Panis (Ligier) | Coulthard (McLaren) | Herbert (Sauber) | Frentzen (Sauber) | Salo (Tyrrell) | Hakkinen (McLaren) |
| 1997 | M.Schumacher (Ferrari) | Barrichello (Stewart) | Irvine (Ferrari) | Panis (Prost) | Salo (Tyrrell) | Fisichella (Jordan) |

## Qualifying

| 1997 | 1996 | 1995 |
|------|------|------|
| Frentzen (Williams) | M.Schumacher (Ferrari) | Hill (Williams) |
| 1:18.216 | 1:20.356 | 1:21.952 |

## Notebook

Last year, Michael Schumacher and Heinz-Harald Frentzen were on the front row of the grid – the first time two German drivers had ever occupied the position since the World Championship started. It was Frentzen's first-ever pole position secured by a margin of 0.019 seconds.

By the harbour, two drivers have actually ended up in the drink. In 1955, Alberto Ascari's Lancia took the plunge while leading the race and in 1965, a Lotus driven by Paul Hawkins tried to become amphibious.

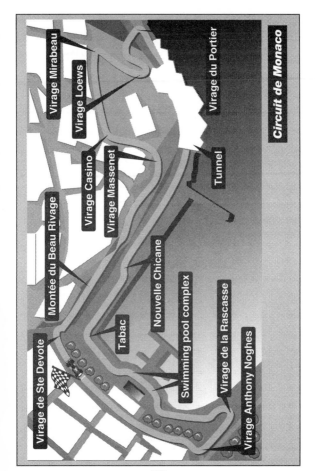

**Circuit de Monaco**

Virage du Portier

Virage Mirabeau

Virage Loews

Virage Casino

Virage Massenet

Montée du Beau Rivage

Tunnel

Virage de Ste Devote

Tabac

Nouvelle Chicane

Swimming pool complex

Virage de la Rascasse

Virage Anthony Noghes

219

# Montreal

**Gilles Villeneuve Circuit**
**Canadian Grand Prix – 7 June 1998**
**Lap Distance:**  2.747 miles/4.421 km – Clockwise
**Race Distance:** 189.543 miles/305.049 km – 69 laps

Located on the Ile Notre Dame, the circuit is within easy reach of the Montreal city centre. It has a picturesque backdrop which includes views of the Lawrence River and the old Olympic Rowing Basin. The Canadian Grand Prix has been staged here since 1978 and the track is part-permanent and part, street circuit. This is the only race to take place on the course each year, so the roads collect a great amount of grit which the wind shifts about causing severe grip problems. It is a high-speed circuit with equally fast chicanes, but it also has slow corners which are fed by straights; as such, braking is paramount and brake performance often proves critical.

## The Circuit

From the starting grid, the cars accelerate to 170 mph and swing quickly through **Turn 1** as the track waves right and left. Once through they brake heavily, pulling -3.8g at the entrance to **Virage Senna.** This hairpin is marked by a tight 90-degree turn to the left before the hairpin itself turns the cars through 180 degrees and it is negotiated at 45 mph in 2nd gear. Cars quickly accelerate to 150 mph and 5th gear as the track curves gently to the right. A series of bends (**Turns 2-6**) see the cars down to 3rd gear and speeds averaging 60 mph as the circuit turns to the right.

**Turn 7** marks the Pont de la Concorde which occupies about a third of the track length. This is a long straight, broken up by a quick right-left turn – **Turn 8** and **Turn 9** – that can be negotiated in 3rd gear. Decelerating from 170 mph, the right bend is entered at 50 mph and then exited at 65 mph.

The lead-up to **Turn 10**, which marks the Virage du Casino, is done at full throttle with a top speed of around 170 mph. This hairpin comes at a point where the entrance and exit run side by side, and so it gives the drivers a chance to see who is behind them. It is a relatively wide portion of the track and it is common to see overtaking manoeuvres here as cars try to out-brake one another. It is also the slowest part of the track, with cars braking down from 180 mph to around 40 mph.

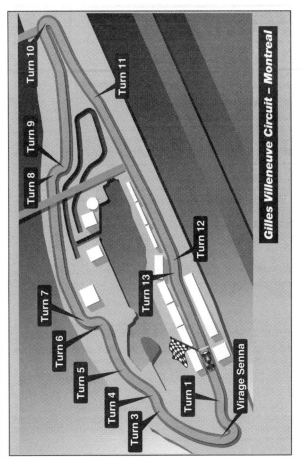

*Gilles Villeneuve Circuit – Montreal*

Patients in the nearby hospital get a good view of the cars accelerating up through the gears along the Casino Straight. This is the fastest section of track with cars hitting speeds of 190 mph in top gear. **Turn 11** marks the hardest braking point on the circuit with drivers experiencing -3.8g. This was modified for the 1996 Grand Prix, from the Casino Bend (**Turn 12** and **Turn 13**) which used to be a chicane, slowing the cars down into the final straight. Now it is much shallower, with cars swinging through it at around 60 mph before accelerating again as they cross the Start-Finish line.

## 3-Year Record

| Year | 1st | 2nd | 3rd | 4th | 5th | 6th |
|------|-----|-----|-----|-----|-----|-----|
| 1995 | Alesi (Ferrari) | Barrichello (Jordan) | Irvine (Jordan) | Panis (Ligier) | M.Schumacher (Benetton) | Morbidelli (Footwork) |
| 1996 | Hill (Williams) | Villeneuve (Williams) | Alesi (Benetton) | Coulthard (McLaren) | Hakkinen (McLaren) | Brundle (Jordan) |
| 1997 | M.Schumacher (Ferrari) | Alesi (Benetton) | Fisichella (Jordan) | Frentzen (Williams) | Herbert (Sauber) | Nakano (Prost) |

## Qualifying

| 1997 | 1996 | 1995 |
|------|------|------|
| M.Schumacher (Ferrari) | Hill (Williams) | M.Schumacher (Benetton) |
| 1:18.095s | 1:21.059 | 1:27.661 |

## Notebook

Olivier Panis broke both legs during the 1997 Canadian Grand Prix when his Prost clipped a wall, coming out of Turn 7, and ploughed into another head-on at around 150 mph. The Safety Car came out three laps later while Panis was dealt with and the race was stopped after only 56 of its scheduled 69 laps. Results were awarded on the basis of cars' positions at the end of lap 54. Ralf Schumacher was more fortunate – he had a spectacular crash on lap 15 at the approach to Virage Senna. A tyre wall cushioned his 120 mph impact.

Alexander Wurz made his F1 debut by being a substitute for Benetton's Gerhard Berger who was sidelined due to a sinus infection. Michael Schumacher notched Ferrari's first pole position of 1997 – it was also the first time a Williams car had not been on the front row of the grid.

Changes in seating arrangements for the 1997 event meant that the 1996 attendance of 101,027 is likely to remain a record for the Canadian Grand Prix for the foreseeable future.

# Monza

## Autodromo Nationale di Monza
## Italian Grand Prix – 13 September 1998
**Lap Distance:**   3.585 miles/5.772 km – Clockwise
**Race Distance:** 191.005 miles/305.908 km – 53 laps

Fifteen miles north-east of Milan, Monza was built in 1922. The modern day autodromo combines fast, sweeping corners and long straights, with Parabolica and Lesmo two of the more famous. The Italian Grand Prix has been staged here for all but one year since the World Championship was introduced in 1950. Downforce requirements are normally low with stiff settings on the car to help ride some of the big bumps that the circuit is notorious for. The low wing levels make grip poor in the low-speed turns, which can create problems for drivers who brake too late into them.

## The Circuit

The **Rettifilio Tribune** is the long start-straight leads to the **Variante Goodyear** (also known as Variante del Rettifilio). This is approached in top gear at around 215 mph and it is marked by the wide pit straight that precedes it. It is a very fast but bumpy left-right-left-right 2nd-gear chicane that's entered in 2nd at 60 mph and exited at 80 mph. Almost immediately after is **Curva Grande**, which is a very bumpy, longish right-hander that is hard work on the steering. Drivers invariably use the kerb at its exit at 185 mph and then it's along the back straight where 200 mph is touched.

The **Variante della Roggia** is also known as 2A Variante. The braking area prior to entering this left-right chicane is both bumpy and slippy. Approached in top gear, it is negotiated in 2nd at 60 mph and exited in 3rd at 85 mph. **Curva di Lesmo** is a contentious sharp right-hander. Invariably taken fast, shifting between 4th and 3rd gears, with speeds ranging between 150 mph and 95 mph. Coming out of the turn, the cars rocket down **Curve del Serraglio**, a long straight that means the driver approaches the next chicane at speeds approaching, and sometimes exceeding, 200 mph.

Drivers hope their brakes are in good order as they approach Curva del Vialone, a left-hander, braking from 200 mph in 6th gear to 4th gear at the 100-metre board. Then, on to **Variante Ascari**, the second part of the chicane, quickly flicking right, then left and changing down into 2nd gear at 85 mph. Exited in 3rd gear at 125 mph, cars accelerate onto the **Rettifilio Centro** straight and attain 200 mph on the approach to the final curve.

The **Curva Parabolica** is a long, looping right-hander that is important to lap-times as the entry and exit to it determine how quickly drivers can get on the gas as they come out of it and on to the longest straight on the circuit. Braking hard at -3.2g, cars decelerate to 100 mph and 3rd gear at its apex. As the curve opens out it is exited in 4th gear at 170 mph as the cars arrive in the long **Rettifilio Tribune** straight, before applying full throttle and crossing the Start-Finish line.

## 5-Year Record

| Year | 1st | 2nd | 3rd | 4th | 5th | 6th |
|------|-----|-----|-----|-----|-----|-----|
| 1993 | Hill (Williams) | Alesi (Ferrari) | Andretti (McLaren) | Wendlinger (Sauber) | Patrese (Benetton) | Comas (Larrousse) |
| 1994 | Hill (Williams) | Berger (Ferrari) | Verstappen (Benetton) | Barrichello (Jordan) | Brundle (McLaren) | Coulthard (Williams) |
| 1995 | Herbert (Benetton) | Hakkinen (McLaren) | Frentzen (Sauber) | Blundell (McLaren) | Salo (Tyrrell) | Boullion (Sauber) |
| 1996 | M.Schumacher (Ferrari) | Alesi (Benetton) | Hakkinen (McLaren) | Brundle (Jordan) | Barrichello (Jordan) | Diniz (Ligier) |
| 1997 | Coulthard (McLaren) | Alesi (Benetton) | Frentzen (Williams) | Fisichella (Jordan) | Villeneuve (Williams) | M.Schumacher (Ferrari) |

## Qualifying

| 1997 | 1996 | 1995 |
|------|------|------|
| Alesi (Benetton) | Hill (Williams) | Coulthard (Williams) |
| 1:22.990 | 1:24.204 | 1:24.462 |

## Notebook

Jean Alesi gained his first and only pole position of 1997 at Monza – it was only the second of his career, the other also coming at Monza in 1994. The Italian Grand Prix, along with the British Grand Prix are the only two races that have formed part of the World Championship every year since it was started.

The stacks of tyres that were placed at the exit to two chicanes for 1996 had created numerous problems for drivers and they were thankfully removed for the 1997 event.

Jacques Villeneuve received a one-race ban, suspended for nine races, after he ignored waved yellow flags during the Sunday warm-up. David Coulthard received a similar ban until the end of the 1997 season for a similar incident.

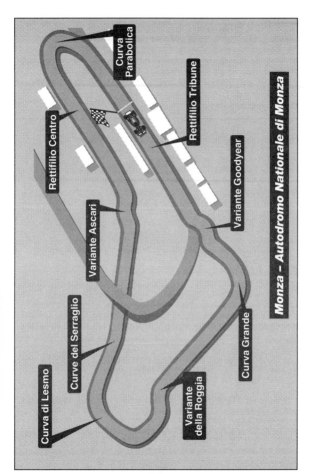

Monza – Autodromo Nationale di Monza

Curva Parabolica

Rettifilio Tribune

Rettifilio Centro

Variante Goodyear

Variante Ascari

Curve del Serraglio

Curva di Lesmo

Curva Grande

Variante della Roggia

# Nurburgring

**Nurburgring (Germany)**
**Luxembourg Grand Prix – 27 September 1998**
**Lap Distance**   2.831 miles/4.568 km – Clockwise
**Race Distance**  190.079 miles/306.027 km – 67 laps

Despite being situated in Germany, about 55 miles south-west of Cologne, the Nurburgring is staging the Luxembourg Grand Prix. The circuit was opened for Grand Prix action in 1984, when Alain Prost won the European event. This was followed by the German Grand Prix, which was the last for some time. Then, after ten years of Grand Prix inactivity, the circuit was used for the European Grand Prix in 1996, which gave Jacques Villeneuve his first win in Formula One.

Situated in beautiful countryside, the Nurburgring is both fast and forgiving with wide run-off areas and large gravel traps. Its twelve corners and curves make for an exciting race, especially as cars generally suffer with understeer problems which can make handling problematic. Medium downforce settings are normally employed.

## The Circuit

Out of the blocks and into top gear at 180 mph towards the **Castrol 'S'** bend and hard on the brakes at the entry to the right-left at 80 mph in 3rd gear. The curve is exited at 100 mph as drivers change up. Quickly up to 6th gear and accelerating to 165 mph for the approach to **Valvoline Kurve** which is entered at 105 mph in 3rd gear and leads directly into the **Ford Kurve** at 65 mph in 2nd gear. Then, hard on the throttle, the cars approach the Dunlop Kurve at 170 mph in 5th gear.

The **Dunlop Kurve** is a right-hand 190-degree loop, making it the second-slowest part of the circuit at under 60 mph in 2nd gear. Provided cars have managed a good line through the loop, they can get on to the gas quickly and through 135 mph as the track swings gently left and right. Out of here the approach to the **Yokohama Kurve** (also known as the RTL Kurve) sees the cars in top gear at 170 mph, which is halved to 3rd gear at 85 mph through the near 90-degree left-hand turn. Having swept left, the **Bit Kurve** sweeps another 90 degrees through a right-hand turn, again in 3rd gear at around 100 mph.

On to the straight, taken full-out in top gear at 180 mph, cars brake to the **Veedol Chicane**, which is the slowest part of the course as cars brake down

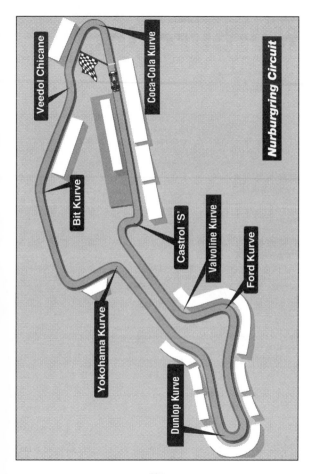

*Nurburgring Circuit*

Veedol Chicane

Coca-Cola Kurve

Bit Kurve

Castrol 'S'

Valvoline Kurve

Ford Kurve

Yokohama Kurve

Dunlop Kurve

227

to 60 mph and sweep left and then right in 2nd gear, before accelerating to 135 mph in 4th gear. Out of here comes the sharp left-hand turn through 160 degrees which marks the **Coca-Cola Kurve.** This is taken in 2nd gear at 70 mph before accelerating out into the finishing straight at top speed.

## 5-Year Record

| Year | 1st | 2nd | 3rd | 4th | 5th | 6th |
|------|-----|-----|-----|-----|-----|-----|
| 1996 | Villeneuve (Williams) | M.Schumacher (Ferrari) | Coulthard (McLaren) | Hill (Williams) | Barrichello (Jordan) | Brundle (Jordan) |
| 1997 | Villeneuve (Williams) | Alesi (Benetton) | Frentzen (Williams) | Berger (Benetton) | Diniz (Arrows) | Panis (Prost) |

*1993-95 – No Grands Prix on this circuit. 1996 – European Grand Prix.*

## Qualifying

| 1997 | 1996 |
|------|------|
| Hakkinen (McLaren) | Hill (Williams) |
| 1:16.602 | 1:18.941 |

## Notebook

Last year, Michael Schumacher celebrated his 100th Grand Prix appearance when he competed in the Luxembourg Grand Prix. Schumacher lasted only two laps though. Mika Hakkinen celebrated his first-ever pole position in what was his 94th Grand Prix. He finished just 0.089 seconds in front of Jacques Villeneuve. Heinz-Harald Frentzen finished third for the fourth successive time following podium finishes at Spa, Monza and the A1-Ring.

Olivier Panis returned to F1 action at the Luxembourg Grand Prix last year after a three month lay-off, having broken both his legs in a crash at the Canadian Grand Prix.

Pedro Diniz secured his first points of the season when he finished fifth in last year's race.

# Silverstone

**Silverstone Circuit**
**British Grand Prix – 12 July 1998**
**Lap Distance:**   3.194 miles/5.142 km – Clockwise
**Race Distance:** 191,634 miles/308.52 km – 60 laps

Silverstone is Britain's longest continually used race circuit and staged the first-ever British Grand Prix in 1926. Although not used for all British Grands Prix, it has held the event since 1987. The circuit is located in the Northamptonshire countryside near the village of the same name.

Operated and owned by the British Racing Drivers' Club, Silverstone held the first-ever round of the World Championship in 1950. It has undergone design revisions in recent years, with changes made to a number of corners. The surface is smooth and teams generally opt for a mid-range set-up to take advantage of good grip.

## The Circuit

From the grid, cars pull away and the straight allows speeds of 175 mph to be reached on the approach to **Copse**. This right-hand corner is blind but, at 140 mph, very fast, so fast in fact that drivers don't normally brake – just change down a gear. Switching back up, cars thunder on towards **Maggots** at 175 mph and shift down twice as they wave their way first through Maggotts and then **Becketts** – as the track wiggles left-right, left-right, slowing down to 100 mph before **Chapel** ends the series of left-right bends and is accelerated through, coming out at 155 mph in 6th gear.

The **Hanger Straight** is the fastest part of the circuit, at 185 mph in top gear, before braking hard into **Stowe**, a right-hand turn that can be taken in 4th gear and speeds of 105 mph maintained. **Vale** is a quick straight in which the cars go through at something like 160 mph with a 2nd-gear, sharp left into **Club**, a right-hand corner taken at 50 mph and then accelerated through and the cars swing back on themselves at 130 mph. Both Vale and Club present good overtaking opportunities, not least because they are tricky to negotiate and understeer comes into play. Up through two gears into 6th and 170 mph towards **Abbey**, a 3rd-gear, 75 mph corner which flips into Farm at 100 mph and up to 160 mph along **Farm Straight**.

Bridge marks the entrance to the 'Complex', a section of the track containing bends at Priory, Brooklands and Luffield. The corners at **Bridge** and **Priory** are fast, entering the first at 150 mph and exiting the second at 100 mph. Priory, along with **Brooklands**, steer the car through 180 degrees. Brooklands, along with **Luffield**, again turn the car around and are both negotiated in 2nd gear at between 50-80 mph. Luffield used to be two corners called Luffield 1 and Luffield 2 prior to 1996. On exit, it's a quick dash through **Woodcote** at 165 mph and a smooth turn to the right before hitting the Start-Finish straight at 175 mph. At the start of 1998 Silverstone re-named the sequence of corners from Priory to Luffield as 'The Grandstand' and intends to install more grandstand steating in this area.

## 3-Year Record

| Year | 1st | 2nd | 3rd | 4th | 5th | 6th |
|------|-----|-----|-----|-----|-----|-----|
| 1995 | Herbert | Alesi | Coulthard | Panis | Blundell | Frentzen |
| | (Benetton) | (Ferrari) | (Williams) | (Ligier) | (McLaren) | (Sauber) |
| 1996 | Villeneuve | Alesi | Hakkinen | Barrichello | Coulthard | Brundle |
| | (Williams) | (Benetton) | (McLaren) | (Jordan) | (McLaren) | (Jordan) |
| 1997 | Villeneuve | Alesi | Wurz | Coulthard | R.Schumacher | Hill |
| | (Williams) | (Benetton) | (Benetton) | (McLaren) | (Jordan) | (Arrows) |

## Qualifying

| 1997 | 1996 | 1995 |
|------|------|------|
| Villeneuve (Williams) | Hill (Williams) | Hill (Williams) |
| 1:21.598 | 1:26.875 | 1:28.124 |

## Notebook

Last year, Mika Hakkinen looked to be driving his way to his first-ever Grand Prix victory before engine failure denied the McLaren driver just seven laps from the chequered flag. Damon Hill, who had qualified in pole position in his three previous British races, earned his first point of the season in the Arrows when he finished sixth.

Jacques Villeneuve's win was Williams' 100th Grand Prix victory. Coincidentally, their first win also came at Silverstone when Clay Regazzoni won the event in 1979. Villeneuve was handed a one-race suspended ban from the stewards after it was claimed he did not maintain a correct distance behind the safety car when it came out at the start of the race.

Rubens Barrichello made history when he became the first driver to crash while testing the grooved tyres that will be compulsory for 1998.

Alexander Wurz virtually secured a place in Benetton's 1998 line-up with his impressive podium finish in only his third race. He had replaced Gerhard Berger who was recovering from a second sinus operation.

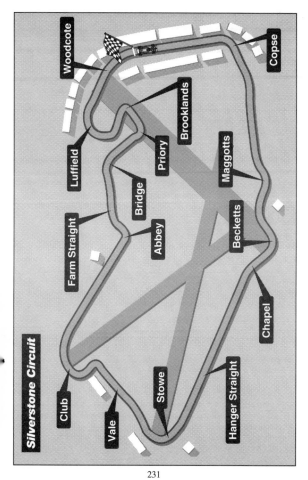

**Silverstone Circuit**

Woodcote

Copse

Brooklands

Luffield

Priory

Maggotts

Bridge

Beckets

Abbey

Farm Straight

Chapel

Club

Stowe

Hanger Straight

Vale

# Spa

## Circuit de Spa-Francorchamps
## Belgian Grand Prix – 30 August 1998
**Lap Distance:**   4.33 miles/6.971 km – Clockwise
**Race Distance:** 190.527 miles/306.7375 km – 44 laps

Lying 30 miles south-east of Liege, Spa-Francorchamps is located in central Belgium. It was first used in 1985 and, at 4.334 miles in length, it is the longest circuit in use in the World Championship. A temporary circuit that makes use of public roads, it remains a firm favourite with most drivers, not least because of its picturesque setting, and because it is demanding enough to present a difficult challenge to those racing. Low to medium downforce settings are used to enable drivers to cope with varied high- and low-speed sections and a number of corners which are all the faster for being downhill.

## The Circuit

From the start, the corner at **La Source** comes very quickly and is a hairpin that is taken in 2nd gear at around 40 mph after which drivers have two long straights that are separated by **Eau Rouge** – which amounts to a small kink in the circuit. Accelerating to 180 mph along the first section, Eau Rouge can be taken in 6th gear with only a slight loss of speed (165 mph) as it goes downhill and then uphill left, right, and left. Cars exit at **Raidillon** and then encounter the fastest part of the course along the **Kemmell** straight at 190 mph.

As the track bears round slowly to the right, there exists good overtaking possibilities at **Les Combes** due to the wide run-off areas. The right-left combination chicane is taken in 3rd gear and 85 mph and is exited at **Malmedy**, which is a right-hander taken at 100 mph.

**Rivage** is a virtual hairpin which, due to being off camber and downhill, causes cars all sorts of steering problems. It is approached in 4th gear at 155 mph, taken in 2nd at 60 mph and exited in 3rd at 110 mph. Out of Rivage the cars sweep along a short straight at 155 mph before the track veers left at 90 mph and on to **Pouhon** at 100 mph, a double left-hander. Also off camber, it is entered and exited in 4th gear at an average of 140 mph. On exit, cars power through the gears to 180 mph before slowing at **Fagnes** – a right-left chicane which is taken in 3rd gear at 100 mph.

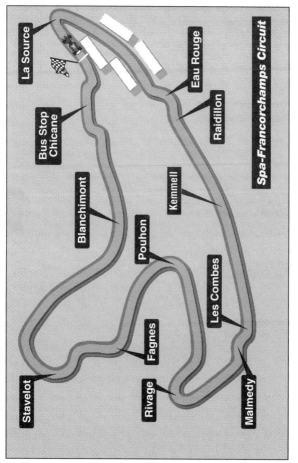

Spa-Francorchamps Circuit

La Source
Eau Rouge
Raidillon
Bus Stop Chicane
Blanchimont
Kemmell
Pouhon
Les Combes
Fagnes
Stavelot
Rivage
Malmedy

**Stavelot** is a double right-hand loop, turning the cars through 180 degrees as they go downhill. Entered in 3rd with 4th (135 mph) being engaged in the middle, but it is bumpy and cars tend to skip about a bit as cars speed-up to 150 mph on exit. **Blanchimont** is a long, sweeping left-hander taken full-out in 6th gear at 185 mph. With the Start-Finish line almost in sight, **Bus Stop Chicane** appears, a sharp right-left-right chicane that slows the cars right down to a 2nd gear 45 mph before they emerge on to the pit straight at 170 mph.

## 5-Year Record

| Year | 1st | 2nd | 3rd | 4th | 5th | 6th |
|------|-----|-----|-----|-----|-----|-----|
| 1993 | Hill (Williams) | M.Schumacher (Benetton) | Prost (Williams) | Senna (McLaren) | Herbert (Lotus) | Patrese (Benetton) |
| 1994 | Hill (Williams) | Hakkinen (McLaren) | Verstappen (Benetton) | Coulthard (Williams) | Blundell (Tyrrell) | Morbidelli (Arrows) |
| 1995 | M.Schumacher (Benetton) | Hill (Williams) | Brundle (Ligier) | Frentzen (Sauber) | Blundell (McLaren) | Barrichello (Jordan) |
| 1996 | M.Schumacher (Ferrari) | Villeneuve (Williams) | Hakkinen (McLaren) | Alesi (Benetton) | Hill (Williams) | Berger (Benetton) |
| 1997 | M.Schumacher (Ferrari) | Fisichella (Jordan) | Frentzen (Williams) | Herbert (Sauber) | Villeneuve (Williams) | Berger (Benetton) |

## Qualifying

| 1997 | 1996 | 1995 |
|------|------|------|
| Villeneuve (Williams) | Villeneuve (Williams) | Berger (Benetton) |
| 1:49.450 | 1:50.574 | 1:54.392 |

## Notebook

Last year, Michael Schumacher recorded his third successive victory at Spa and his fourth overall. Schumi needs one more win at this event to equal the record of Ayrton Senna who had five wins in the Belgian Grand Prix. In 1998, Jacques Villeneuve will be looking for his third successive pole position and his first-ever win in Belgium.

Arrows competed in their 300th and Minardi their 200th Grand Prix at Spa last season. Neither team have yet won a Grand Prix race. Mika Hakkinen was excluded from the results of last year's race – having finished third – when it was found the fuel used in his car did not match the supplied sample. McLaren were also fined £50,000. Heinz-Harald Frentzen was fined $7,500 for speeding in the pit lane during practice.

# Suzuka

**Suzuka International Racing Course**
**Japanese Grand Prix – 1 November 1998**
**Lap Distance:**   3.642 miles/5.864 km – Figure of Eight
**Race Distance:** 193.026 miles/310.772 km – 53 laps

Located between Osaka and Nagoya, south-west of Tokyo, Suzuka has been a regular stage on the Grand Prix calendar since 1987. The circuit is unique to the Championship in that it follows a figure of eight pattern with numerous turns and straights, thus providing both clockwise and anticlockwise movement for the cars. Cars normally opt for medium to soft settings with stiff suspension to take in the various bumps in what is otherwise a smooth surface.

## The Circuit

The start is downhill and this can help cars get away. Indeed, in 1988, it helped Ayrton Senna get away after he stalled just before the go signal. Once away, the cars approach **First Curve** flat out in top gear at speeds of up to 190 mph with a change down to 5th and 150 mph into the bend and into a second curve that is much tighter than the first and can only be negotiated in 3rd with speed dropping to 95 mph.

The **S Curve** is a left-right-left-right combination that severely taxes any car that is not well balanced. It can usually be taken all the way through in 4th. The sequence is entered at 135 mph, dropping to 85 mph on exit of the final curve. On exiting, the S Curve's 4th gear is maintained for the approach to the **Dunlop Curve**. This long left-hander is extremely bumpy with plenty of understeer at 135 mph.

Accelerating to 160 mph, the **Degner Curve** is a tight right-hander that is taken in 4th gear at 120 mph, down to 3rd as the second part of the corner becomes tighter still, and then generally exited with the use of the kerb. Then it is up to top gear at 170 mph to go under the bridge where the course crosses itself to the **Hairpin Curve**. This is guarded by a short right-hander which slows the cars, but then they have to get down very quickly to 2nd gear for the 45 mph hairpin. Out of the hairpin the circuit curves to the right and on completion of the curve the majority of cars will be in top gear at 170 mph.

**Spoon Curve** awaits at the end of the looping right-hander. It is negotiated in 3rd gear, with speeds dropping from 105 mph on entry to 85 mph on exit. Then it's full on the throttle and it's a 185 mph straight-screamer over the **Crossover** to **130R**, a very fast left-hander which forces a slight deceleration to 155 mph. The **Casino Chicane** (Triangle Chicane) guards the entrance to the finishing straight. The right-left combination is taken in 2nd gear at 40 mph, with the cars having to brake hard from 175 mph as they approach it. Once through, the cars swing right at 120 mph and onto the Start-Finish straight for the next lap.

## 5-Year Record

| Year | 1st | 2nd | 3rd | 4th | 5th | 6th |
|---|---|---|---|---|---|---|
| 1993 | Senna (McLaren) | Prost (Williams) | Hakkinen (McLaren) | Hill (Williams) | Barrichello (Jordan) | Irvine (Jordan) |
| 1994 | Hill (Williams) | M.Schumacher (Benetton) | Alesi (Ferrari) | Mansell (Williams) | Irvine (Jordan) | Frentzen (Sauber) |
| 1995 | M.Schumacher (Benetton) | Hakkinen (McLaren) | Herbert (Benetton) | Irvine (Jordan) | Panis (Ligier) | Salo (Tyrrell) |
| 1996 | Hill (Williams) | M.Schumacher (Ferrari) | Hakkinen (McLaren) | Berger (Benetton) | Brundle (Jordan) | Frentzen (Sauber) |
| 1997 | M.Schumacher (Ferrari) | Frentzen (Williams) | Irvine (Ferrari) | Hakkinen (McLaren) | Villeneuve (Williams) | Alesi (Benetton) |

## Qualifying

| 1997 | 1996 | 1995 |
|---|---|---|
| Villeneuve (Williams) | Villeneuve (Williams) | M.Schumacher (Benetton) |
| 1:36.071 | 1:38.909 | 1:38.023 |

## Notebook

Michael Schumacher has not finished outside the first two places in Suzuka in the previous four races. Jacques Villeneuve clinched his ninth pole position of the season and will be looking for his third successive pole at the 1998 Japanese Grand Prix. Villeneuve raced under a suspended ban last year and was ultimately disqualified from the race after finishing fifth.

The World Championship has been decided at the Japanese Grand Prix on seven occasions. Williams secured their eighth Constructors' Championship at Suzuka last year.

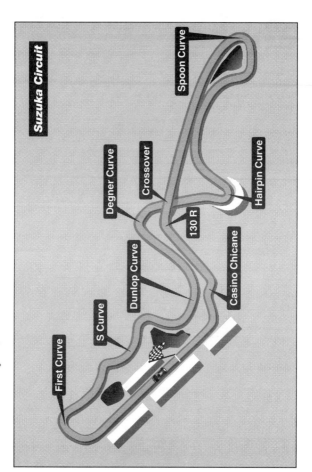

Suzuka Circuit

Spoon Curve

Degner Curve

Crossover

Hairpin Curve

130 R

Casino Chicane

Dunlop Curve

S Curve

First Curve

# Zhuhai

**Zhuhai International Circuit**
**Chinese Grand Prix – Reserve Grand Prix**
**Lap Distance:**    2.683 miles/4.32 km
**Race Distance:** tbc

The Zhuhai International Circuit is located some ten km from the centre of Zhuhai City, sixty km west of Hong Kong and fifteen km north-east of Macau. Constructed on a 1,000 acre site, it includes an 11,000-seat grandstand and 36-hole golf course.

The site was constructed after a street circuit race in Zhuhai City in 1993 had attracted over 100,000 spectators and a national TV audience. With the support of the FIA, the Grand Prix circuit was built and opened in 1996. Being named as a reserve circuit in 1998, it seems certain that F1 races at Zhuhai will soon be a regular occurrence.

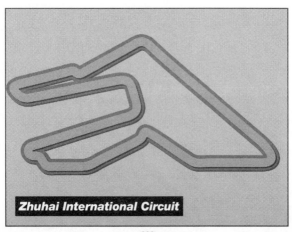

**Zhuhai International Circuit**

# 107% Times

To qualify for the starting grid, cars must finish within 107% of the pole position qualifying time. The simple table below provides a rough 107% guide for potential qualifying times.

| Qualifying Time | 107% Time | Qualifying Time | 107% Time |
|---|---|---|---|
| 1m 15.00s | 1m 20.25s | 1m 53.00s | 1m 60.91s |
| 1m 16.00s | 1m 21.32s | 1m 54.00s | 1m 61.98s |
| 1m 17.00s | 1m 22.39s | 1m 55.00s | 1m 63.05s |
| 1m 18.00s | 1m 23.46s | 1m 56.00s | 1m 64.12s |
| 1m 19.00s | 1m 24.53s | 1m 57.00s | 1m 65.19s |
| 1m 20.00s | 1m 25.60s | 1m 58.00s | 1m 66.26s |
| 1m 21.00s | 1m 26.67s | 1m 59.00s | 1m 67.33s |
| 1m 22.00s | 1m 27.74s | 2m 00.00s | 2m 08.40s |
| 1m 23.00s | 1m 28.81s | 2m 01.00s | 2m 09.47s |
| 1m 24.00s | 1m 29.88s | 2m 02.00s | 2m 10.54s |
| 1m 25.00s | 1m 30.95s | 2m 03.00s | 2m 11.61s |
| 1m 26.00s | 1m 32.02s | 2m 04.00s | 2m 12.68s |
| 1m 27.00s | 1m 33.09s | 2m 05.00s | 2m 13.75s |
| 1m 28.00s | 1m 34.16s | 2m 06.00s | 2m 14.82s |
| 1m 29.00s | 1m 35.23s | 2m 07.00s | 2m 15.89s |
| 1m 30.00s | 1m 36.30s | 2m 08.00s | 2m 16.96s |
| 1m 31.00s | 1m 37.37s | 2m 09.00s | 2m 18.03s |
| 1m 32.00s | 1m 38.44s | 2m 10.00s | 2m 19.10s |
| 1m 33.00s | 1m 39.51s | 2m 11.00s | 2m 20.17s |
| 1m 34.00s | 1m 40.58s | 2m 12.00s | 2m 21.24s |
| 1m 35.00s | 1m 41.65s | 2m 13.00s | 2m 22.31s |
| 1m 36.00s | 1m 42.72s | 2m 14.00s | 2m 23.38s |
| 1m 37.00s | 1m 43.79s | 2m 15.00s | 2m 24.45s |
| 1m 38.00s | 1m 44.86s | 2m 16.00s | 2m 25.52s |
| 1m 39.00s | 1m 45.93s | 2m 17.00s | 2m 26.59s |
| 1m 40.00s | 1m 47.00s | 2m 18.00s | 2m 27.66s |
| 1m 41.00s | 1m 48.07s | 2m 19.00s | 2m 28.73s |
| 1m 42.00s | 1m 49.14s | 2m 20.00s | 2m 29.80s |
| 1m 43.00s | 1m 50.21s | 2m 21.00s | 2m 30.87s |
| 1m 44.00s | 1m 51.28s | 2m 22.00s | 2m 31.94s |
| 1m 45.00s | 1m 52.35s | 2m 23.00s | 2m 33.01s |
| 1m 46.00s | 1m 53.42s | 2m 24.00s | 2m 34.08s |
| 1m 47.00s | 1m 54.49s | 2m 25.00s | 2m 35.15s |
| 1m 48.00s | 1m 55.56s | 2m 26.00s | 2m 36.22s |
| 1m 49.00s | 1m 56.63s | 2m 27.00s | 2m 37.29s |
| 1m 50.00s | 1m 57.70s | 2m 28.00s | 2m 38.36s |
| 1m 51.00s | 1m 58.77s | 2m 29.00s | 2m 39.43s |
| 1m 52.00s | 1m 59.84s | 2m 30.00s | 2m 40.50s |

# Race Diary '98

Listed below are provisional dates and venues for the 1998 Formula One season and were awaiting final FIA confirmation at the time of going to press. As such they are subject to change and alteration.

| Date | Grand Prix | Circuit | Laps | Start GMT |
|------|-----------|---------|------|-----------|
| 8 March | Australian | Melbourne | 58 | 04.00 hours |
| 29 March | Brazilian | Interlagos | 71 | 16.00 hours |
| 12 April | Argentinian | Buenos Aires | 72 | 16.00 hours |
| 26 April | San Marino | Imola | 62 | 12.00 hours |
| 5 May | Spanish | Catalunya | 65 | 12.00 hours |
| 24 May | Monaco | Monte Carlo | 78 | 13.30 hours |
| 7 June | Canadian | Montreal | 69 | 18.00 hours |
| 28 June | French † | Magny-Cours | 72 | 12.00 hours |
| 12 July | British | Silverstone | 60 | 13.00 hours |
| 26 July | Austrian | A1-Ring | 71 | 12.00 hours |
| 2 August | German | Hockenheim | 45 | 12.00 hours |
| 16 August | Hungarian | Hungaroring | 77 | 12.00 hours |
| 30 August | Belgian * | Spa | 44 | 12.00 hours |
| 13 Sept | Italian | Monza | 53 | 12.00 hours |
| 27 Sept | Luxembourg | Nurburgring | 67 | 12.00 hours |
| 1 Nov | Japanese | Suzuka | 53 | 04.00 hours |
| Reserve | Kyalami | South Africa | | |
| Reserve | Zhuhai | China | | |

*† Not on official calendar at time of going to press but likely to be re-instated if a TV contract problem is resolved in time. * Subject to tobacco-advertising ban restrictions being eased.*